PETR KOPL
COMIC SKETCH BOOK

A MANUAL OF A PROFESSIONAL COMIC BOOK MAKER

A WICKEDLY DRAWING CO — AUTHOR OF THIS BOOK IS

....

Zoner PRESS

CARTOONING

THIS BOOK CONSISTS OF THREE MAIN CHAPTERS. I ADVISE YOU: DO NOT SKIP. COMIC BOOK MAKING IS SIMPLE AT FIRST SIGHT. DO NOT MISS ANY SINGLE DETAIL BECAUSE THE SOUL OF A COMIC BOOK IS RIGHT IN THEM. THE MOST IMPORTANT THINGS THAT HAPPEN IN A COMIC BOOK ARE NOT VISIBLE. YOU NEED TO GO THROUGH EVEN THE STUFF YOU THINK YOU KNOW, IN ORDER TO UNDERSTAND THE ESSENCE.

THERE ARE A LOT OF MYTHS AND HALF-TRUTHS ABOUT MAKING COMIC BOOKS. I WILL TRY TO GUIDE YOU THROUGH THIS FORREST. BE FOCUSED. IT WILL NOT BE AN EASY JOURNEY AND SOMETIMES IT WILL HURT.

HOWEVER, I PROMISE THAT IF YOU CARRY ON REALLY THOROUGHLY, I WILL GUIDE YOU THROUGH FIRE AND, ON THE OTHER SIDE, YOU WILL SEE A COMIC BOOK FROM ANOTHER PERSPERCTIVE.

INTRODUCTION	4
WARNING	6
NOTES ABOUT A COMIC BOOK I.	12
TOOLS	13
CARTOONING RULES	14
INTRODUCTION TO CARTOONING	15
EXPLANATION OF TERMS	17
INSIDE OUT	18
DOOR PERSONIFICATION	20
STORYTELLING DOORS	22
STORYTELLING INTERIOR	28
SOMETHING ABOUT PERSPECTIVE	30
MORE ABOUT PERSPECTIVE	32

SOME TASKS ARE MARKED WITH THIS ICON

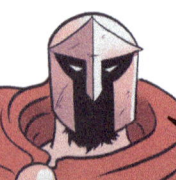

IN CASE YOU GET LOST OR YOU WANT TO TAKE A LOOK AT HOW THE AUTHOR HIMSELF GOT ON WITH THE TASKS, DOWNLOAD THE PICTURES FROM THE FOLLOWING ADDRESS:

http://soubory.zonerpress.cz/zrk1711/

LINK AVAILABLE ALSO ON PAGE
www.petrkopl.cz

Board 2

CHARACTER DESIGN

INTRODUCTION TO ARCHETYPE	34
NEUTRAL HERO	36
ROBIN'S HEAD	38
MAIN ANGLES OF A HEAD	40
TABLOID REVELATION OF AN EYBALL	42
FROM THE CRADDLE TO THE GRAVE	44
DRAWING AN ARM	46
EVERYTHING IS IN THE PALMS	48
LEGS ARE ESSENTIAL	50
SHAPEABLE FACES	52
COMBINATION OF EMOTIONS	54
LEVELS OF EMOTIONS	56
CONTRADICTORY LANGUAGE OF THE BODY AND FACE	60
POLARIZE YOUR HERO	62
IT NEVER RAINS IN THE HERO'S FACE	64
SOMETIMES IT RAINS IN HERO'S FACE	66
PERSONIFICATION OF ANIMALS	68
DOG IKAR	70
SPARROW PEEP	72
NEUTRAL HORSE	74
POLARITY OF A HORSE	76
POLARITY OF GUNS	78
SYMBOLS	80
ATTRIBUTES	82
CHILDREN	84
MODERN VILLAIN	86
A PAIR OF HENCHMEN	88
WITCH AND ENCHANTRESS	92
BARBARIANS AND BANDITS	94
SUPERHERO	96
INTRODUCTION TO A COMIC BOOK	98
COMIC BOOK TEST – QUESTIONS	99

COMICS

COMIC BOOK TEST – ANSWERS	100
COMIC BOOK BASIC TERMS	101
PANELS	102
BUBBLES	104
LETTERING	106
SOUNDS AND SCREAMS	108
EXPRESSIVE LOOK OF SOUNDS	110
INSPIRATION	112
STORY CONSTRUCTION	114
COMIC BOOK STRIP	116
USEFULNESS VS LAZINESS	118
DYNAMICS IN A COMIC BOOK	120
MOVEMENT IN RELATION TO A STORY	122
GRAPHIC OUTLINE OF A STORY	124
HOW TO WRITE A GOOD STORY	126
SCENARIO	128
ABSTRACT AND SYNOPSIS	134
10 LIES ABOUT COMIC BOOK MAKING	136
GENERAL TIPS FOR COMIC BOOK MAKERS	137
FIRST DRAFT	138
ACCURATE DRAFT	140
PULLING OUT	142
COLOUR	144
WAYS OF COLOURING A COMIC BOOK	145
PRACTICAL THEORY OF COLOURS IN PRINTING	146
SYMBOLISM OF COLOURS	148
HOW TO DEAL WITH PUBLISHERS	150
NOTES ABOUT COMIC BOOK	152
LAST TASK	156
COLLEAGUES' COMMENTS	158
ACKNOWLEDGEMENT	160

INTRODUCTION

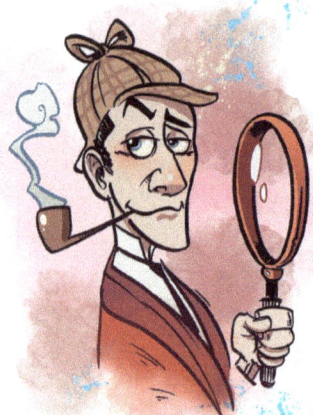

"IT IS EASIER TO READ A COMIC BOOK THAN A BOOK." IT IS ONE OF THE BIGGEST LIES EVER. ANOTHER LIE IS, "A COMIC BOOK IS SOMETHING BETWEEN A BOOK AND A MOVIE." I KNOW A LOT OF ADULTS WHO CLAIM SUCH THINGS. THEY APPROVE READING COMIC BOOKS AND THEY GIVE THEM TO THEIR CHILDREN HOPING THAT COMIC BOOKS WILL LEAD THEM TO READING "TRUE BOOKS". IT IS A GENERAL WIDESPREAD ERROR. THERE ARE COMIC BOOKS WHICH ADULTS DO NOT READ THOUGH. THEY SAY IT IS BORING. IN FACT IT IS BECAUSE THEY DO NOT KNOW WHAT IS EXPECTED FROM THEM IN A COMIC BOOK. IT IS EITHER BECAUSE THEY FORGOT IT OR THEY SIMPLY NEVER LEARNT IT. AS THEY ARE USED TO READING BOOKS, THE ILLUSTRATIONS DISTURB THEM, BECAUSE SOME ARTISTS IMPOSE SOME IMAGINATION WHICH THEY CAN MAKE ON THEIR OWN.

WHILE YOU ACTIVELY USE YOUR OWN IMAGINATION WITH BOOKS, AND WORDS ARE FLUENTLY CHANGING INTO MEMORIES, IN A MOVIE YOU PASSIVELY RECEIVE A FOREIGN IMAGINATION FROM SOMEONE ELSE ABOUT VISUAL PART. UNTIL THIS PART IT COULD SEEM THAT A COMIC BOOK IS SOMETHING BETWEEN A MOVIE AND A BOOK. HOWEVER, THE INSIDERS KNOW THAT IT IS NOT TRUE. YOU NEED TO GO TO MEET A COMIC BOOK. MORE THAN ANY OTHER MEDIA. THERE ARE WRITTEN WORDS TOGETHER WITH VISUAL INTERPRETATION FROM THE ARTIST. THESE ARE COMPLETELY DIFFERENT THINGS WHICH MUST BE PUT TOGETHER BY THE READER'S BRAIN. YOU WILL BE HOLDING NOT A COMPLETE PIECE OF ART BUT SOMETHING LIKE A CONCEPT. THE READER BECOMES A DIRECTOR, EDITOR, SOUND ENGINEER AND CAMERAMAN.

TO MAKE IT SIMPLE, SWORN BOOK READERS KNOW THAT WORDS ON THE PAPER CHANGE INTO IMAGES. WHILE READING, THEY USE JUST ONE BRAIN HEMSPHERE AND THE SECOND ONE RUNS ON NETURAL GEAR. WHILE WATCHING A MOVIE WE ENGAGE THE SECOND HEMISPHERE AND THE FIRST ONE JUST FOLLOWS. DURING READING A COMIC BOOK, OUR BRAIN GOES AT FULL SPEED! EACH SIDE OF A COMIC BOOK IS AN ADVENTUROUS PLAN FOR A READER WHICH IS OVERLOOKED FIRST AND THEN IT COMES BACK AND THE READER BECOMES THEIR OWN EXPERIENCE COMPOSER. AS GREAT AS THEY WANT. A COMIC BOOK MAKER IS JUST THE BACKGROUND. THEY KNOW THAT THEY SHOULD JUST PROMPT AND THAT THEY DO NOT HAVE TO LEAD THE READER.

THE ABILITY TO SWITCH ON BOTH BRAIN HEMISPHERES AND FULLY EMERGE INTO THE CREATIVE ACTIVITY IS USUALLY LINKED TO CHILDREN AND YOUNG PEOPLE. IT DISAPPEARS ALONG WITH AGEING, UNLESS PRACTISED. IT IS NECESSARY TO KNOW HOW TO READ COMIC BOOKS. A COMIC BOOK MAKER ALREADY KNOWS WHERE TO SLOW DOWN THE STORY, WHERE MUSIC WILL SOUND AND WHERE A PARTICULAR SOUND WILL BE HEARD. THEN HE OR SHE WONDERS THEMSELVES BY THEIR CREATIVITY WHICH THEY PUT INTO THEIR PIECE OF ART. IT IS BLATANTLY OBVIOUS THAT READING COMIC BOOKS...IS A SKILL.

I DO NOT WANT TO SAY THAT WATCHING MOVIES OR READING BOOKS IS SOMETHING INFERIOR OR EVEN BAD, FOR GOD'S SAKE NO! ONCE AND FOR ALL: IT IS REALLY DIFFERENT STORY.

"READING A COMIC BOOK IS ART"

THIS BOOK IS SUPPRISINGLY NOT A GUIDEBOOK FOR CARTOONISTS. I CONSIDER MYSELF MORE AS A STORYTELLER THAN A CARTOONIST. PLEASE ACCEPT THIS SKETCHBOOK AS A NARRATING TECHNIQUE GUIDE, WITH THE HELP OF CARTOONING WHICH I USE AND AT THE SAME TIME AN INTRODUCTION TO THE WORLD OF COMIC BOOKS MAKING AND ALSO, HOW TO READ IT. THIS BOOK WILL NOT TEACH YOU HOW TO DRAW. IT EXPECTS YOU TO HAVE ALREADY MASTERED THE BASICS. IN CARTOONING, IT IS ABOUT DRAWING FOR CHILDREN, IT IS A DISCIPLINE THAT IS REALLY COMPLEX THAT LOOKS SIMPLE AT FIRST SIGHT. SO, IF YOU HAVE NOT MASTERED THE BASICS OF THE ANATOMY FOR ARTISTS, PERSPECTIVE, SHADING AND THEORY OF COLOURS, THIS BOOK WILL NOT TEACH YOU THEM.

WHAT YOU WILL **LEARN** THEN? IT WILL TRY TO ADVANCE YOU TO THE NEXT LEVEL OF PERCEPTION OF IMAGES AND SYMBOLS IN THEIR SHAPE.

IT WILL REVEAL SECRETS OF CARTOONING SHORTCUT AND FORCE YOU TO STOP COPYING THE REALITY AND START TO ILLUSTRATE IT.

IN THIS SKETCHBOOK I DO NOT PROCEED JUST FROM MY OWN EXPERIENCE. ON MY JOURNEY I HAVE STUDIED A LOT OF PIECES OF ART MADE BY VARIOUS AUTHORS AND I AM GRATEFUL TO THEM. HERE, THERE ARE SOME NAMES WHO HELPED ME TO GET WHERE I AM NOW. ADOLF BORN, KAREL FRANTA, ONDŘEJ SEKORA, FRANTIŠEK KOBÍK, KÁJA SAUDEK, SCOTT MCCLOUD, BEN CALDWELL, STAN LEE, STEVE DITKO, DISNEY, DON ROSA, ALBERT UDERZO, RENÉ GOSCINNY, JAROSLAV NĚMEČEK AND SO ON...

AT THE END OF THIS BOOK, WE WILL TRY TO DRAW UP OUR OWN COMIC BOOK. EVERYTHING WHAT WE WILL BE DOING BEFOREHAND, IS A DEVELOPMENT AND PREPARATION FOR ITS MAKING.

WE WILL CREATE CHARACTERS, DETERMINE THEIR APPEARANCE, EXPLAIN WHY THEY LOOK THE WAY THEY DO, WHY THEIR CLOTHES, TOOLS AND EVEN HENCHMEN HAVE RULES FOR THEIR APPEARANCE. WE WILL GENERATE THE ENVIRONMENT AND WILL HAVE A LOOK AT EXAMPLES ABOUT HOW CARTOONING WORKS IN PRACTICE.

EVERYTHING YOU WILL SEE AND READ IN THIS BOOK ARE **MY** OPINIONS AND **MY** BELIEVES WHICH ACQUIRED THANKS TO MY LONG-STANDING EXPERIENCE AND STUDYING OF OTHER AUTHORS. SO MY EXPERIENCE TELLS ME TO POINT OUT THAT MY OPINIONS ARE JUST OPINIONS AND NOT GENERAL FACTS. FIRST OF ALL I AM THE ONE WHO WANTS TO SAY THAT NOT EVERYTHING THAT I HAVE MADE WAS CORRECT, FLAWLESS OR PERFECT. I AM TRYING TO PROVIDE YOU AN ADVANTAGE. ORDER TO DEVOTE TO THIS CREATIVE ACTIVITY IS A GIVEN SKILL MAINLY TO CHILDREN AND THE YOUTH. DUE TO AGING, IF NOT PRACTISED, IT LEAVES. READING A COMIC BOOKS IS A SKILL. AS AN EXPERIENCED COMICBOOK AUTHOR, I'M TRYING TO OFFER YOU TO LEARN FROM MY OWN MISTAKES EVEN BEFORE YOU MAKE THEM BY YOURSEVES.

SO GOOD LUCK!

"AN OPINION IS NOT A GENERAL FACT"

PETR KOPL

TASK

THIS IS YOUR BOOK. DRAW YOURSELF HOW YOU ARE DRAWING IN YOUR STUDY. USE ALL OF YOUR FANTASY, BUT STILL IT MUST BE RECOGNIZABLE THAT IT IS YOUR STUDY. AT THE END OF THE BOOK AND BY THE TIME WE WILL HAVE GONE THROUGH ALL LESSONS; WE WILL DRAW THE SAME PICTURE TO SEE IF THERE IS SOME ADVANCEMENT. TRY YOUR BEST IN YOUR OWN INTEREST THEN.

WARNING

IF YOU PURCHASED THIS BOOK, IT MEANS THAT YOU BELIEVED THE LURING COVER. IT SEEMS YOU DO NOT WANT JUST CONSUME COMIC BOOKS BUT YOU WANT TO BECOME THEIR AUTHOR AS WELL. SO WELCOME DEAR FRIENDS. YOU HAVE JUST COME TO NEVER ENDING THIN ICE AND NEVER ENDING HARD WORK. I CAN SEE THAT YOU DO NOT MISS COURAGE INDEED. I LIKE IT. IT IS AN HONOUR THAT IS JUST ME, PETR KOPL WILL GUIDE YOU ON YOUR FIRST STEPS, THE ONE WHO WILL OPEN THE CURTAINS AND YOU WILL SEE A TREASURE OF INCALCULABLE VALUE. THIS BOOK WILL NOT TEACH YOU HOW TO DRAW...ALTHOUGH IT WILL SEEM FROM TIME TO TIME THAT IT WILL, BUT WE WILL NOT DEAL WITH SUCH THINGS.

ARE YOU A LAYMAN? I NEED TO GIVE YOU A SOLEMN WARNING. IF YOU REALLY GO THROUGHLY THROUGH THIS COURSE, THE SECRETS OF AN ART CALLED CARTOONING AND COMIC BOOKS WILL BE REVEALED TO YOU. HOWEVER, NOT ALL OF THEM. NO WORRIES. YOU WILL STILL BE DISCOVERING NEW THINGS. YOU WILL NOT BE AN AMATEUR, WHO JUST CONSUMES COMIC BOOKS, ANY LONGER. JUST LOOK BEHIND THE SCENES AT HOW COMIC BOOKS ARE MADE IN ORDER TO MAKE YOU LAUGH, TOUCH OR MAKE YOU CRY. THIS COULD SPOIL A BIT OF THE READING EXPERIENCE.

LET´S PROMISE SOMETHING TO EACH OTHER. OR MAYBE NOT. LET'S TAKE OATH! IF YOU DO NOT TAKE IT SERIOUSLY, IT IS YOUR FAULT. I WARNED YOU.

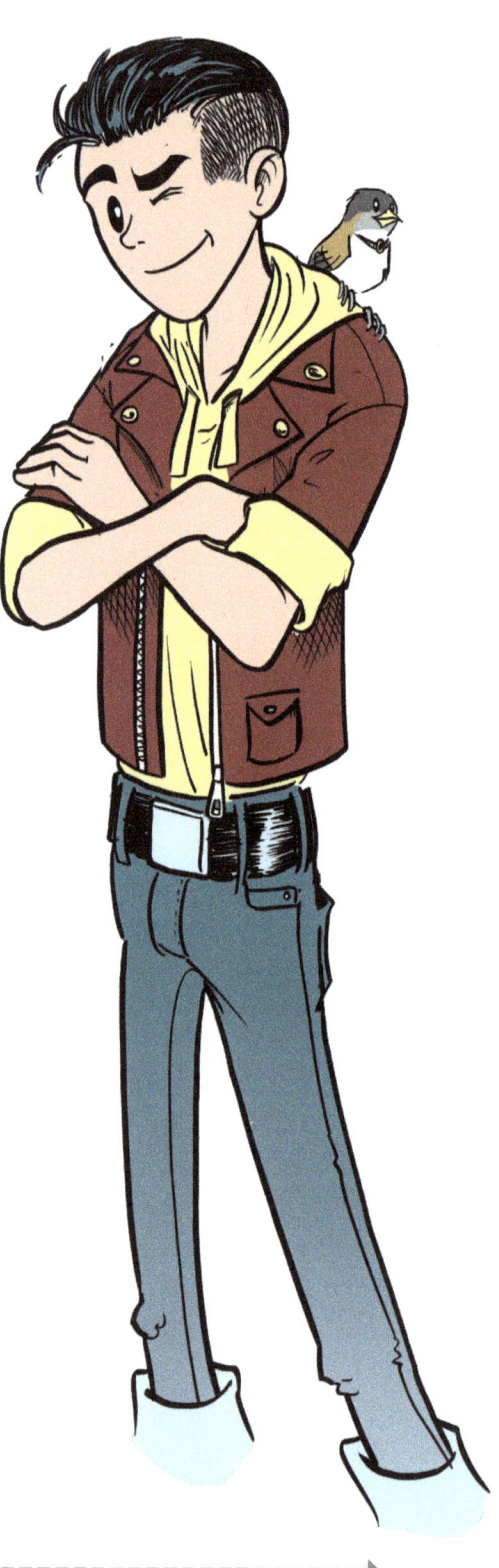

OATH:
I TAKE AN OATH THAT EVERYTHING AND ANY SECRETS THAT I COME TO KNOW IN THIS BOOK WILL NEVER AFFECT THE MANNER OF HOW I READ COMIC BOOKS AND ALTHOUGH I WILL BE WALKING IN THE VALLEY OF TEMPTATION, I WILL ENJOY THE COMIC BOOK FIRST AND THEN EVALUATE IT.

STILL HAVEN'T QUIT? I CAN SEE THAT THE FORCE IS WITH YOU. ON THE FOLLOWING PAGES THERE IS JUST A MERE SAMPLE FROM A 30 PAGE COMIC BOOK, BUT IT IS A PROLOGUE WITH A DRAMATIC PLOT. THEREFORE, YOU ARE GETTING A COMPLETE STORY. ITS MISSION IS TO PRESENT THE MAIN HERO AND HIS ABILLITIES. THIS STORY IS HERE BECAUSE I WILL ILLUSTRATIVELY SHOW YOU HOW TO MAKE HIM AND WHAT TRICKS I USED YOU WILL BE INITIATED THEN. SO, LET´S GO TO THE NEVER ENDING STORY!

FIRST TASK
WELL THEN, MY FAITHFUL APPRENTICES, READ THE FOLLOWING FIVE PAGES WITH THE AWARENESS THAT IT IS THE LAST COMIC BOOK STORY YOU WILL BE READING AS LAYMEN. WHEN YOU FINISH WITH THIS BOOK, COMIC BOOKS WIILL NEVER BE THE SAME AS BEFORE. YOU WILL BECOME PROFESSIONALS.

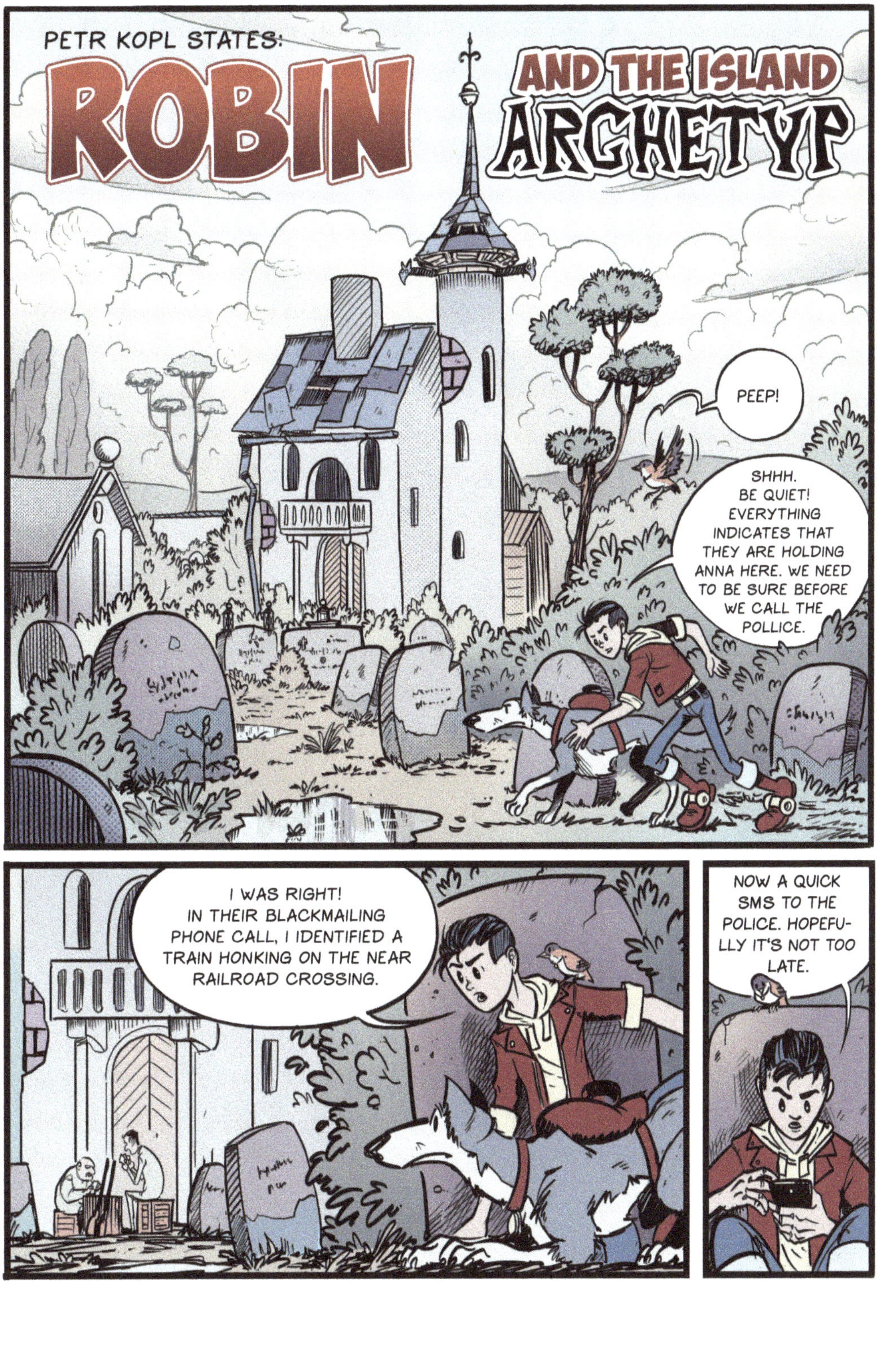

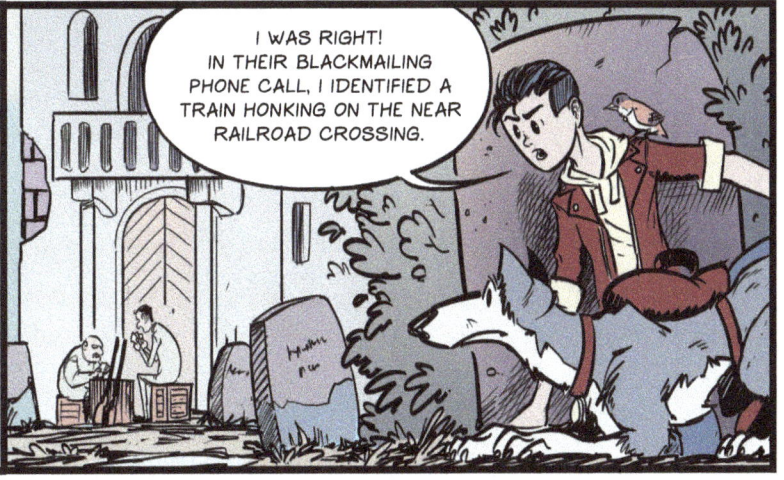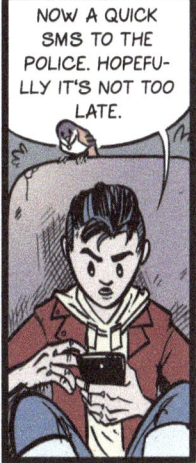

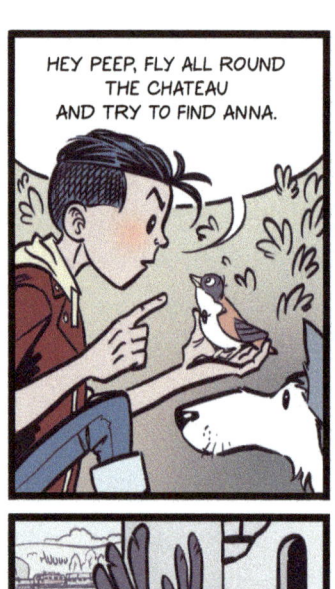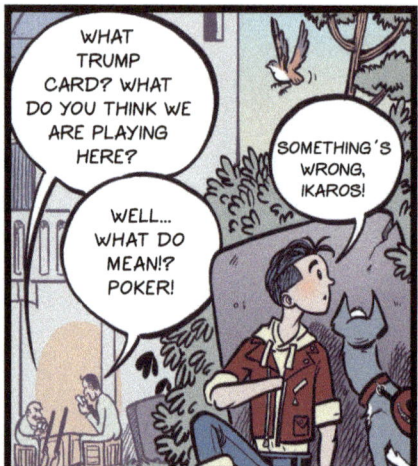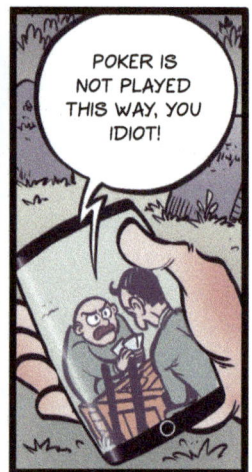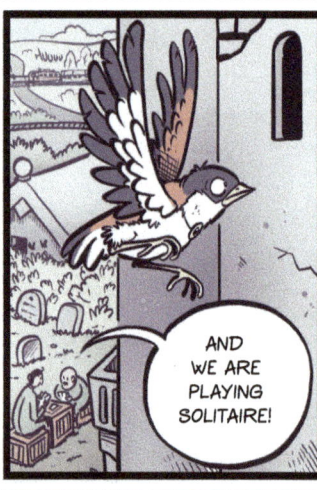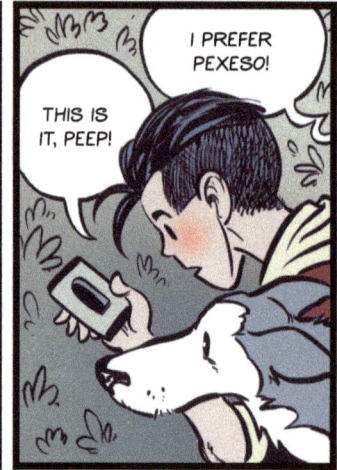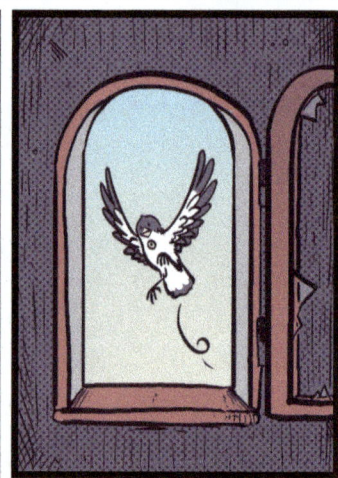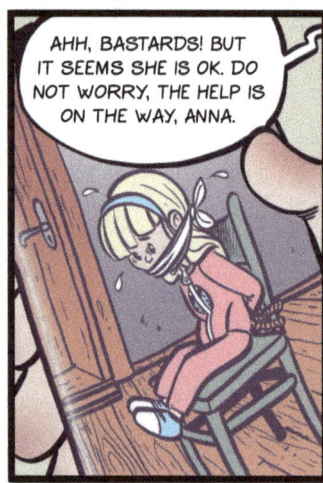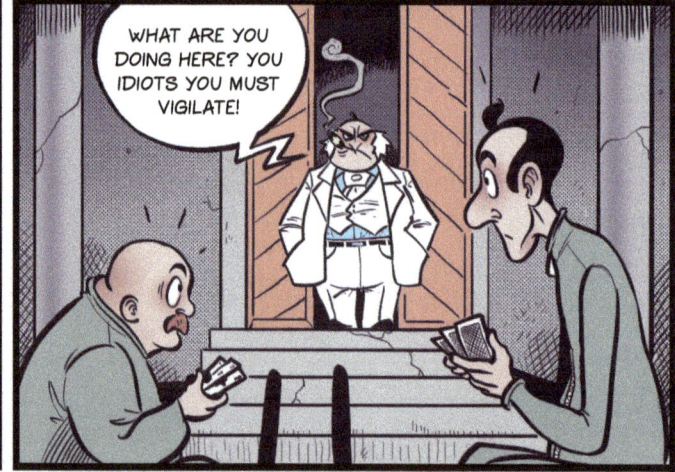

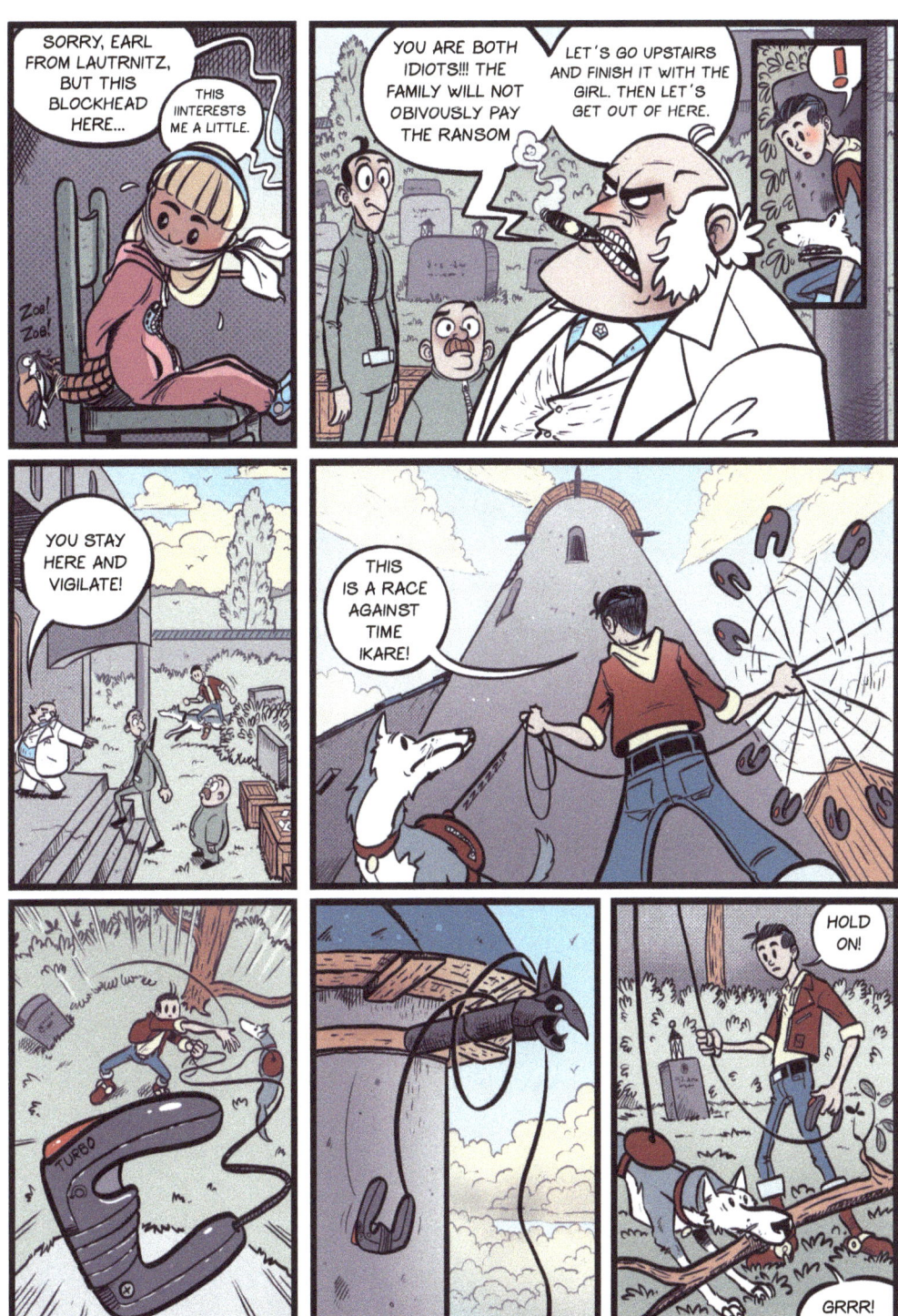

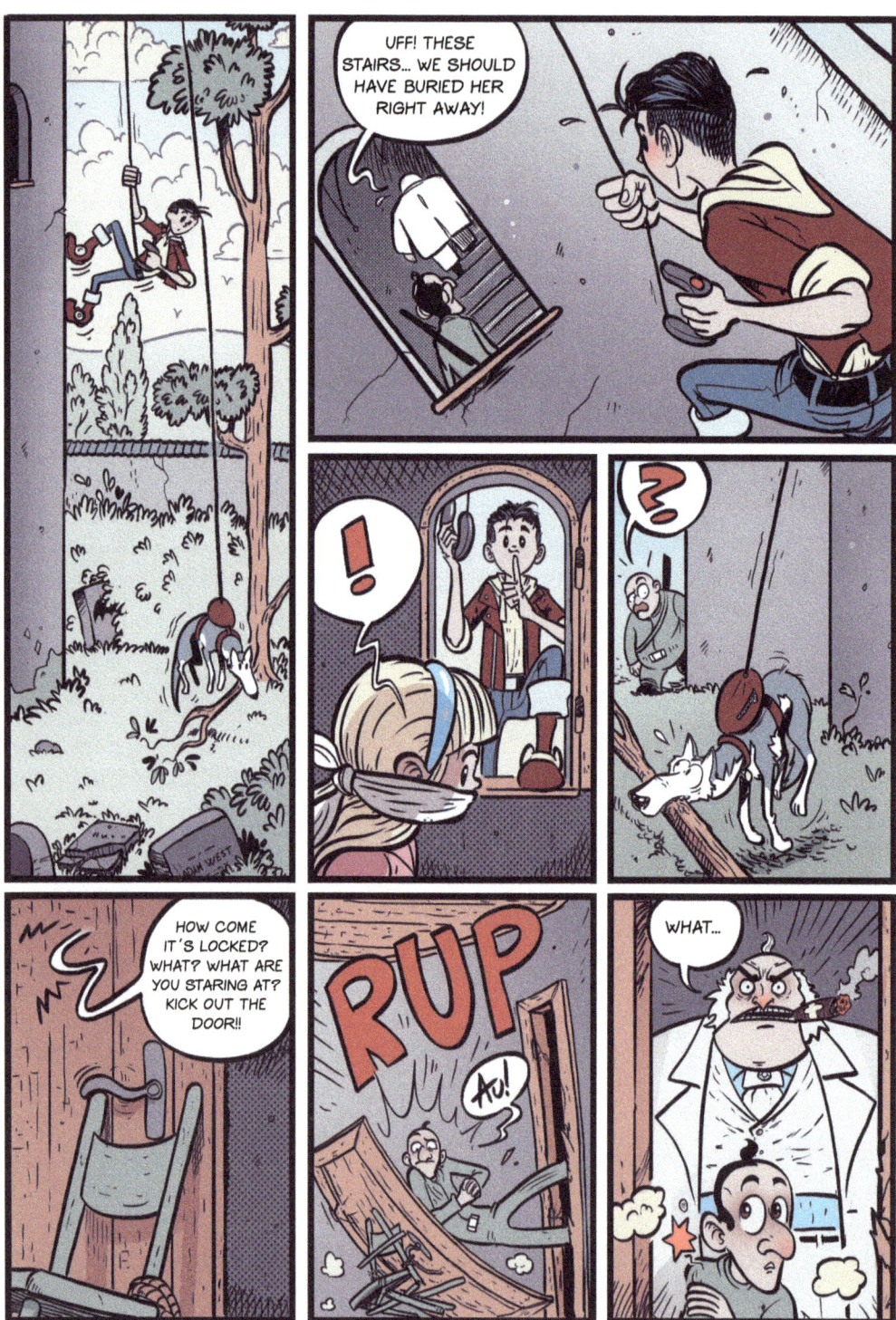

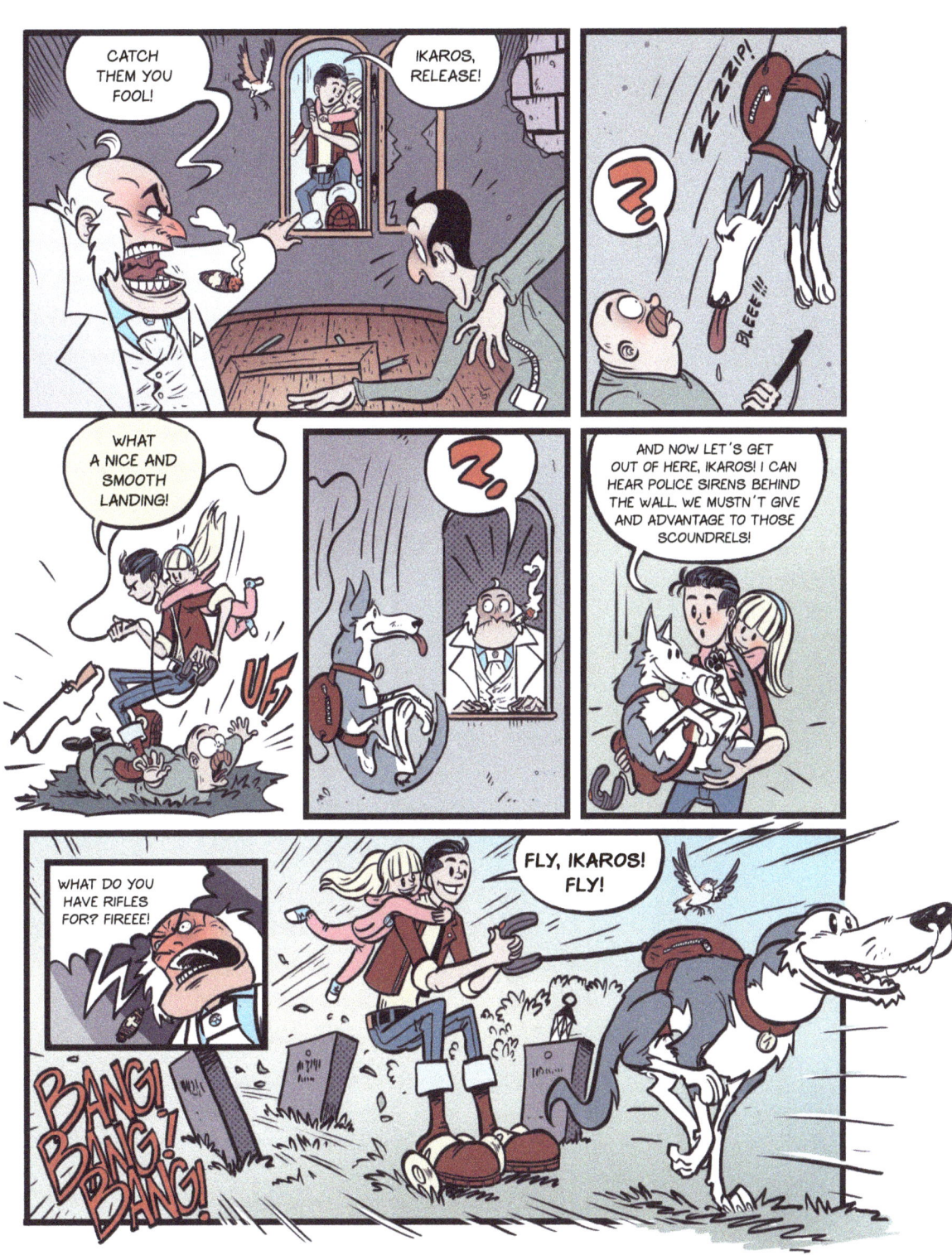

COMIC BOOK NOTES I.

WRITE DOWN YOUR IDEAS FROM THE COMIC STORY WHICH YOU HAVE JUST READ. ON EACH PAGE AND ALMOST ON EVERY PANEL I USED ONE OF THE TECHIQUES WHICH WILL BE TEACHING YOU. IT IS THE LANGUAGE YOU NEED TO BE LEARN TO BE ABLE TO MASTER NARRATION WITH THE HELP OF THIS MEDIA. PUTTING PICTURE BY PICTURE AS THE PLOT GOES IS AN EASY TASK AND ANYBODY CAN MAKE IT. HOWEVER, I WANT YOU TO CARRY THE READER AWAY, TO IDENTIFY THEMSELVES WITH THE STORY AND MOREOVER, YOU TO BRING AND HAVE THE READER'S CURRENTLY EXPERIENCED EMOTIONS UNDER CONTROL. WRITE DOWN EVERYTHING WHAT COMES UP TO YOUR MIND EVEN IF IT LOOKS LIKE A BANALITY. AT THE END OF THE BOOK, YOU WILL COME TO KNOW EVERYTHING WHAT YOU WILL HAVE MISSED.

BOARD 7

BOARD 8

BOARD 9

BOARD 10

BOARD 11

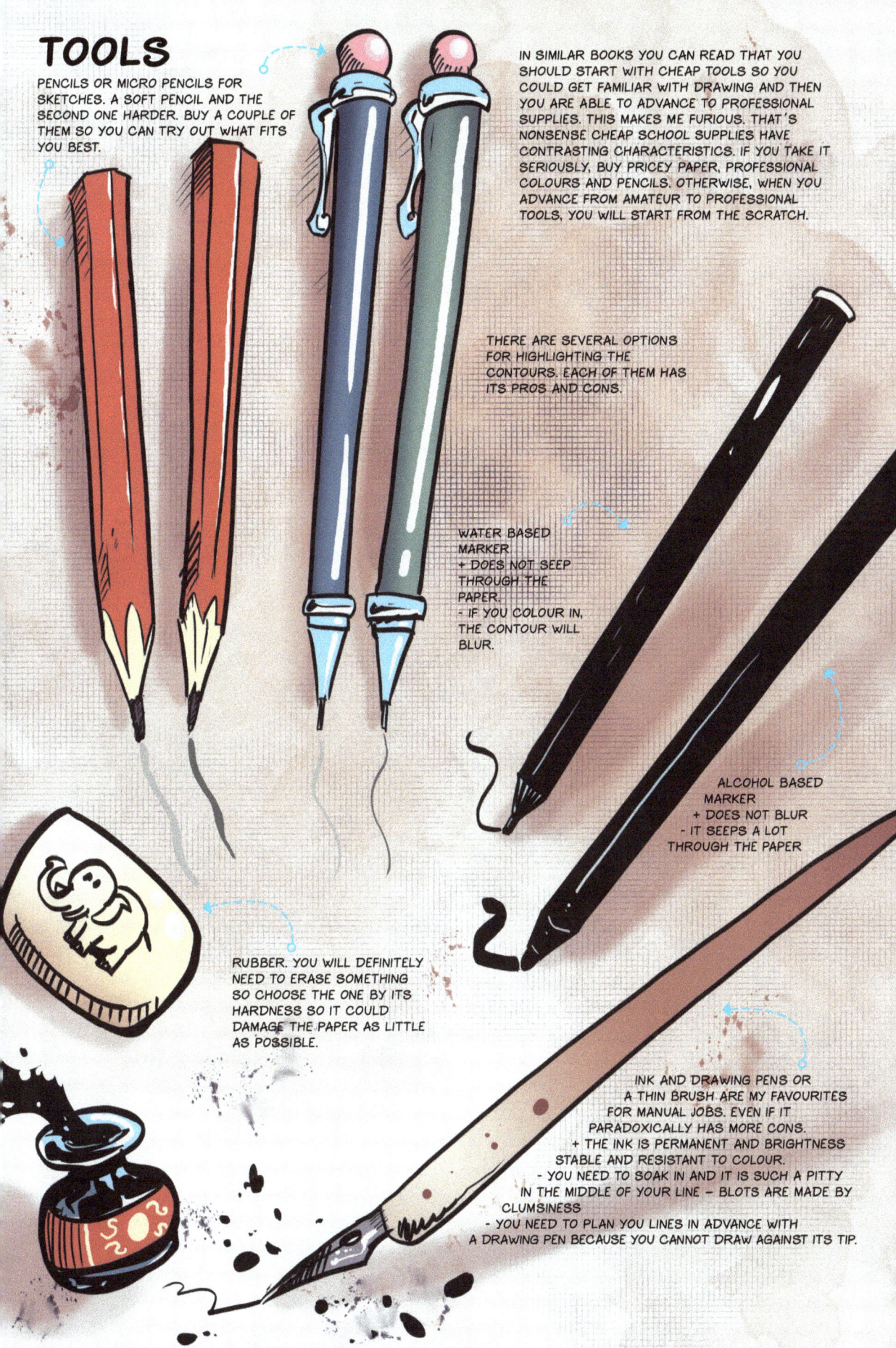

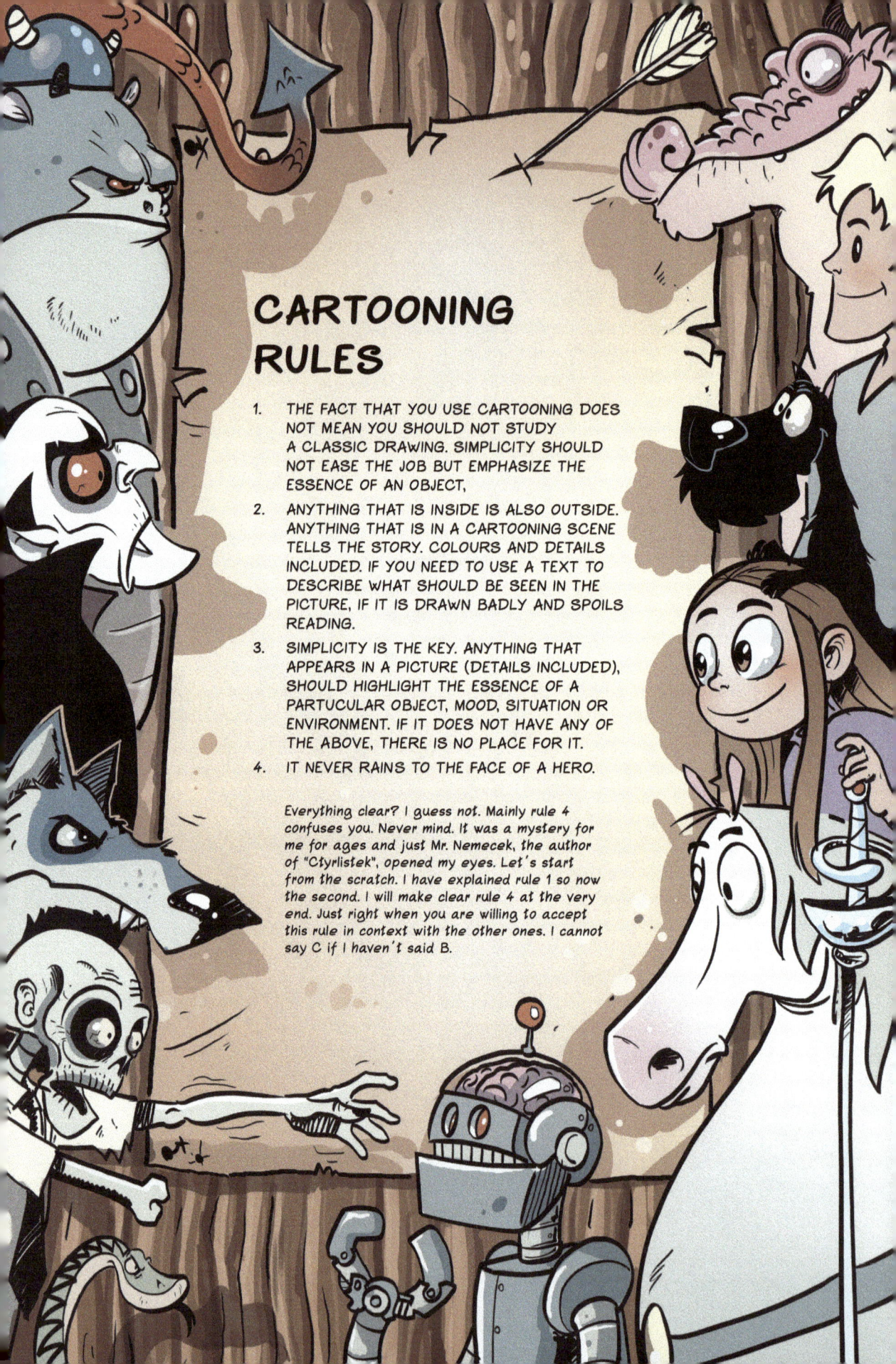

CARTOONING RULES

1. THE FACT THAT YOU USE CARTOONING DOES NOT MEAN YOU SHOULD NOT STUDY A CLASSIC DRAWING. SIMPLICITY SHOULD NOT EASE THE JOB BUT EMPHASIZE THE ESSENCE OF AN OBJECT.

2. ANYTHING THAT IS INSIDE IS ALSO OUTSIDE. ANYTHING THAT IS IN A CARTOONING SCENE TELLS THE STORY. COLOURS AND DETAILS INCLUDED. IF YOU NEED TO USE A TEXT TO DESCRIBE WHAT SHOULD BE SEEN IN THE PICTURE, IF IT IS DRAWN BADLY AND SPOILS READING.

3. SIMPLICITY IS THE KEY. ANYTHING THAT APPEARS IN A PICTURE (DETAILS INCLUDED), SHOULD HIGHLIGHT THE ESSENCE OF A PARTUCULAR OBJECT, MOOD, SITUATION OR ENVIRONMENT. IF IT DOES NOT HAVE ANY OF THE ABOVE, THERE IS NO PLACE FOR IT.

4. IT NEVER RAINS TO THE FACE OF A HERO.

Everything clear? I guess not. Mainly rule 4 confuses you. Never mind. It was a mystery for me for ages and just Mr. Nemecek, the author of "Ctyrlistek", opened my eyes. Let´s start from the scratch. I have explained rule 1 so now the second. I will make clear rule 4 at the very end. Just right when you are willing to accept this rule in context with the other ones. I cannot say C if I haven´t said B.

INTRODUCTION TO CARTOONING

WHAT IS THAT CARTOONING? A NEW WORD FOR AN OLD THING. IT IS AN ESPECIALLY DEVELOPED STYLE OF DRAWING WHICH SHOULD HAVE, IN ITS BEGINNINGS, EASE THE WORK OF ANIMATORS. THEREFORE, THE MONEY OF FILM STUDIOS.

LONG BEFORE DISNEY, FLEISCHER BROTHERS WERE HERE. THEY WERE REAL PIONEERS OF ANIMATED MOVIES. THEY SOON FOUND OUT THAT CONVERTING CHARACTERS INTO GEOMETRICAL SHAPES REALLY HELPED ANIMATORS. THEIR ADAPTATION ON THE TECHNIQUE OF THE DRAWING WAS GIVEN PRECISION THEN AND THEY MADE ANIMATIONS MORE ATRACTIVE.

LET'S GO OVER DISNEY. LET'S LOOK AT THE SIXTIES OF THE 20TH CENTURY. ONCE UPON THE TIME THERE WAS A STUDIO CALLED HANNA-BARBERA.

THE STUDIO HAD ALREADY HAD A LOT OF THINGS DONE. THE CARTOON WAS STILL REALLY EXPENSIVE AND REQUIERED WHOLE ARMIES OF CARTOON MAKERS. FOR TRADITIONAL STUDIOS, IT WAS NOT WORTH MAKING THESE FILMS, SO THE CARTOON WAS STRUGLING ON THE EDGE OF GENERAL INTEREST. THE FAME OF TOM AND JERRY, WHICH HAS BECOME CLASSIC, WAS NOT HELPING THEN. THE STUDIO WAS STANDING BEFORE A CHALLENGE HOW TO MAKE THE PRODUCTION OF FUNNY CARTOONS CHEAPER IN ORDER TO MAKE THEM QUICKLY. MOREOVER, CHEAPLY FOR THE TV PRODUCTION.

THEY CAME WITH SOMETHING WHICH HAS DOUBTED UP TODAY BY PURITANS. IT IS CALLED SAVING ANIMATION. IT WORKS MAINLY WITH STATIC PICTURES AND JUST THE PART OF A CHARACTER WHICH IS NECESSARY IS ANIMATED. THE DRAWING SUBMITED TO IT AND IT HAS BECOME SIMPLIER THANKS TO IT. SO INSTEAD OF RICH ANIMATIONS, SOMETHING LIKE SQUARED PICTURES IN MOTION.

> "CARTOONING SHOULD ORIGINALLY EASE THE JOB BUT IT HAS BECOME SOMETHING FAR BIGGER."

LONG SHOTS ON THE FACES OF CHARACTERS. JUST THEIR LIPS MOVE. IF THE CHARACTER SHOULD START RUNNING, INSTEAD OF FLUENT ACCELERATION THEY JUST DISSAPEAR IN A CLOUD OF DUST. FIGHTS TOOK PART IN OUT OF THE PICTURE OR AGAIN IN A CLOUD OF DUST AND STARS. IN SIMPLE WORDS, A NIGHTMARE OF CARTOON LOVERS... IT WORKED! WHAT LOOKED LIKE A SACRILEGE TURNED OUT AN INCREDIBLY EFFICIENT SHORTCUT. ALL OF THESE EDIATIONS SUPPORTED THE FUN AND SITUATIONAL JOKES WHICH COULD BE COMPLEMENTED BY CONVERSATIONAL JOKES.

SO A VIRTUE CAME OUT OF NEED, THE AUDIENCE LOVED IT AND THE COMIC MAKING FACTORY STARTED MAKING THEM AT FULL SPEED. SERIES SUCH AS THE FLINTSTONES OR SCOOBY DOO ARE MADE BY THIS METHOD. THEY HAVE BECOME CLASSICS ANAD WE ALL KNOW THEM.

HOWEVER, BE CAREFUL. AT HANNA-BARBERA, THEY KNEW WHERE TO STOP. IF THEY HAD REDUCED THE ANIMATION, THEY WOULD HAVE COME TO THE BORDER OF TOLERABILITY AND FUN. THIS IS WHAT HAPPENED TO OTHER STUDIOS WHICH HAD TRIED TO GO A BIT FURTHER AND COMBINED THE DRAWINGS AND PHOTOGRAPHY. INSTEAD OF MOUTH ANIMATION, THEY INSERTED CUT HUMAN MOUTH INTO THE PICTURE AND SIMILAR THINGS AND THIS WAS ALREADY REALLY YUCK.

WHAT CARTOONING REALLY IS? IT IS A SHORTCUT. IT COULD BE SAID THAT IT WAS CARICATURE. HOWEVER, IT IS NOT EXACT. IT IS A MAXIMAL SIMPLIFICATION OF AN ANIMATED OBJECT BUT NOT JUST FOR US TO BE ABLE TO EASE THE JOB. IT IS TO SIMPLIFY THE INNER AND OUTER ESSENCE OF AN OBJECT.

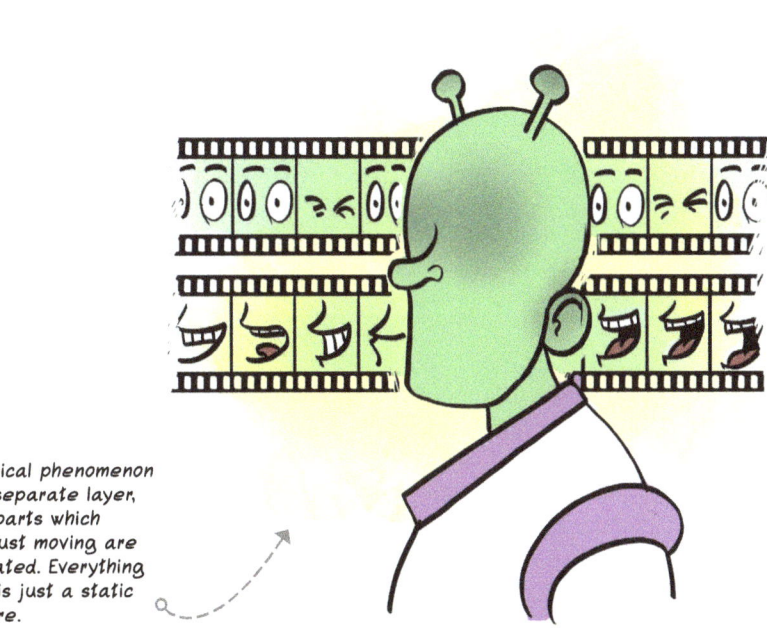

A typical phenomenon in a separate layer, just parts which are just moving are animated. Everything else is just a static picture.

AN ETERNAL RULE APPLIES HERE: IF YOU WANT TO TAKE A SHORTCUT, YOU NEED TO KNOW THE LONGER WAY. THE FACT THAT YOU DRAW SIMPLIFIED CHARACTERS DOES NOT LIBERATE YOUR FROM STUDYING PATTERNS. THERE IS NO OTHER WAY TO CAPTURE THEIR ESSENCE.

TODAY, THERE IS ALREADY NO PREASSURE ON ANIMATION SIMPLIFICATION BECAUSE THE TECHNOLOGY HAS ADVANCED AND COMPUTER PROGRAMS MANAGE THINGS WHICH WOULD HAVE NEEDED ARMIES OF PEOPLE FOR. INSPITE OF THIS FACT, CARTOONING IS STILL USED. IT IS NOT A QUESTION OF NEED ANY LONGER. IT IS A QUESTION OF CHOICE. CARTOONING HAS OUTLIVED ITS UTILITY. WE DO NOT NEED IT ANY LONGER. WE WANT IT!

CARTOONING HAS BECOME A FULLY FLEDGED ARTISTIC MOVEMENT AND THANKS TO WHICH, GREAT NAMES SUCH AS DARWYN COOKE, STAN SAKAI, JEFF SMITH, BILL WATTERSON, JIM DAVIS COULD ARISE AND MANY MORE OF THE ONES WHO I HAVE JUST OFFENDED BECAUSE I DID NOT MENTION.

A SHORTCUT WHICH IS CHARACTERISTIC FOR CARTOONING TURNED OUT INTO SOMETHING REALLY USEFUL RULE AND JUST THE SPELL WHICH IS IN ITS SIMPLICITY GIVES IT AN INCREDIBLE FREEDOM OF EXPRESSING EVEN REALLY COMPLEX, SERIOUS OR ARTISTIC QUESTIONS IN THEIR FULL ABSTRACTION.

> "IF YOU WANT TO TAKE A SHORTCUT, YOU NEED TO KNOW THE LONGER WAY."

HOWEVER, JUST IN THE CASE WHEN YOU STRICTLY STICK TO THE GIVEN CARTOONING RULES. THIS IDEA WAS DEVELOPED TO ITS MASTERY BY SCOTT MC CLOUD. FROM HIS TREATISE OF A COMIC BOOK IN COMIC FORM, THIS BOOK IS ALSO RELEASED.

HOWEVER, THE REASON WHY I LOVE CARTOONING IS BECAUSE ITS SECOND RULE. EVERYTHING WHAT YOU CONVERT INTO THE DRAWING STYLE LOOKS AS IT IS FROM THE INSIDE. AT FIRST SIGHT, YOU CAN RECOGNISE WHO THE HEROES AND VILLAINS ARE, WHO IS GOOD AND WHO IS SICK, WHO IS STRONG, STUPID OR SNEAKY. YES, EVERYTHING CAN BE DISTINGUISHED IN CARTOONING AT FIRST SIGHT.

AND IT IS NOT EVERYTHING, YET YOU CAN DRAW A SINGLE DOOR AND JUST BY ITS SHAPE, YOU CAN MAKE THE READER BELIEVE WHAT IS BEHIND IT WITHOUT OPENING! JUST WITH A MERE COLOUR OF CLOTHES YOU CAN INDICATE IN THE CHARACTERS WHO THE INNOCENT AND TRAITORS ARE. THE SHAPE OF LINES SHOWS THE INNER CHARACTERICTICS OF THE HEROES...

HOWEVER, JUST IF YOU UNDERSTAND ITS NATURE AND SUBCONSCIOUS PERCEPTION OF A HUMAN BRAIN. I WILL TRY TO TEACH YOU ALL OF THAT.

WHAT DO I NEED FROM YOU? TRY TO FORGET ABOUT ALL PREJUDICE WHICH YOU HAVE AGAINST CARTOONING. NO MATTER IF YOU LOVE IT OR HATE IT. (ALTHOUGH, WHY WOULD YOU BUY THIS BOOK, RIGHT?). TRY NOT TO BE A TABULA RASA FOR A WHILE. SO LET´S GET DOWN TO BUSINESS.

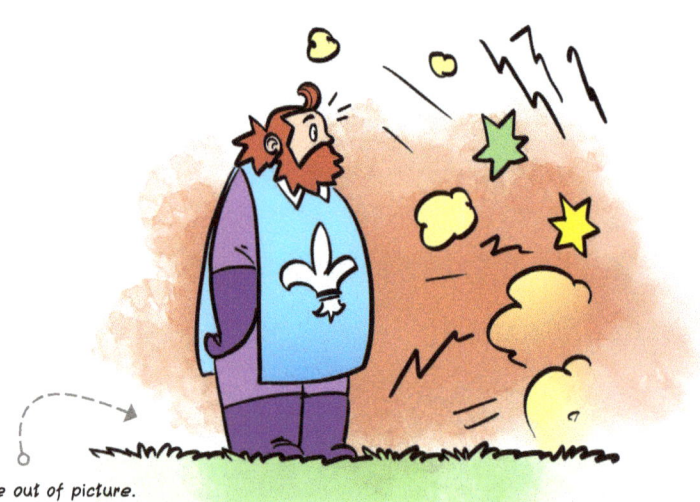

Action scene out of picture. The reaction of the observer is often mostly funnier than the scene itself. Just prepare that there will always be a fool who will say that you did it by this manner because you had not wanted to draw the fight.

TERM EXPLANATION

THERE ARE NOT SO MANY OF THEM, HOWEVER, IT IS IMPORTANT TO MAKE CLEAR SOME WORDS WHICH WE WILL USE, SKETCH EDGES, YOU CAN SEE AROUND, ARE INCLUDED.
IF WANT TO EVER BE SERIOUS WITH ILLUSTRATIONS OR COMIC BOOKS, YOUR PUBLISHER WILL USE SIMILAR SKETCH FOR PRINT PRODUCTION ILLUSTRATION. YOU WILL GET USE TO IT. FOR PROFESIONALS IT IS IMPORTANT.

BOARD – THIS IS A SHEET OF PAPER THAT YOU WILL BE CREATING COMIC BOOKS ON. JUST BEFORE YOU START DRAWING, THE PAPER WILL CONSIST OF A BLEED, PROTECTIVE ZONE AND EDGES – A MIRROR.

BLEED - IF YOUR COMIC BOOK ALWAYS HAS WHITE EDGES, THE BLEED IS NOT NECESSARY. HOWEVER, IF THE DRAWING, AS WITH MODERN COMIC BOOKS, OVERLAPSES THE PAGE EDGES, IT IS NECESSARY TO CREAT A PRINTED EDGE. THIS EDGE WILL NOT EVENTUALLY BE IN THE FINAL VERSION BECAUSE THE PAPER CUTTER WILL CUT IT IN THE PRINTING - OFFICE. WHY TO MAKE IT THEN? BECAUSE DUE TO TODAY´S TECHNOLOGY, NO PRINTER WILL GUARRANTEE THAT THEY CAN CUT OFF THE EDGES COMPLETELY ACCURATELY. SO, FROM TIME TO TIME IT CAN HAPPEN THAT THAT THEY CUT AN IMPORTANT PIECE OF THE DRAWING, OR THEY CAN MISS THE RIGHT MEASUREMENT AND CUT THE BOOK A MILLIMETER BEHIND THE DRAWING. THEN, AN UNPLEASANT THIN WHITE LINE WILL APPEAR. WE DO NOT WANT THIS, OF COURSE. TODAY´S TECHNOLOGY IS REALLY PRECISE BUT IT WILL NOT GUARANTEE LESS THAN 3 MILLIMETRES OF SECURITY SO, IF YOU DO A 5 MILLIMETRE BLEED ON EACH SIDE OF THE BOARD, YOU WILL BE ABSOLUTELLY SURE THAT ANY MISTAKES MADE WILL BE A PRINTER´S MISTAKE.

PROTECTIVE ZONE – FOR THE SAME REASON AS WITH THE BLEED, YOU HAVE TO COUNT ON THE PROTECTIVE ZONE AROUND THE BOARD. THIS PLACE WILL BE SEEN IN THE PRINTED VERSION BECAUSE THE PRINTER CANNOT TECHNICALLY GUARANTEE THAT THE PAPER DOES NOT MOVE BY A MILLIMETRE. NO IMPORTANT THINGS MUST BE IN THIS ZONE. TEXT NOT AT ALL

MIRROR – THIS BOOK HAS DIMENSIONS OF 178 X 254 MM. DUE TO THE BOOK UNIFICATION, THE EDGES ARE SET 10 MILLIMETRES FROM THE EDGE. ALTHOUGH, SOME PICTURES OVERLAP INTO THE BLEED, TEXT AND THE COMIC STORY ARE STUCK TO THIS SETTING. PAGE NUMBERING IS AN EXEPTION. THE MIRROR DIMENSIONS CAN DIFFER DEPENDING ON THE THICKNESS OF THE BOOK, WHERE IT IS CONSIDERED THAT THE EDGE AT THE SPINE OF THE BOOK WILL BE WIDER JUST FOR THE COMFORT OF THE READER OR FOR ESTHETIC REASONS. IN ADDITION, THE THICKER THE BOOK IS, THE MORE LIMITED THE MIRROR IS AT THE SPINE.
BESIDES THE MIRROR, I DREW THE BLEED AND THE EDGES FOR YOU TO MAKE YOU GET USED TO THEM. IF YOU DRAW PROFESSIONALLY, THESE THINGS SHOULD BE A COMPLETE ROUTINE FOR YOU. WE DRAW THESE THINGS WITH A PENCIL IN ORDER TO ERASE THEM EVENTUALLY REALLY EASILY.

Protective zone - no text - 5 mm
Bleed 5 mm

INSIDE OUT

AS I HAVE ALREADY WRITTEN, THIS SKETCH BOOK WILL NOT TEACH YOU THE BASICS OF DRAWING. ON THE OTHER HAND, IT ASSUMES THAT YOU ALREADY MASTER AT LEAST PARTIALLY THE PERSPECTIVE AND PROPORCIONAL DRAWING BECAUSE WE WILL BREAK THE RULES WHICH YOU HAVE ALREADY LEARNT. YOU MAY ASK, WHY DID YOU LEARN THESE RULES TO FORGET THEM NOW? JUST BECAUSE BREAKING THE RULES MUST HAVE PRECISE REASON. WE ARE NOT GOING TO COPY REALITY. WE ARE GOING TO ILLUSTRATE IT AND IT REQUIRES ITS MODIFICATION. I WILL BE HAPPY TO EXPLAIN THIS ISSUE ON DOORS. TRY TO FIND ANY DOOR IN YOUR SURROUNDING AND DRAW THEM THE WAY THEY LOOK.

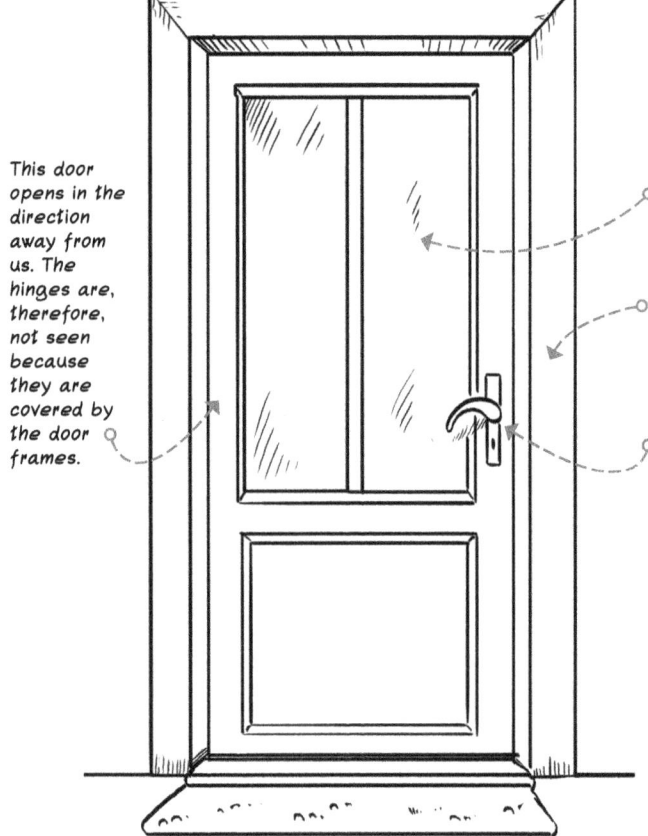

This exercise is the first step to the understanding cartooning. Examine the door, which you will be drawing, thoroughly and note the details of it. Other people will not notice these things but these details and trivial things are extremely important for achieving the photographical truth for the cartoonist.

This door opens in the direction away from us. The hinges are, therefore, not seen because they are covered by the door frames.

The glass should let the space behind the door in or reflect the space in front of it.

The door frames and body of this door are made of wood and painted by a white lacquer. The drawing of the wood fades but we need to notice the shine of the lacquer used and how it reacts on light.

Metal handles and all metallic surfaces and reflect the crooked shape of its surroundings

SHOCK! CARTOONING WILL MAKE US LOSE ALL OF THESE DETAILS. WHY? IF THEY ARE NOT IMPORTANT FOR EXPRESSING THE ATMOSPHERE OR STORY, THEY ARE RATHER UNDESIRABLE. IN CARTOONING, WE RATHER WORK WITH SYMBOLS THAN PICTURES. AND THEREFORE WE HAVE NEUTRAL DOOR WHICH DO NOT PROVIDE US ANY INFORMATION COMPLEMENTING THE STORY. FROM THE CARTOONING POINT OF VIEW, THESE DOORS ARE DRAWN BADLY.

THIS IS WHAT THE DOOR TO MY STUDY LOOKS LIKE. IT IS A COPIED REALITY AND NOTHING INDICATES WHAT OBJECTS ARE BEHIND IT. HOWEVER, WE NEED THE PICTURE TO TELL MORE SO WE DO NOT NEED TO ATTACH ANY TEXT TO IT. HOW DO WE DO THAT? FIRST OF ALL WE NEED TO ANSWER THE FOLLOWING THREE THINGS AND LIKE THIS DEFINE AN ANIMATED PICTURE. YOU WILL NOT FORGET ABOUT THEM BECAUSE YOU WILL NEED THEM, IN CARTOONING, ALL THE TIME. THEY ARE:

1. What is it?
2. What does it look like?
3. What is it used for?

TASK
COME UP WITH A GENEREAL DEFINITION OF A DOOR AND THEN DRAW IT, OR THE ONE YOU HAVE CHOSEN, IN A MANNER TO BE ABLE SEE SOMETHING POSITIVE BEHIND IT, THEN SOMETHING NEGATIVE, THEN SOMETHING MYSTERIOUS OR MAYBE CREEPY. BE CAREFUL! THE DOOR MUST REMAIN CLOSED.
SHOW THE PICTURES TO YOUR FRIENDS THEN AND ASK THEM WHAT IMPRESSION IT GIVES TO THEM. MAKE THEM GUESS WHAT IS BEHND THE DOOR. THEY SHOULD FIND IT OUT. THE KEY IS ON THE NEXT PAGE BUT TRY TO PUZZLE OVER.

DOOR PERSONIFICATION

BEFORE YOU CARRY ON READING, LOOK AT THESE THREE DOORS BELOW. WHICH OF THEM LOOKS POSITIVE AND WHICH NEGATIVE? IF YOUR WERE IN A FAIRY TALE AND YOU WERE TOLD THAT BEHIND SOME DOOR THERE WOULD BE THE ROUND TABLE OF KING ARTHUR, WHICH DOOR YOUR WOULD CHOOSE?

THIS IS ONE OF THE APPROACHES FREQUENTLY USED IN CARTOONING. PERSONIFICATION IS MATCHING A CHARACTER WITH AN UNLIVING OBJECT, NATURAL POWER, ELEMENT OR ANIMAL. THESE PICTURES ARE ONE OF THE SOLUTIONS FROM THE PREVIOUS PAGE. YOU SHOULD ALREADY KNOW WHAT I HAVE DONE WITH THEM.

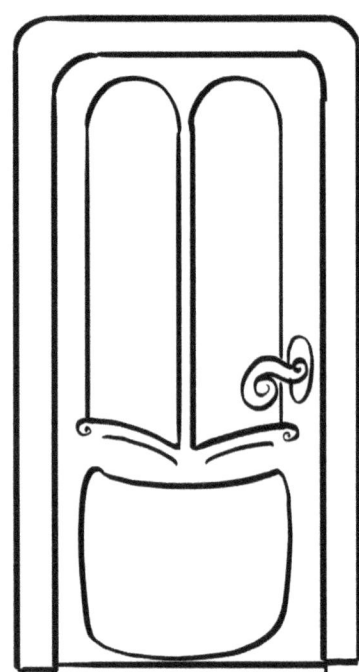 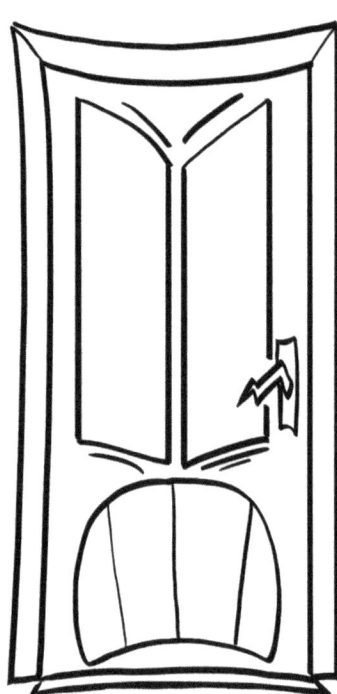 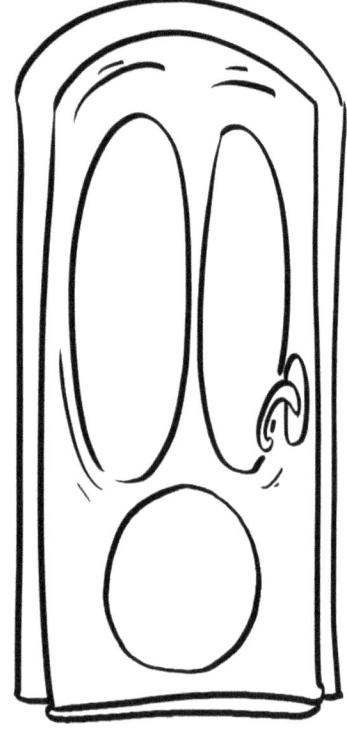

I BET EVERYTHING WHAT I HAVE, THAT YOU OPENED THE FIRST ONE. YOU SHOULD BE COMPLETELY CERTAIN NOW ON HOW I ACHIEVED IT. I MODIFIED THE REALITY IN A WAY THAT IT IS STILL THE DOOR FROM THE PREVIOUS PAGE. AND MATCHED WITH A CHARACTER. I GAVE THEM A FACE TO LET THEM EXPRESSS EMOTIONS. THEREFORE, THE SECOND DOOR FROWNS AT YOU AND LOOKS FURIOUS AND SQUARED. THE THIRD ONE TREMBLES WITH FEAR AND INDICATES THAT THERE IS SOMETHING CREEPY BEHIND. THE FIRST DOOR SMILES AND WELCOMES YOU. IT INVITES YOU TO ENTER.

DISNEY USES THIS TRICK A LOT. LOOK AT THE ANIMATED VERSION OF THE BEAUTY AND BEAST. IT IS A FILM WHEN DISNEYS' MOVIES WERE ALWAYS PIONEERS IN SOMETHING AND USPSCALING THE CARTOONS ONE STEP FORWARD.

Door definition:

1. **What is it?** – A door.
2. **What does it look like?** – It is an entrance to the throne hall / hell / tomb.
3. **What is it used for?** – It is used for connecting or dividing two rooms.

ALWAYS ASK YOURSELF THESE QUESTIONS WHEN YOU DRAW EITHER CLASSIC DRAWINGS OR A CARTOON. THEY WILL HELP YOU UNDERSTAND AN ANIMATED OBJECT.

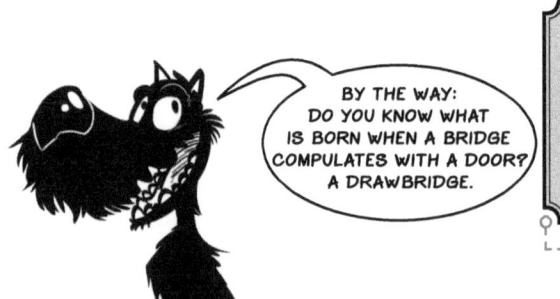

BY THE WAY: DO YOU KNOW WHAT IS BORN WHEN A BRIDGE COMPULATES WITH A DOOR? A DRAWBRIDGE.

TASKS
DRAW A DOOR FROM YOUR SURROUNDINGS AND MATCH IT WITH WITH CHARACTERS JUST LIKE I HAVE DONE IN MY PICTURES.
TRY TO THINK ABOUT HOW YOU WOULD ILLSUTRATE A DOOR, WHICH YOU DO NOT WANT TO OPEN, AND MATCH IT WITH A CHARACTER.

STORY TELLING DOOR

DOORS WHICH, WITHOUT A NEED OF PERSONIFICATION, ALREADY TELL A STORY ARE SEEN BELOW. DOOR, IT IS JUST ONE OF THE INFINITE NUMBER OF SOLUTIONS OF THIS ISSUE.

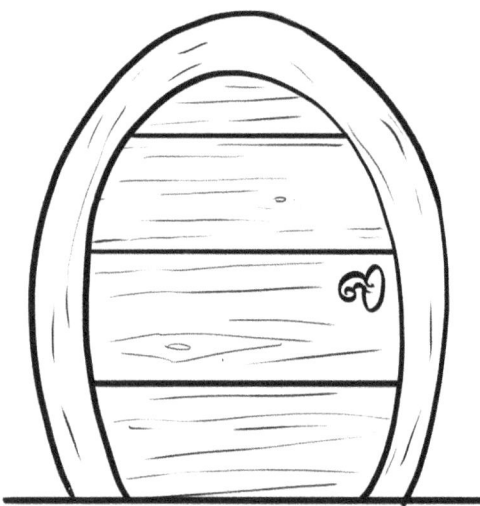

A COMPLETELY NEUTRAL DOOR. BESIDES, IT IS MADE OF WOOD, WE DO NOT ABOSOLUTELY KNOW ANYTHING ABOUT IT. IN ADDITION, WE DO NOT EVEN KNOW WHETHER WE ARE INSIDE OR OUTISDE, WHETHER IT IS LOCKED OR OPENED WITH THE HANDLE. REALLY NOTHING.

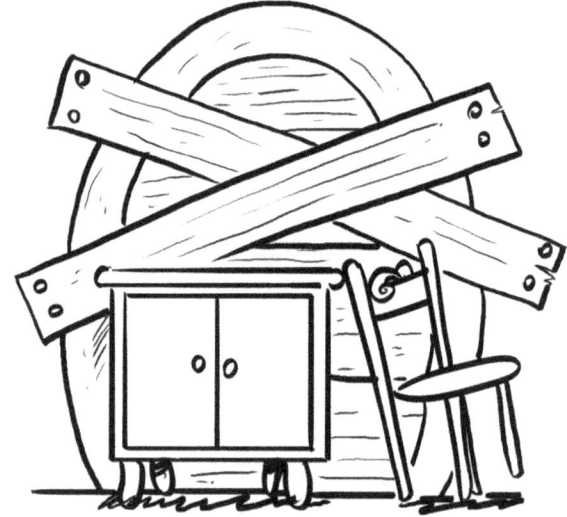

HOWEVER, THIS IS A DIFFERENT STORY. WE STILL DO NOT KNOW MUCH. WHETHER WE ARE STANDING OUTSIDE OR INSIDE, OR WHAT IS BEHIND THE IT. ON THE OTHER HAND WE ARE SURE THAT WE DO NOT WANT ANYTHING BEHIND THE DOOR TO GO THROUGH IT. THIS DOOR HIDES A THREAT. IT TELLS A STORY AND RAISES CURIOSITY.

IMPORTANT NOTE:

DRAW PICTURES WITH THE AGE OF THE READER IN MIND! AS YOU WORK WITH SYMBOLS, YOU HAVE TO CONSIDER THE AGE, CULTURE AND BACKGROUND OF THE SPECTATOR. SYMBOLS BEHAVE LIKE IDIOMS, THEREFORE, BOOKS FOR CHILDREN ARE WRITTEN IN A DIFFERENT MANNER THAN ONES FOR ADULTS. THE SAME THING HAPPENS WITH COMIC BOOKS. LET ME EXPLAIN THIS ON A SIMPLE SENTENCE.

"DADDY WAS SITTING BEHIND A PILE OF NEWSPAPER AND MEANWHILE, MUM WAS PIERCING HIM WITH HER SIGHT."

A CHILD (10+) WHEN HE OR SHE READS THIS, CORRECTLY IMAGINES IMAGES LIKE THIS.

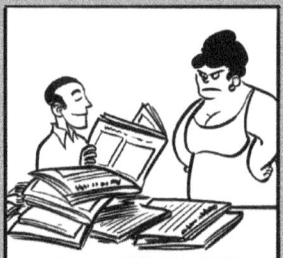

HOWEVER, A CHILD (5-) SEES THIS PICTURES IN THEIR HEAD AND THEY ARE COMPLETELY CONFUSED.*

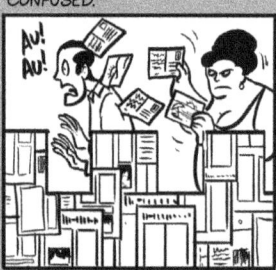

* THIS IS A REALLY EXTREME EXAMPLE, I DO NOT UNDERSTAND KIDS SO MUCH. BUT YOU KNOW WHAT I AM TALKING ABOUT, RIGHT?

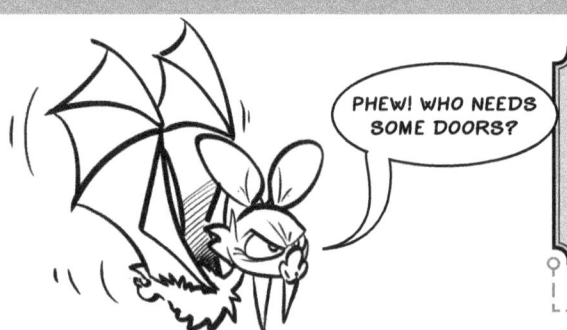

PHEW! WHO NEEDS SOME DOORS?

TASK
LET'S LEAVE THE DOORS. DRAW A CHEST. DRAW MORE OF THEM. ONE WHICH HIDES A PLEASANT SECRET OR, ON THE OTHER HAND, SOMETHING DANGEROUS. OR BOTH! THE KEY IS ON THE NEXT PAGE, BUT FIRST OF ALL TRY IT ON YOUR OWN. THEN SHOW IT TO YOUR FRIENDS, TO SEE IF IT WORKS LIKE YOU HAD INTENDED.

A CHEST WITH NO SECRET

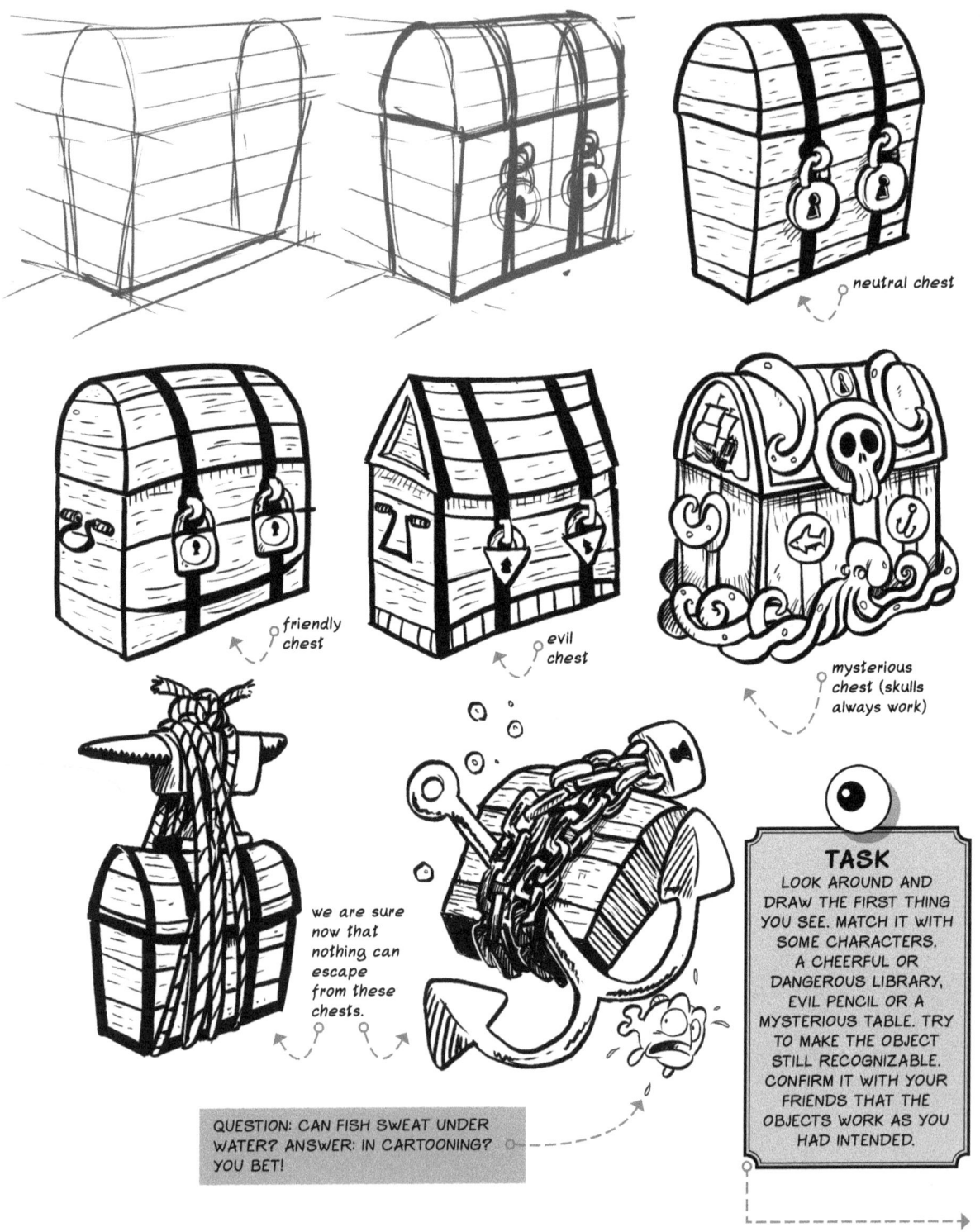

neutral chest

friendly chest

evil chest

mysterious chest (skulls always work)

we are sure now that nothing can escape from these chests.

QUESTION: CAN FISH SWEAT UNDER WATER? ANSWER: IN CARTOONING? YOU BET!

TASK
LOOK AROUND AND DRAW THE FIRST THING YOU SEE. MATCH IT WITH SOME CHARACTERS. A CHEERFUL OR DANGEROUS LIBRARY, EVIL PENCIL OR A MYSTERIOUS TABLE. TRY TO MAKE THE OBJECT STILL RECOGNIZABLE. CONFIRM IT WITH YOUR FRIENDS THAT THE OBJECTS WORK AS YOU HAD INTENDED.

INMEDIATE ENVIRONMENT

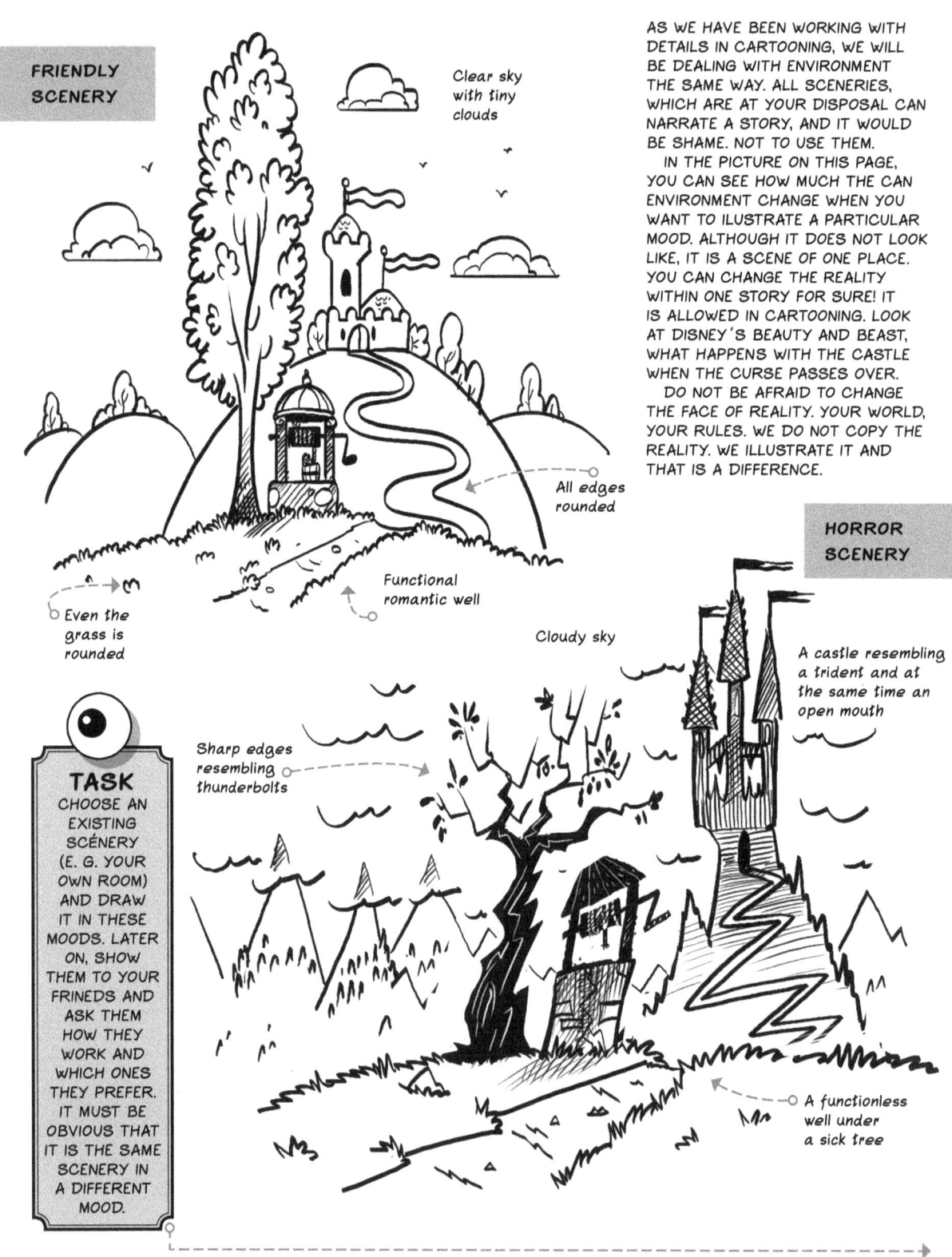

AS WE HAVE BEEN WORKING WITH DETAILS IN CARTOONING, WE WILL BE DEALING WITH ENVIRONMENT THE SAME WAY. ALL SCENERIES, WHICH ARE AT YOUR DISPOSAL CAN NARRATE A STORY, AND IT WOULD BE SHAME. NOT TO USE THEM.

IN THE PICTURE ON THIS PAGE, YOU CAN SEE HOW MUCH THE CAN ENVIRONMENT CHANGE WHEN YOU WANT TO ILUSTRATE A PARTICULAR MOOD. ALTHOUGH IT DOES NOT LOOK LIKE, IT IS A SCENE OF ONE PLACE. YOU CAN CHANGE THE REALITY WITHIN ONE STORY FOR SURE! IT IS ALLOWED IN CARTOONING. LOOK AT DISNEY'S BEAUTY AND BEAST, WHAT HAPPENS WITH THE CASTLE WHEN THE CURSE PASSES OVER.

DO NOT BE AFRAID TO CHANGE THE FACE OF REALITY. YOUR WORLD, YOUR RULES. WE DO NOT COPY THE REALITY. WE ILLUSTRATE IT AND THAT IS A DIFFERENCE.

FRIENDLY SCENERY

Clear sky with tiny clouds

All edges rounded

Even the grass is rounded

Functional romantic well

HORROR SCENERY

Cloudy sky

Sharp edges resembling thunderbolts

A castle resembling a trident and at the same time an open mouth

A functionless well under a sick tree

TASK
CHOOSE AN EXISTING SCÉNERY (E. G. YOUR OWN ROOM) AND DRAW IT IN THESE MOODS. LATER ON, SHOW THEM TO YOUR FRINEDS AND ASK THEM HOW THEY WORK AND WHICH ONES THEY PREFER. IT MUST BE OBVIOUS THAT IT IS THE SAME SCENERY IN A DIFFERENT MOOD.

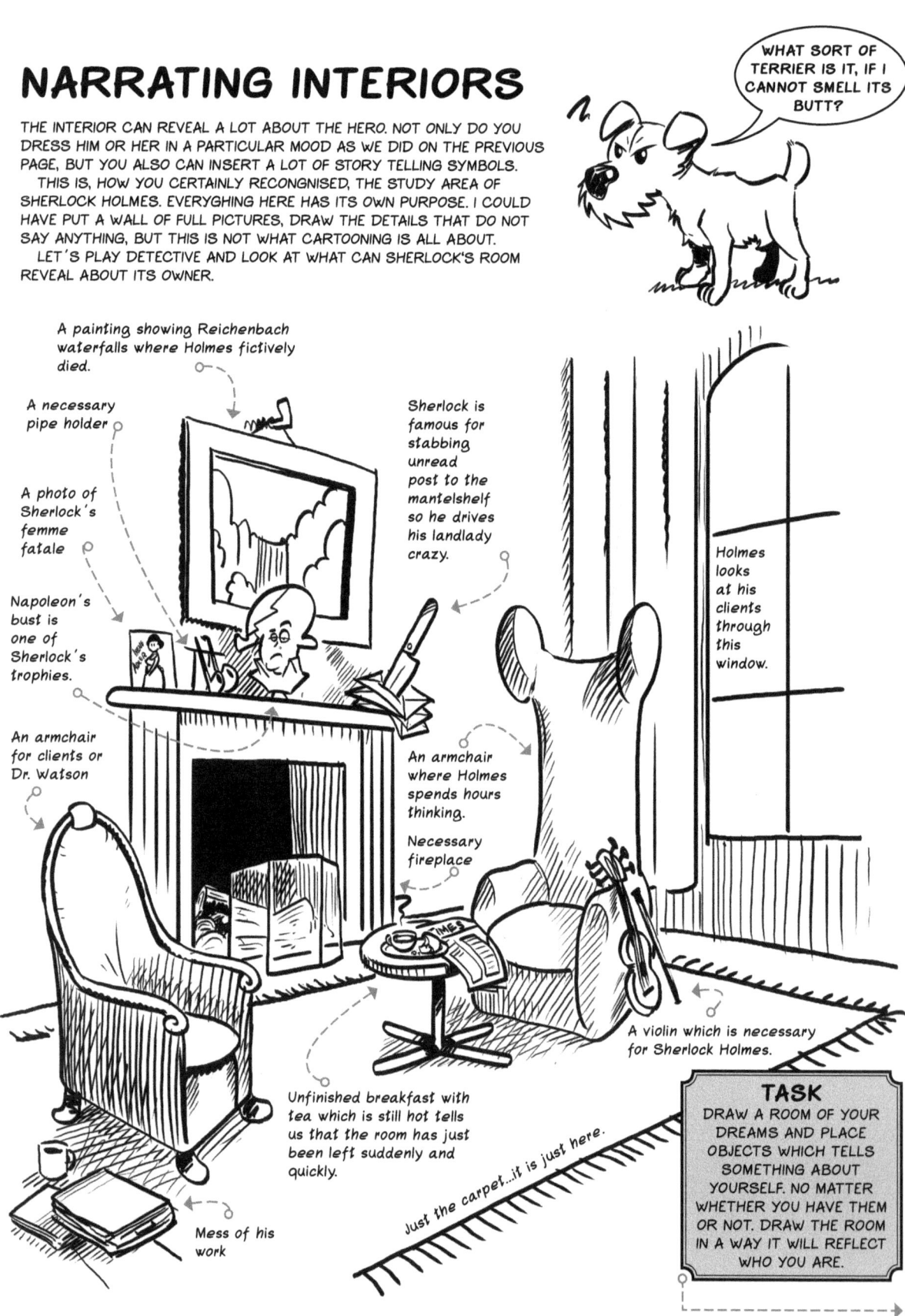

SOMETHING ABOUT PERSPECTIVE

THIS AND THE FOLLOWING CHAPTER SHOULD HAVE NOT BEEN IN THIS BOOK BECAUSE ITS PURPOSE IS NOT TO TEACH YOU HOW TO DRAW. MY AMBITION IS TO TEACH YOU HOW TO NARRATE WITH PICTURES. THEREFORE I SUPPOSE THAT YOU ALREADY MASTER THE BASICS AS THE PERSPECTIVE. NEVERTHELESS, WHEN I TESTED THIS BOOK ON MY WORKSHOPS, I FOUND THAT MY PUPILS ARE ON VARIOUS LEVELS OF MASTERING THE CRAFT, SO I DIVIDED THEM INTO TWO GROUPS. FIRST GROUP WAS BEFORE UNDESRTANDING THE PERSPECTIVE, AND THE OTHER ONE, AFTER UNDERSTANDING. AS THE PERSPECTIVE WAS SOMETHING LIKE INITIATION. **UNDERSTANDING THE PESRPECTIVE, FOR CARTOONISTS, IS THE BASICS OF PERCEPTION OF THREE-DIMENSIONAL SPACE IN A PICTURE.** IF DO NOT GET THE PREVIOUS SENTENCE, CLOSE THIS BOOK AND GO PRACTISE THE PERSPECTIVE. ON YOUTUBE, YOU WILL FIND A MILLION TUTORIALS AS HOW TO DO IT. IN THESE TWO CHAPTERS, I CAN EXPLAIN TO YOU THAT SOME PERSPECTIVE EXISTS. THOSE OF YOU WHO ARE MORE ADVANCED CAN TRY THE TASKS WHICH I GIVE TO YOU. FOR THE REST OF YOU, I ORDER YOU TO SELF-STUDY!

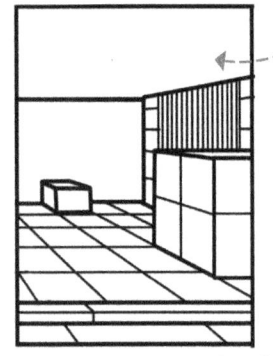

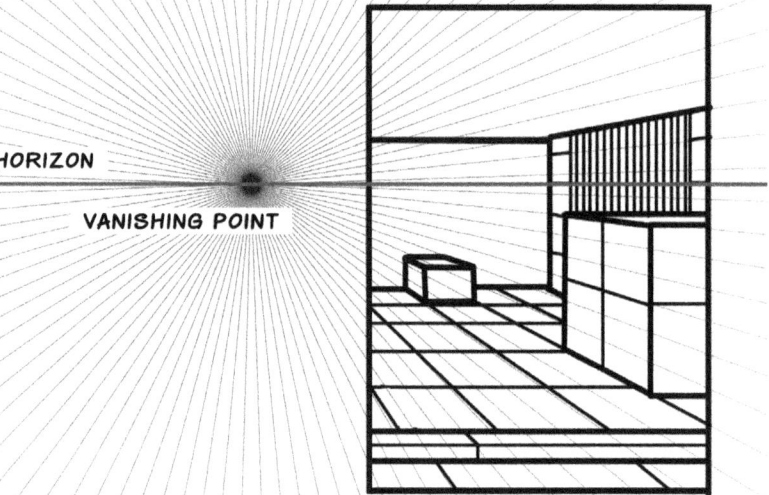

LET'S SAY THAT WE NEED A PICTURE OF THIS ROOM. AS YOU CAN SEE, ALL ITEMS SUCCUMB TO SPACE PERSPECTIVE AND CREATE AN ILLUSION OF THREE-DIMENSIONAL SPACE. THIS IS THE EASIEST PERSPECTIVE AND IT IS NOT HARD TO ACHIEVE IT IF YOU KNOW HOW TO DO IT. SO, HOW DO WE ACHIEVE IT SO THAT ALL ITEMS FIT IN THE INTERIOR AND DO NOT LOOK WEIRD?

START WITH OUTLINING THE HORIZON. IT IS A STRAIGHT LINE AT THE LEVEL OF THE EYE SIGHT OF A WATCHER.

THEN WE DETERMINE THE VANISHING POINT. IT IS A PLACE WHERE ALL LINES COME TOGETHER AT A RIGHT ANGLE TO THE WATCHER. LIKE YOU STAY ON A RAILWAY AND YOU SEE THE RAILS COME TOGETHER IN THE DISTANCE. IN THIS PICTURE, THE VANISHING POINT IS OUT OF THE PICTURE AND THIS IS QUITE COMMON.

NOW YOU CAN HAPPILY DRAW ANY ITEM. DO NOT FORGET THAT ALL SHAPES WILL SUCCUMB TO THIS DISTORTION. IF YOU HAVE NOT USED THE PERSPECTIVE UNTIL NOW, YOU PICTURES WILL SUDDENLY JUMP UP A COUPLE OF LEVELS. BE CAREFUL THOUGH. BEGINNERS OFTEN FORGET THAT NOT ONLY THINGS, BUT ALSO LIVING BEINGS SUCCUMB TO THE PERSCPECTIVE. SEE THE PICTURES BELOW. MEANWHILE, IN THE SECOND PICTURE, THERE IS ROBIN DEPENDING ON THE PERSPECTIVE, DRAWN CORRECTLY, IN THE FIRST PICTURE HE SEEMS LIKE HE DOES FIT IN THERE. LIKE HE HAS BEEN ADDED FROM A DIFFERENT PICTURE. IT IS JUST BECAUSE ALL ITEMS IN THE PICTURE MUST BE IN COMPLIANCE WITH THE PERSPECTIVE. IN OTHER WORDS, IF YOU CREATE A SPACE, YOU MUST CREATE ALL CHARACTERS UNDER SAME CONDITIONS.

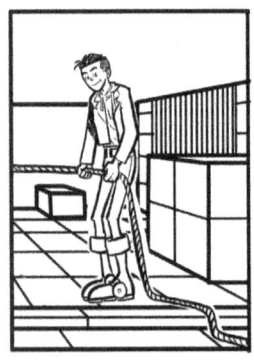 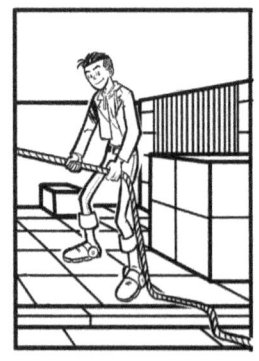 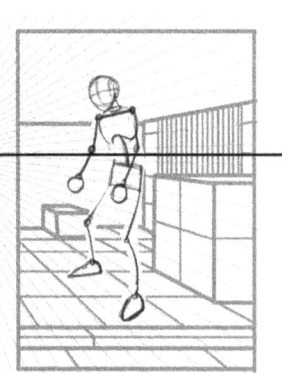

TASK
DRAW YOUR ROOM AGAIN WITH THE FOCUS ON PERSPECTIVE.

Board 30

SOMETHING MORE ABOUT PERSPECTIVE

YOU MIGHT CORRECLY ASSUME THAT NOT EVERYTHING CAN BE ABOUT PERSPECTIVE. THIS WHOLE TEXTBOOK COULD BE ABOUT PERSPECTIVE AND IT STILL WOULD NOT COVER THE ENTIRE TOPIC. IN THE PICTURE BELOW, YOU CAN SEE HOW IT IS DONE, WHEN WE WANT TO TURN THE OBJECT TO THE VIEWER IN A DIFFERENT WAY THAN BY ITS STRAIGHT EDGE.AS WE SAW ON THE PREVIOUS PAGE. IN THIS CASE, THERE WILL BE TWO VANISHING POINTS. BOTH OF THEM WILL BE LOCATED ON THE SAME HORIZON LINE.

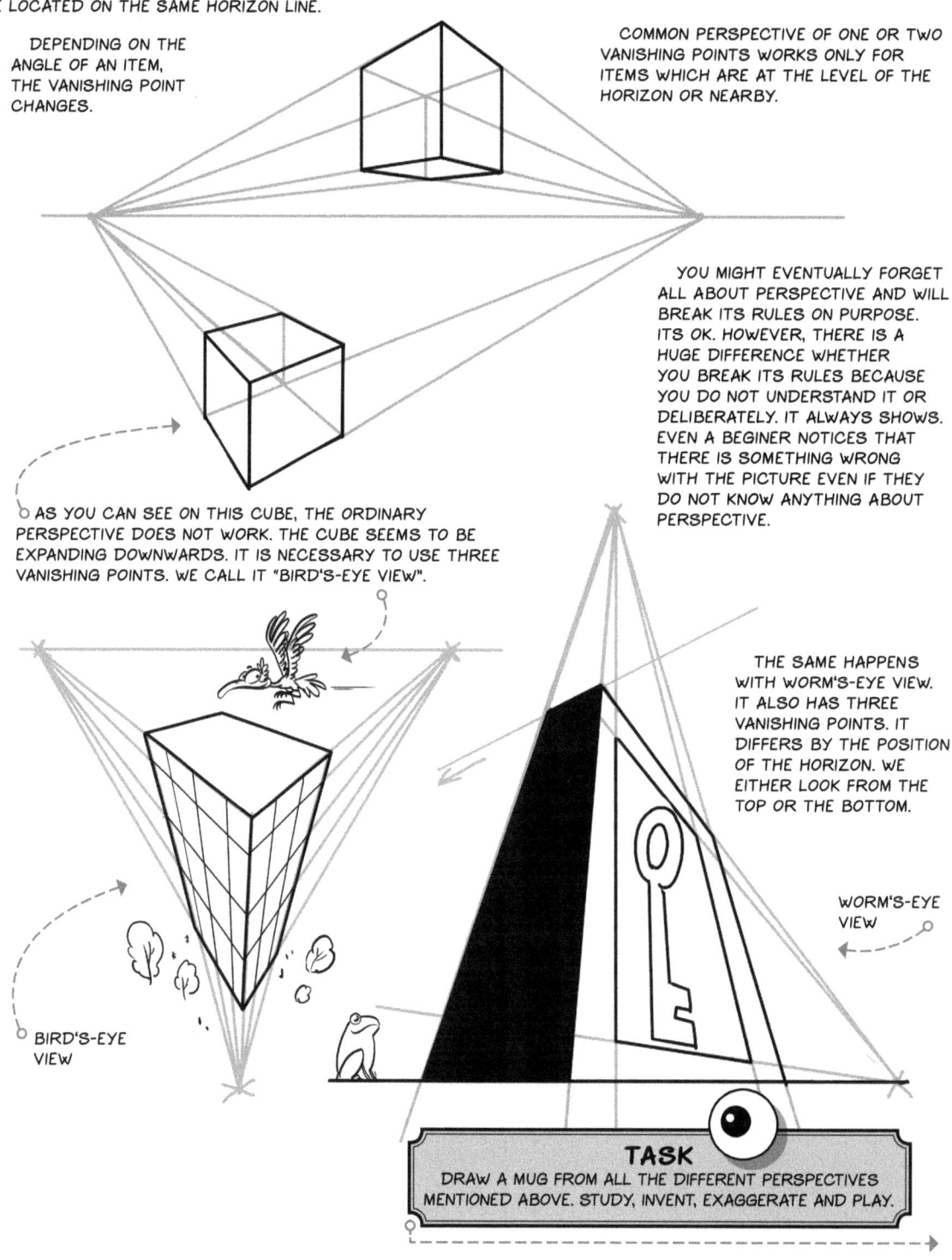

DEPENDING ON THE ANGLE OF AN ITEM, THE VANISHING POINT CHANGES.

COMMON PERSPECTIVE OF ONE OR TWO VANISHING POINTS WORKS ONLY FOR ITEMS WHICH ARE AT THE LEVEL OF THE HORIZON OR NEARBY.

AS YOU CAN SEE ON THIS CUBE, THE ORDINARY PERSPECTIVE DOES NOT WORK. THE CUBE SEEMS TO BE EXPANDING DOWNWARDS. IT IS NECESSARY TO USE THREE VANISHING POINTS. WE CALL IT "BIRD'S-EYE VIEW".

YOU MIGHT EVENTUALLY FORGET ALL ABOUT PERSPECTIVE AND WILL BREAK ITS RULES ON PURPOSE. ITS OK. HOWEVER, THERE IS A HUGE DIFFERENCE WHETHER YOU BREAK ITS RULES BECAUSE YOU DO NOT UNDERSTAND IT OR DELIBERATELY. IT ALWAYS SHOWS. EVEN A BEGINER NOTICES THAT THERE IS SOMETHING WRONG WITH THE PICTURE EVEN IF THEY DO NOT KNOW ANYTHING ABOUT PERSPECTIVE.

THE SAME HAPPENS WITH WORM'S-EYE VIEW. IT ALSO HAS THREE VANISHING POINTS. IT DIFFERS BY THE POSITION OF THE HORIZON. WE EITHER LOOK FROM THE TOP OR THE BOTTOM.

BIRD'S-EYE VIEW

WORM'S-EYE VIEW

TASK
DRAW A MUG FROM ALL THE DIFFERENT PERSPECTIVES MENTIONED ABOVE. STUDY, INVENT, EXAGGERATE AND PLAY.

INTRODUCTION TO ARCHETYPES

EVERYTHING THAT WE HAVE BEEN LEARNING ABOUT PERSONIFICATION OF THINGS UNTIL NOW ALSO WORKS WITH CHARACTERS THAT WE WILL BE USING IN OUR COMICS.

NOW SERIOUSLY. AS WE SAID, THE INSIDE-OUT RULE ALSO WORKS IN CARTOONING. IT IS A BIT MORE COMPLICATED WITH CHARACTERS. PEOPLE, UNLIKE THINGS, CAN TELL LIES. SO WE NEED TO EXPRESS THIS DIFFERENCE.

HOWEVER, IN ANY CASE, WE WILL BE WORKING WITH A TERM CALLED **ARCHETYPE**. WHAT DOES IT MEAN?

ARCHETYPE IS A TYPICAL CHARACTER, IMAGINATION OR A STORY OF A PARTICULAR GENRE. WE BASICALLY FOCUS ON CHARACTERS, SO LET'S FOCUS ON THEM.

THIS DOES NOT WORK IN REAL LIFE, SO DO NOT APPLY ARCHETYPES ON REAL PEOPLE, PLEASE. DO NOT CONFUSE ARCHETYPES WITH STEREOTYPES. MEANWHILE, IN COMIC BOOKS, A WEAK NERD IS USUALLY SLEEK AND SLENDER, A BIG MUSCLED GUY IS A STUPID DUMMY. IN REAL LIFE YOU COULD GET INTO HOT WATER WITH SOMEONE FOR THIS. SO BE CAREFUL.

IN CARTOONING, WE EXPRESS THE INSIDE NATURE OF CHARACTERS ON THEIR OUTER LOOK. IT IS IN CONTRADICTION ONLY WHEN IT IS THE INTENTION OF THE STORY (IN A DETECTIVE STORY THE MURDERER WILL BE THE LEAST SUSPECTED ONE).

A CHARACTER SHOULD BE PREDICTABLE. WHEN YOU LOOK AT A POINTED HAT, MAGIC STAFF AND LONG BEARD, YOU AUTOMATICALLY SAY: "A WIZARD!" WHEN YOU SEE A BEAUTIFUL GIRL WITH LONG BLOND HAIR AND A CROWN ON HER HEAD, YOU PROBABLY WOULD NOT SAY: "THAT'S AN EVIL WITCH."

AND THIS IS HOW CARTOONING WORKS. NICE AND SIMPLE. ARCHETYPES ARE MADE NOT ONLY OF THEIR ATRIBUTES (THINGS AND SYMBOLS) BUT ALSO BY THE CHARACTER PHYSIOLOGY. ALL OF THAT ALSO DEPENDS ON THEIR POLARITY. IT MEANS WHETHER THEY ARE GOOD OR EVIL. YOU DRAW A GOOD DRAGON DIFFERENTLY FROM AN EVIL ONE. CARTOONING DEALS WITH ALL OF THAT.

IN ORDER TO GO THROUGH ALL ARCHETYPES, THIS BOOK WOULD HAVE TO HAVE AT LEAST A MILLION ISSUES. I WILL TRY TO SHOW YOU SOME BASIC ONES AND THEN IT IS UP TO YOU IF YOU STUDY OTHER ONES.

FIRST OF ALL, HOWEVER, WE WILL DO SOMETHING ELSE. WE WILL COME UP WITH OUR MAIN HERO WHO WILL BECOME THE GUIDE THROUGH THIS BOOK.

> ### TASK
> COME UP WITH A CHARACTER OF A NEUTRAL HERO. THEY MUST BE UNBIASED BECAUSE WE WANT OUR READER TO IDENTIFY WITH THEM EASILY. THE HERO MUST INCLINE TO NEITHER GOOD NOR EVIL. WE WILL BE ABLE TO SEND THEM TO SPACE, DEEP OCEANS, WILD WEST OR DESERTED ISLANDS. IF THEY ARE NOT BURDENED WITH THEIR PAST AND AFFECTED BY THEIR CHARACTER OR LOOK, WE WILL CREATE A UNIVERSAL CHARACTER FOR ANY ADVENTURE.
>
> I LIKE EXPLAINING THIS ISSUE ON HERGÉ'S TINTIN. HOW COME THAT ALL CHARACTERS OF HIS ADVENTURES ARE SO PRECISELY PSYCHOLOGICALLY AND VISUALLY DESCRIBED AND THE MAIN HERO DOES NOT HAVE STRONG QUALITIES? EVEN HIS FACE IS JUST OUTLINED AS IF HE WOULD HAVE AN EMOJI ICON INSTEAD. IT INFORMS US ABOUT HIS MOOD BUT NOT ABOUT HIS LOOK. WHY DID HERGÉ DO IT THIS WAY? WHEN I, AS A READER, READ TINTIN, I AM TINTIN. TINTIN DOES NOT NEED HIS PAST, HE HAS MINE. HE DOES NOT NEED A FACE BECAUSE I KNOW HOW I LOOK. I JUST WANT THE INFORMATION ABOUT HIS MOOD AND HERGÉ MAKES THIS TASK REALLY ILLUSTRATIVELY. DO YOU ALREADY UNDERSTAND WHAT I ASK FROM YOU? FIRST OF ALL, TRY IT ON YOUR OWN.
>
> THE HERO SHOULD BE YOUNG BUT NOT OF A SPECIFIC AGE. IDEALLY, SOMEWHERE BETWEEN 16 AND 30 YEARS OLD. ANYTHING THAT WOULD DETERMINE THEIR NATURE MUST BE LEFT OUT OR BALANCED. THAT MEANS CLOTHES, FIGURE AND FACE. EVERYTHING IS NEUTRAL. THEY CAN ALSO HAVE ANY SUPERIOR ABILITIES. THAT DOES NOT CONTRADICT OUR GOAL. THE CHARACTER SHOULD NOT BE THAT EASY AND THEIR FACE THAT SIMPLE. WE NEED THE READER TO IDENTIFY WITH THEM AS MUCH AS POSSIBLE.
>
> P.S.: YOU CAN OBVIOUSLY CREATE A HEROINE! IT IS UP TO YOU! IT IS YOUR CHARACTER!

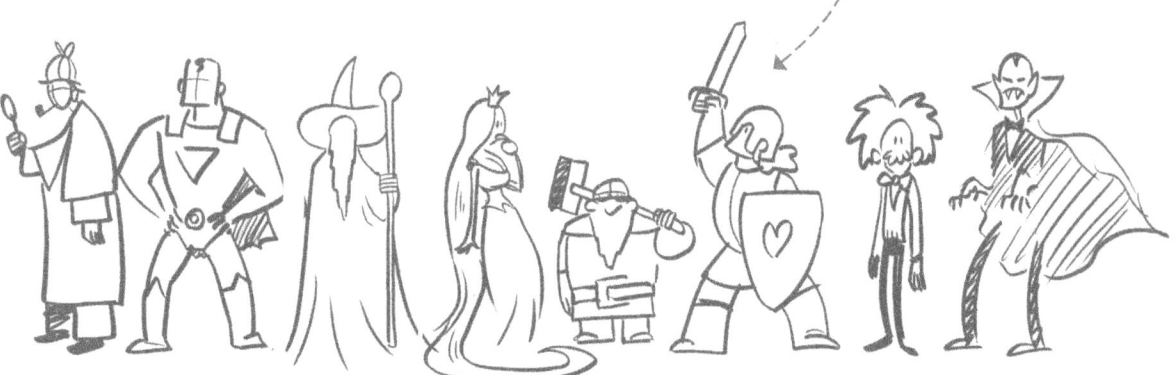

Just from these brief sketches, we can recognise the outlined archetypes.

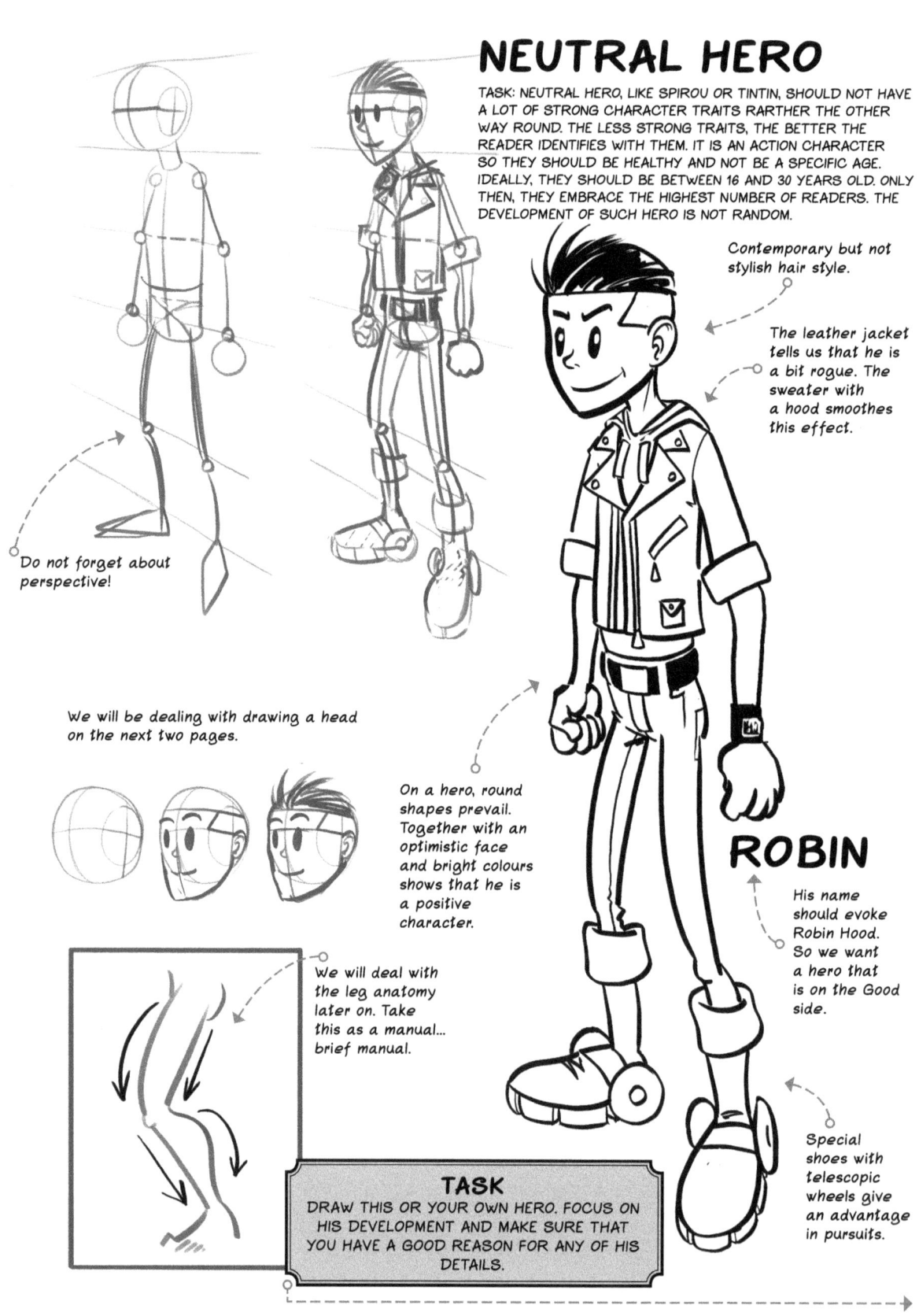

ROBIN'S HEAD

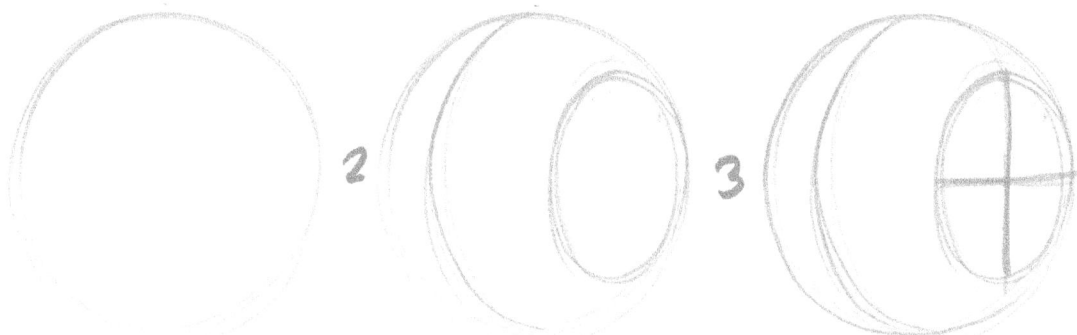

1. We make a rough draft really softly. Start with the most precise circle possible. Try to draw it just with your hand.

2. Now the more difficult part comes. Imagine the circle as a sphere, then divide it in the middle and cut it on the sides.

3. Draw a cross on the cut part according to the head inclination. Our head will be inclined from a half profile and will be looking ahead, so the cross on the side is straight.

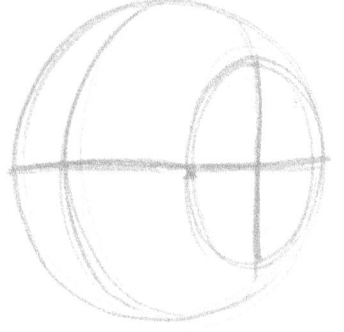
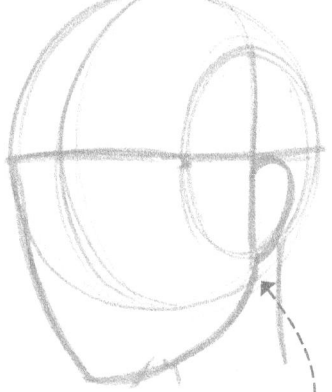
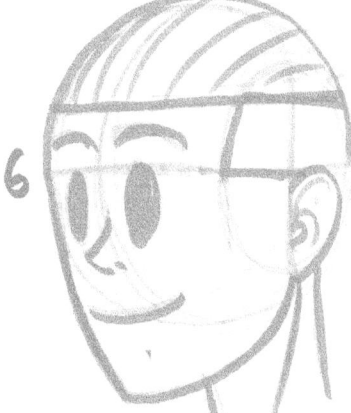

4. Add a line which crosses both hemispheres.

5. Mark the chin by two curves. It will go from the bottom ends of the cross on the sides. You can already mark the ear and neck.

6. Now we can create the face...

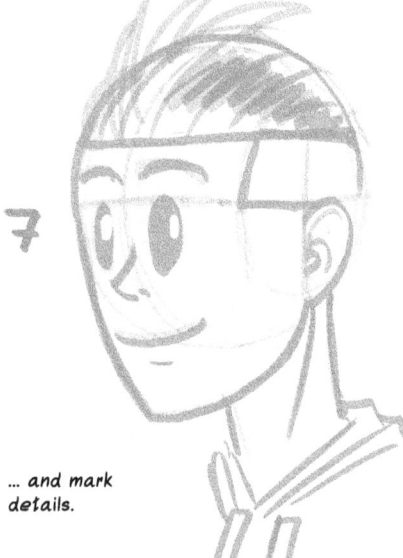
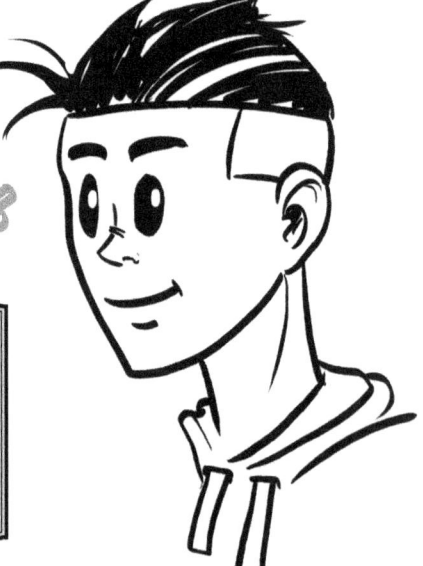

7. ... and mark details.

Outline the contours with ink or marker and rubber the pencil.

TASK
DRAW ROBIN OR YOUR OWN HERO'S HEAD. BE THOROUGH. IN THE NEXT LESSON WE WILL FIND OUT IF THE SHAPE WORKS.

Board 38

MAIN ANGLES OF A HEAD

THE DEVELOPMENT OF A CHARACTER'S APPEARANCE IS NOT THAT SIMPLE, ESPECIALLY IN CARTOONING. IT IS A REALLY TRICKY THING. YOU WILL OFTEN COME UP WITH A BEAUTIFUL FACE BUT IF YOU DO NOT TRY TO DRAW FROM DIFFERENT ANGLES, YOU WILL SOON REALISE THAT YOUR HERO SOMETIMES LOOKS LIKE SOMEBODY COMPLETELY DIFFERENT EVEN IF YOU KEEP THE DIMENSIONS OR, YOU CANNOT DRAW HIM FROM THE FRONT BECAUSE HIS BIG NOSE WILL COVER HIS EYES. HAVE YOU EVER THOUGHT WHY YOU KNOW ASTERIX JUST IN PROFILE, FROM THE BACK OR HALF PROFILE... BUT YOU WILL HARDLY EVER SEE HIM FROM THE FRONT? IN ORDER TO GET OVER THESE OBSTACLES, TRY TO DRAW YOUR CHARACTER FROM ALL POSSIBLE ANGLES. YOU WILL BECOME AWARE OF ALL POSSIBLE ISSUES.

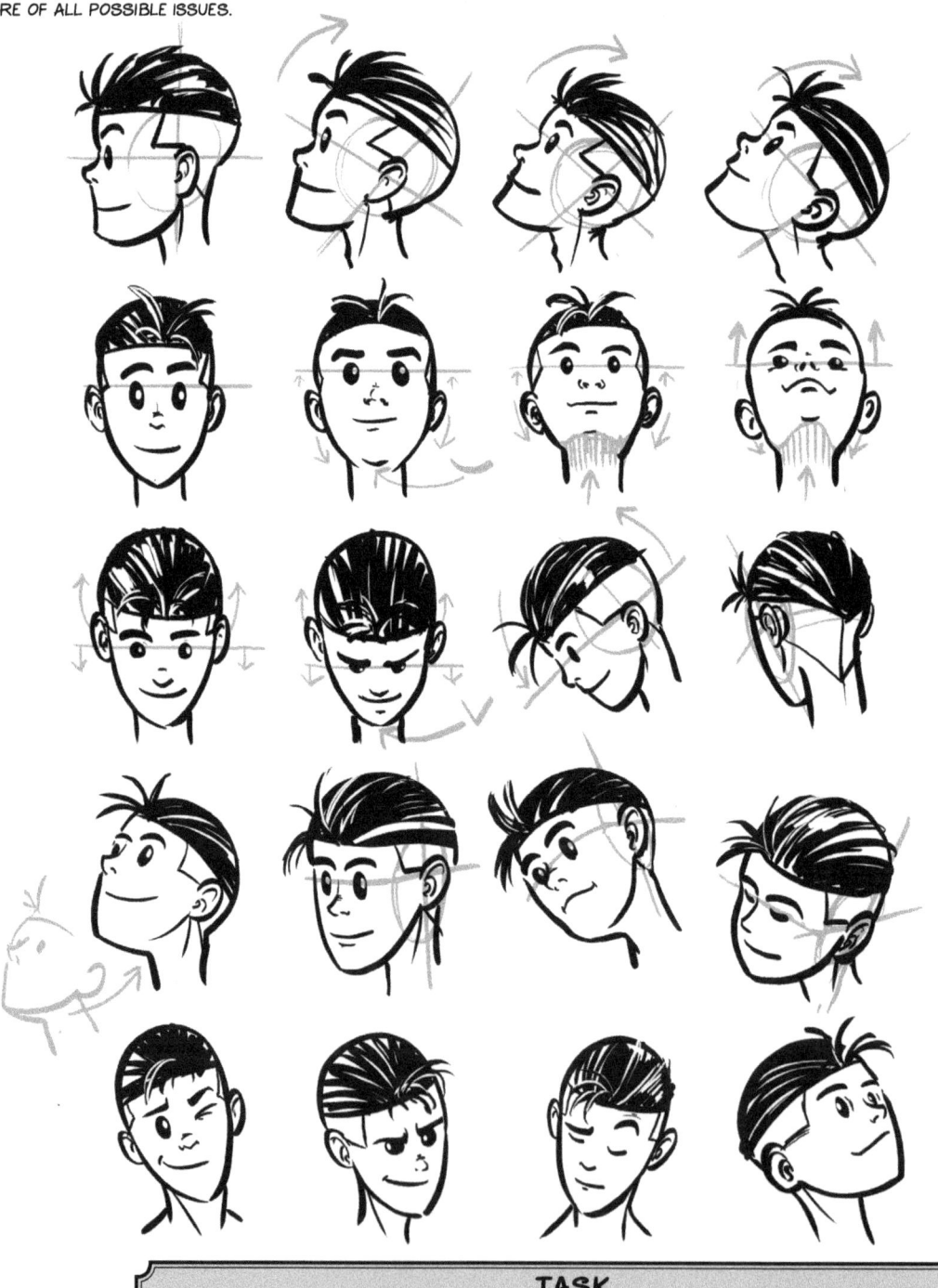

TASK
DRAW ROBIN OR YOUR OWN HERO'S HEAD FROM ALL POSSIBLE ANGLES.

TABLOID REVELATION OF AN EYBALL

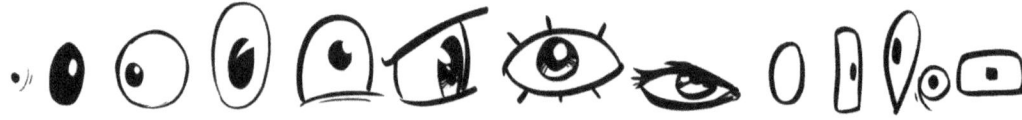

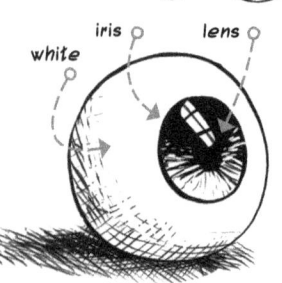

THERE ARE A LOT OF POSSIIBLE EYEBALL ILLUSTRATIONS. IT IS A QUESTION OF STYLE AND FASHION. IN COMICS, WE CAN EVEN COMBINE MORE APPROACHES (E. G. SPIROU OR LUCKY LUCK). HOWEVER, I DO NOT RECOMMEND COMBINING THAN TWO APPROACHES, AND IN ANY CASE, MORE APPROACHES ON ONE HEAD.

CENTURIES AGO, CLASSICAL PAINTERS DISCOVERED THAT AN EYEBALL IS AN ESSENTIAL CENTRE OF A PORTRAIT.

IN ADDITION, THEY FOUND OUT WHY. THE VIEW OF A SPECTATOR IS SUBCONCIOUSLY ATTRACTED TO THE HIGHEST CONTRAST IN THE PAINTING, AND THAT IS NATURALY THE EYBALL OF THE PERSON PORTRAYED WHICH IS REALLY DESIRABLE, OF COURSE. THIS IS WHY, EVEN IF THE PORTRAYED PERSON WEARS A LOT OF GOLD OR DIAMONDS, THE STRONGEST SHINE IS IN THEIR EYES THIS RULE IS WELL KNOWN BY TODAY'S PROFESSIONALS, SO THEY THOROUGHLY RETOUCH THE SHINE ON THE JEWELS AND CUFFLINGS ON THEIR MODELS.

LOOKING AT SOMEBODY'S EYES FROM A SHORT DISTANCE IS LIKE WATCHING FLAMES OR GLIMMERING WATER HOWEVER, WHAT MAKES AN EYE SO CONTRASTING? HOW COME WE FIND SHINE EVEN IN ITS DARKEST PLACE? HOW IS IT POSSIBLE?

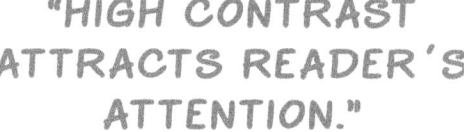

"HIGH CONTRAST ATTRACTS READER'S ATTENTION."

Let´s start with a sphere. Even if an eyeball is not a perfect sphere, it does not matter now. It is about the principle. Firstly, we determine where the light comes from and we shade the sphere.

We must imagine the iris such as a deep plate impressed in the eyeball. As a bitten apple.

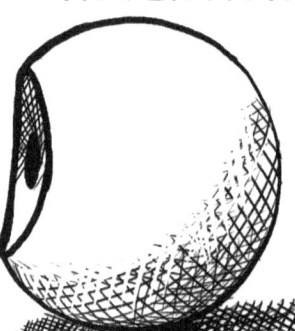

The cornea covers this plate, which complements the round shape of the eye that was taken by the plate. It is like a lid made of glass which darkens the iris a bit.

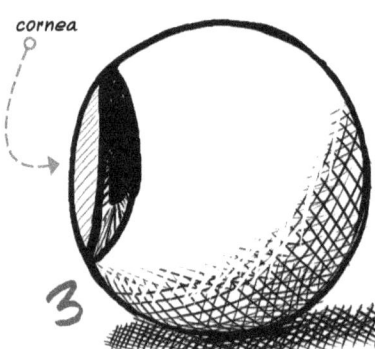

THE SHAPE OF IRIS NATURALLY CASTS A SHADOW OVER A PLACE WHERE THE CORNEA CONCENTRATES A SHARP LIGHT REFLECTION.

This is how a required contrast emerges, which makes the eye a hypnotically beautiful thing.

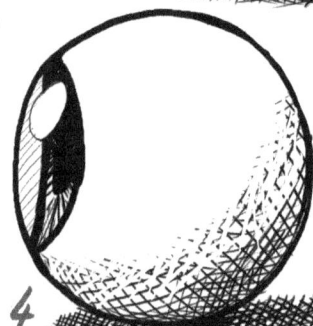

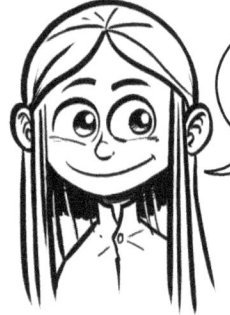

YOU HAVE JUST CAUGHT MORGAN GHOSTREING'S EYE!

TASK
DRAW AN EYBALL FROM A SHORT DISTANCE AND THEN TRY TO DEVELOP YOUR OWN STYLE OF YOUR COMIC HEROES' EYES. THEY ARE THE MOST IMPORANTANT PART OF A FACE AND IF YOU DRAW THEM WELL, THEIR EYES WILL BE THE FIRST THING THE READER WILL NOTICE IN YOUR PICTURES. HOWEVER, IT'S ALL UP TO YOU.

FROM THE CRADDLE TO THE GRAVE

AGE TRAITS RECOGNISING IS A BASIC SKILL OF A CARTOONIST. IN ONE SUBJECT, LET'S TAKE A LOOK AT THE MAIN ONES THAT PUTS A PERSON INTO SOME AGE CATEGORIES.

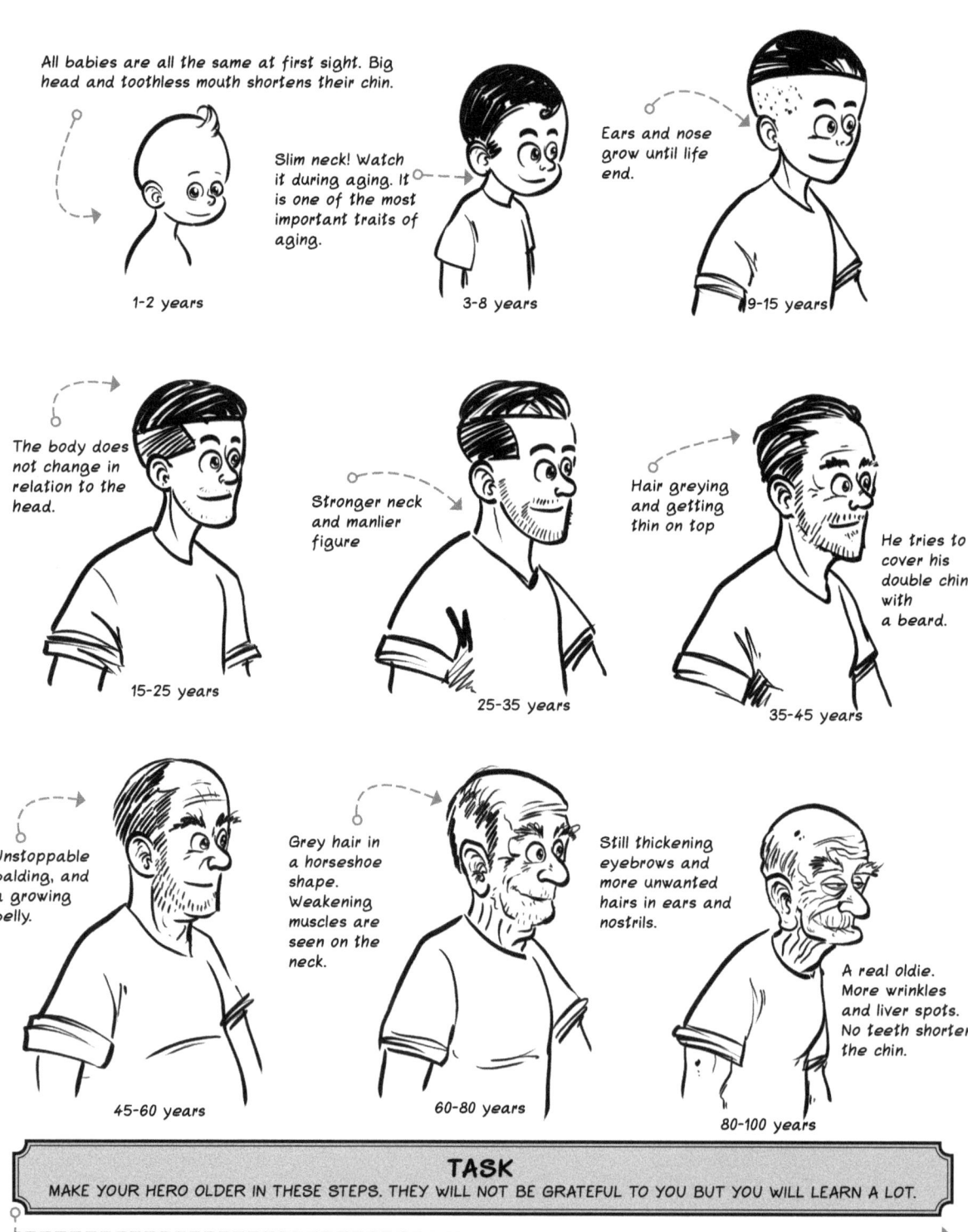

TASK
MAKE YOUR HERO OLDER IN THESE STEPS. THEY WILL NOT BE GRATEFUL TO YOU BUT YOU WILL LEARN A LOT.

DRAWING AN ARM

AS I HAVE MENTIONED, JUST THE FACT THAT WE WILL BE DEALING WITH CARTOONING DOES NOT LIBERATE YOU FROM A NEED OF STUDYING CLASSICAL DRAWINGS. CARTOONING IS SIMPLIFICATION. YOU CANNOT SIMPLIFY SOMETHING THAT YOU DO NOT UNDERSTAND. LET'S GET DOWN TO BUSINESS! DRAW AND STUDY MUSCLES EVEN THOUGH YOU MIGHT EVENTUALLY DRAW ARMS THIS WAY.

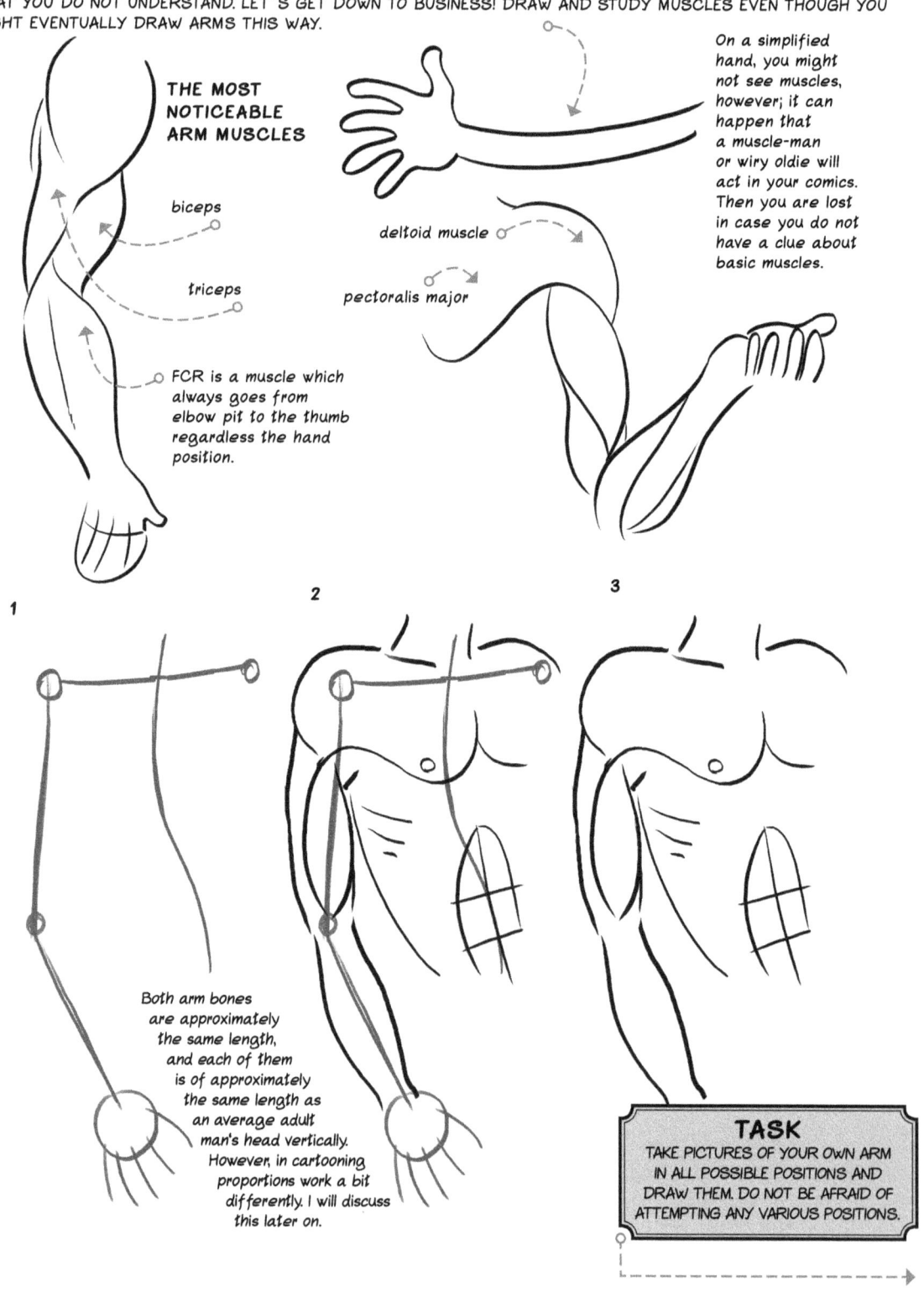

THE MOST NOTICEABLE ARM MUSCLES

biceps

triceps

deltoid muscle

pectoralis major

FCR is a muscle which always goes from elbow pit to the thumb regardless the hand position.

On a simplified hand, you might not see muscles, however; it can happen that a muscle-man or wiry oldie will act in your comics. Then you are lost in case you do not have a clue about basic muscles.

Both arm bones are approximately the same length, and each of them is of approximately the same length as an average adult man's head vertically. However, in cartooning proportions work a bit differently. I will discuss this later on.

TASK
TAKE PICTURES OF YOUR OWN ARM IN ALL POSSIBLE POSITIONS AND DRAW THEM. DO NOT BE AFRAID OF ATTEMPTING ANY VARIOUS POSITIONS.

Board 46

EVERYTHING IS IN PALMS

PALMS ARE ONE OF THE MOST IMPORTANT PARTS OF YOUR CHARACTERS. HERE, BE EXTREMELY CAREFUL SO THAT THE GESTURES WOULD LOOK NATURAL. OF COURSE, YOU NEED TO STUDY THE CLASSICAL DRAWINGS OF A HAND SO THAT YOU COULD ADVANCE TO ADEQUATE STYLISATION SOME CARTOONISTS SIMPLIFY THE HAND BY DRAWING JUST 4 FINGERS. I DO NOT HAVE ANYTHING AGAINST IT. HOWEVER, I HAVE ALWAYS CLINGED TO FIVE.

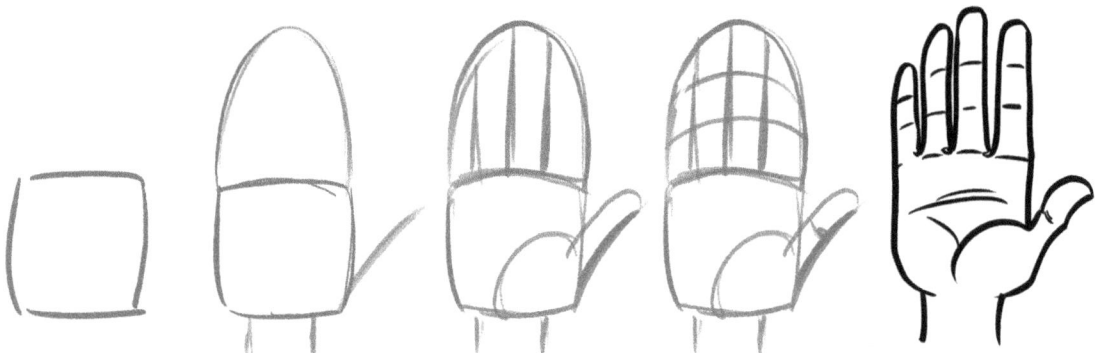

I ALWAYS START WITH A SQUARE AND THEN ADD PARTS OF THE HAND AS YOU CAN SEE IN THE PICTURES. I ALWAYS GO FROM THE SIMPLE TO THE MORE DIFFICULT. JUST LIKE THIS YOU MAKE SURE THAT YOU DID NOT MAKE A MISTAKE AT THE BEGINNING.

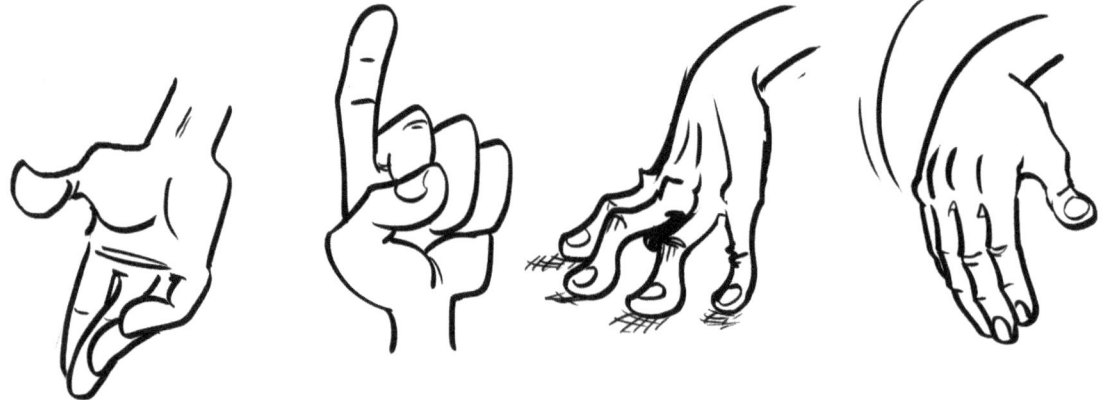

YOU MUST DRAW HUNDREDS OR THOUSANDS OF HANDS UNTIL YOU FIND OUT HOW THEY REALLY WORK. THE MOMENT YOU GET FAMILIAR WITH THAT, YOU WILL NEVER FORGET IT.

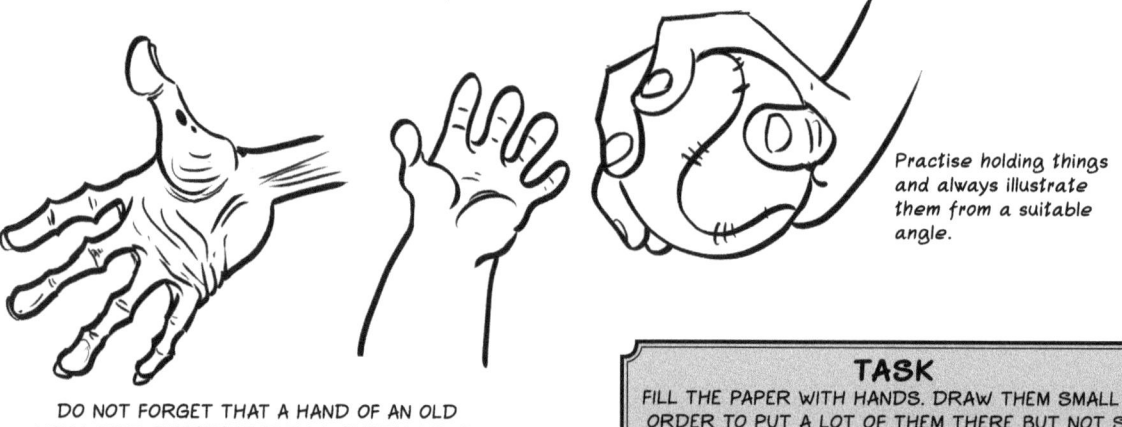

Practise holding things and always illustrate them from a suitable angle.

DO NOT FORGET THAT A HAND OF AN OLD MAN LOOKS DIFFERENT FROM A CHILD'S HAND. A HAND OF MAN DIFFERS FROM A WOMAN'S, A FATSO'S FROM A SCRAWNY'S.

TASK
FILL THE PAPER WITH HANDS. DRAW THEM SMALL IN ORDER TO PUT A LOT OF THEM THERE BUT NOT SO SMALL IN ORDER TO KEEP DETAILS. IF YOU FAIL IN DRAWING A PARTICULAR POSITION, BE STUBBORN AND WORK HARD UNTIL YOU MASTER IT.

LEG IS ESSENTIAL

ALL RULES WHICH WORK WITH THE REST OF ANATOMY, WORK ALSO FOR LEGS. IF YOU WANT TO SIMPLIFY, YOU NEED TO UNDERSTAND THE ISSUE. STUDY THE MUSCLES ON A LEG AND YOU WILL FIND OUT CERTAIN SHORTCUTS WHICH YOU COULD USE IN YOUR PIECES OF WORK

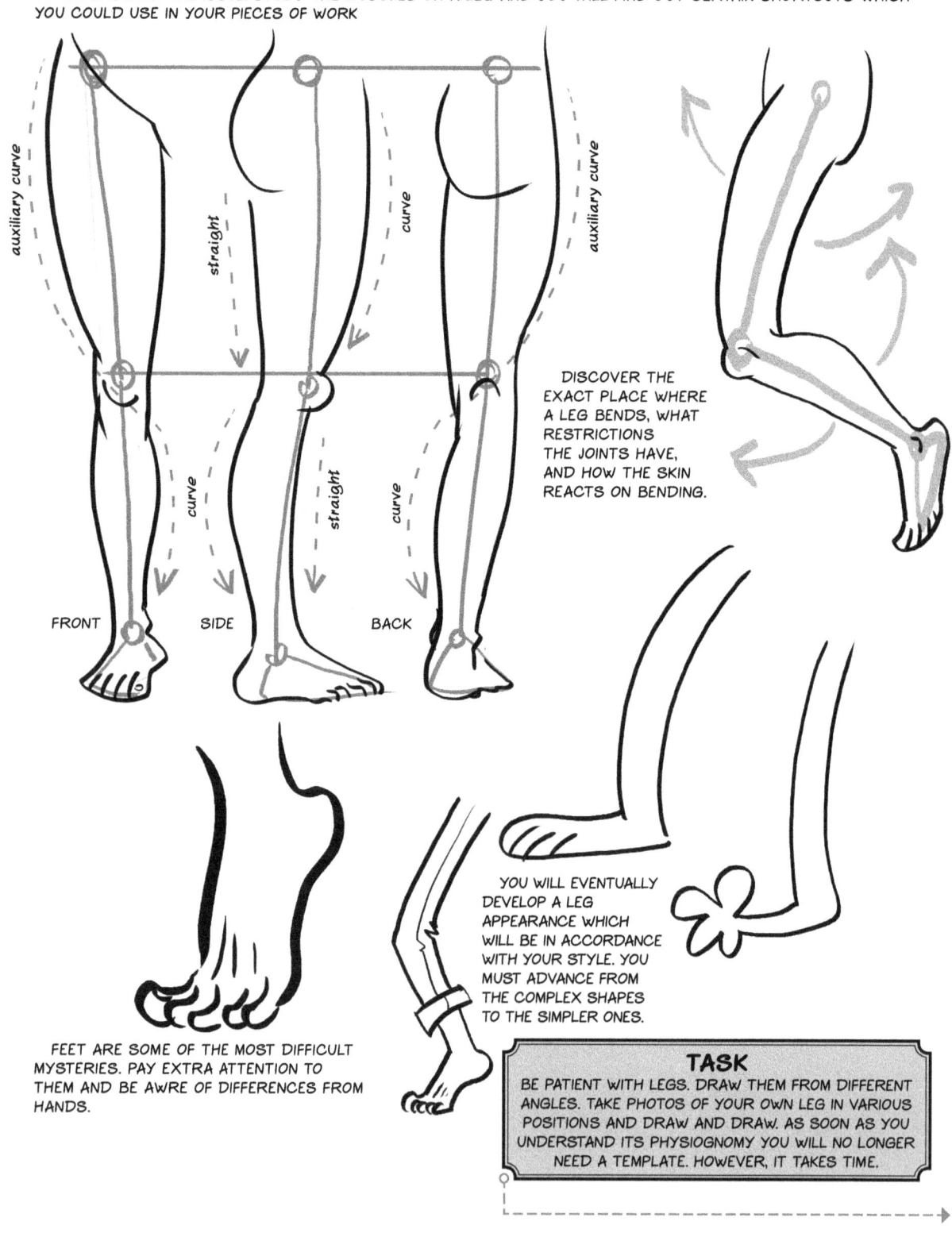

DISCOVER THE EXACT PLACE WHERE A LEG BENDS, WHAT RESTRICTIONS THE JOINTS HAVE, AND HOW THE SKIN REACTS ON BENDING.

YOU WILL EVENTUALLY DEVELOP A LEG APPEARANCE WHICH WILL BE IN ACCORDANCE WITH YOUR STYLE. YOU MUST ADVANCE FROM THE COMPLEX SHAPES TO THE SIMPLER ONES.

FEET ARE SOME OF THE MOST DIFFICULT MYSTERIES. PAY EXTRA ATTENTION TO THEM AND BE AWRE OF DIFFERENCES FROM HANDS.

TASK
BE PATIENT WITH LEGS. DRAW THEM FROM DIFFERENT ANGLES. TAKE PHOTOS OF YOUR OWN LEG IN VARIOUS POSITIONS AND DRAW AND DRAW. AS SOON AS YOU UNDERSTAND ITS PHYSIOGNOMY YOU WILL NO LONGER NEED A TEMPLATE. HOWEVER, IT TAKES TIME.

SHAPEABLE FACES

YOUR CHARACTER MUST SHOW EMOTIONS CLEARLY. HIS FACE MUST NOT EVER BE ILLEGIBLE. THIS DEALS WITH THE CARTOONING RULE, WHICH WAS WEIRD IN THE BEGINNING. IT NEVER RAINS IN THE HERO'S FACE. THE FACE IS A PIECE OF INFORMATION FOR US. IF YOU COVER IT, IT IS LIKE TEARING OUT SOME IMPORTANT PAGES FROM THE READER'S BOOK.

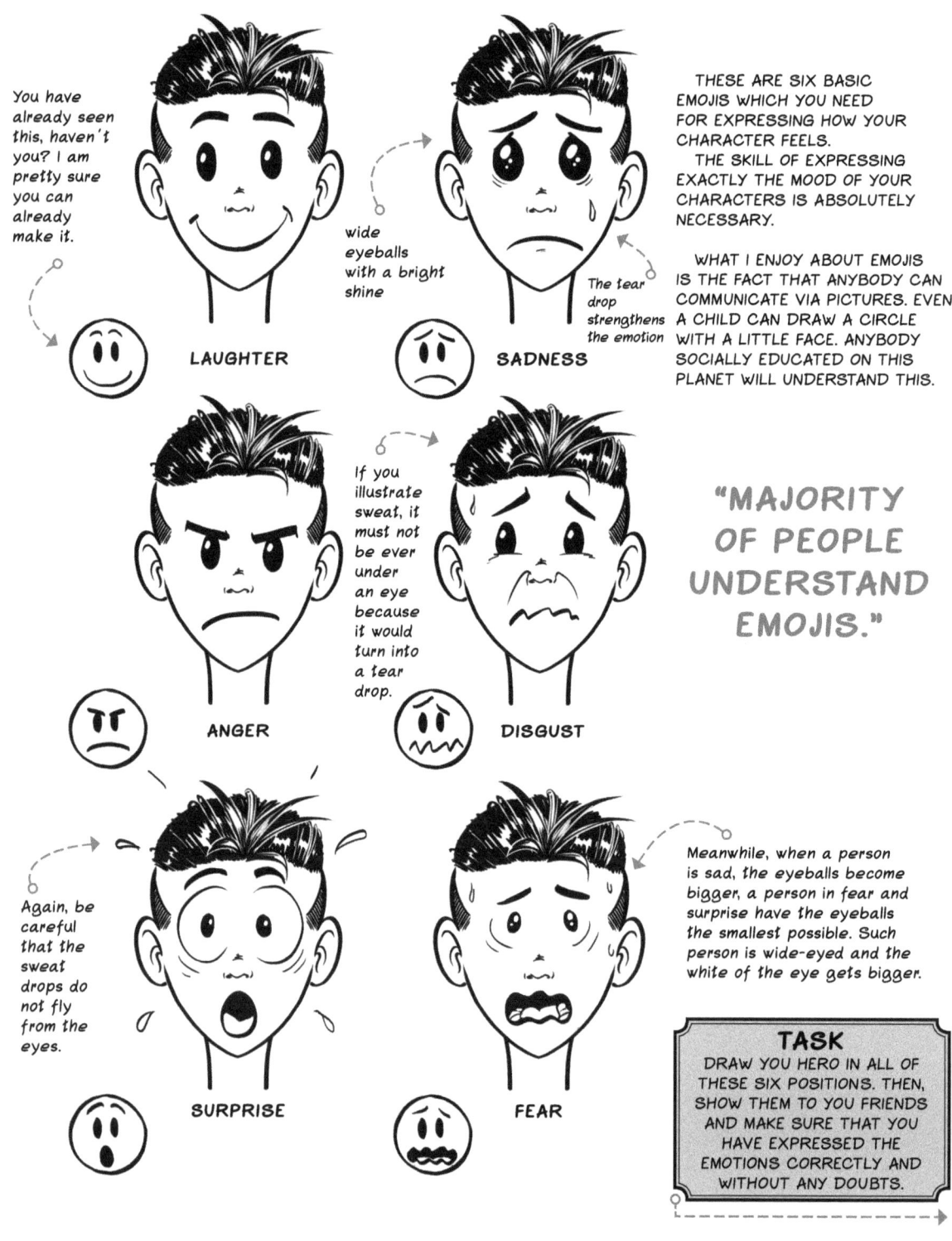

You have already seen this, haven't you? I am pretty sure you can already make it.

LAUGHTER

wide eyeballs with a bright shine

The tear drop strengthens the emotion

SADNESS

THESE ARE SIX BASIC EMOJIS WHICH YOU NEED FOR EXPRESSING HOW YOUR CHARACTER FEELS.

THE SKILL OF EXPRESSING EXACTLY THE MOOD OF YOUR CHARACTERS IS ABSOLUTELY NECESSARY.

WHAT I ENJOY ABOUT EMOJIS IS THE FACT THAT ANYBODY CAN COMMUNICATE VIA PICTURES. EVEN A CHILD CAN DRAW A CIRCLE WITH A LITTLE FACE. ANYBODY SOCIALLY EDUCATED ON THIS PLANET WILL UNDERSTAND THIS.

If you illustrate sweat, it must not be ever under an eye because it would turn into a tear drop.

ANGER

DISGUST

> "MAJORITY OF PEOPLE UNDERSTAND EMOJIS."

Again, be careful that the sweat drops do not fly from the eyes.

SURPRISE

FEAR

Meanwhile, when a person is sad, the eyeballs become bigger, a person in fear and surprise have the eyeballs the smallest possible. Such person is wide-eyed and the white of the eye gets bigger.

TASK
DRAW YOU HERO IN ALL OF THESE SIX POSITIONS. THEN, SHOW THEM TO YOU FRIENDS AND MAKE SURE THAT YOU HAVE EXPRESSED THE EMOTIONS CORRECTLY AND WITHOUT ANY DOUBTS.

COMBINATION OF EMOTIONS

UNTIL NOW, WE HAVE DEALT JUST WITH BASIC EMOTIONS. HOWEVER, YOU MIGHT ALREADY FEEL THAT THERE ARE MORE OF THEM. WOULD YOU BE SURPRISED IF I TOLD YOU THAT YOU CAN EXPRESS OTHER MOODS BY COMBINING THE BASIC ONES? BELIEVE OR NOT! TRY IT ON YOUR OWN. COMBINE THE UPPER AND LOWER PART OF THE FACES. YOU WILL GET SURPRISING COMBINATIONS. SOME OF THEM WILL NOT BE CLEAR BUT IN MOST CASES, YOU WILL GET SOME NEW ONES. ISN'T IT SUCH FUN?

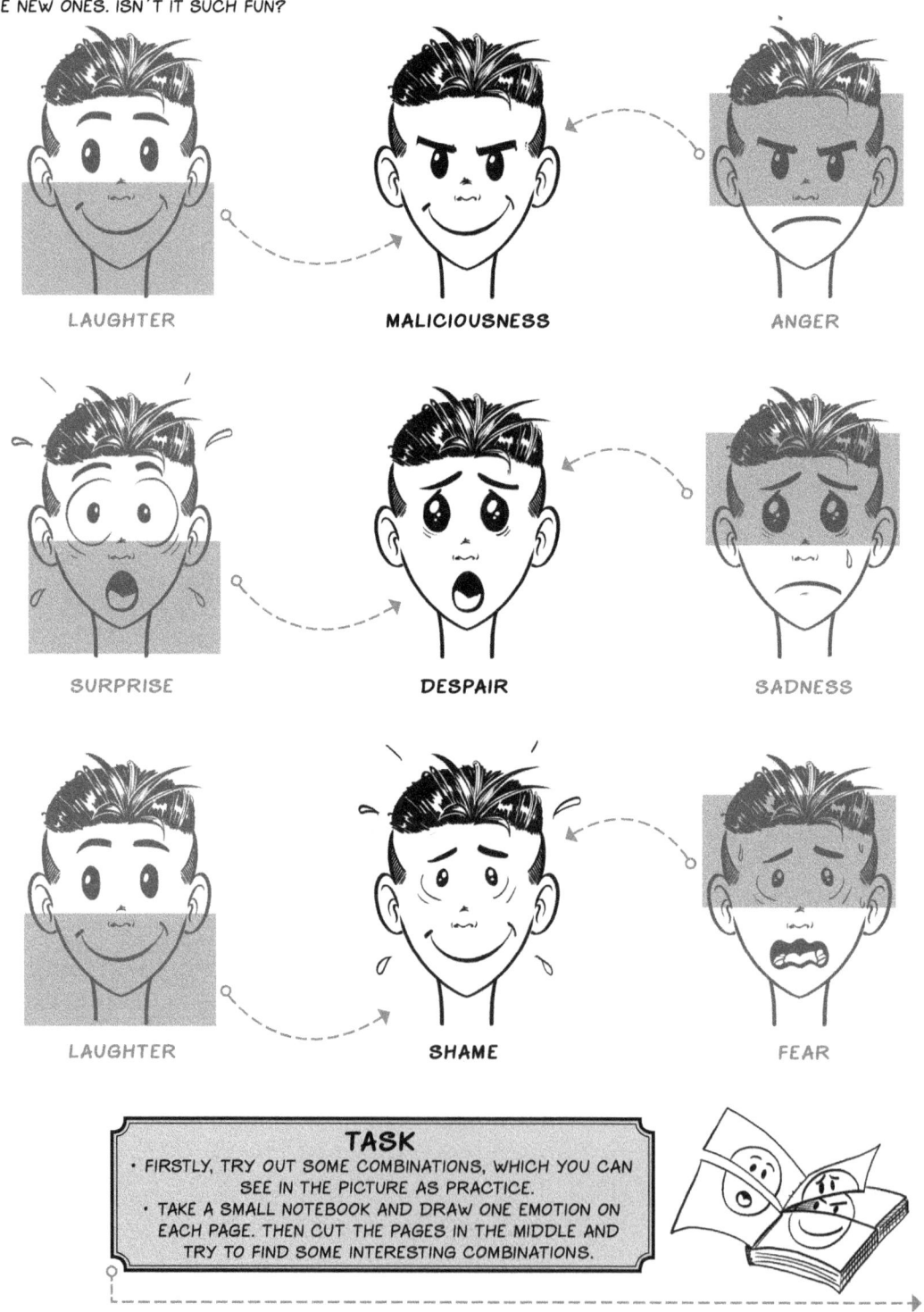

TASK
- FIRSTLY, TRY OUT SOME COMBINATIONS, WHICH YOU CAN SEE IN THE PICTURE AS PRACTICE.
- TAKE A SMALL NOTEBOOK AND DRAW ONE EMOTION ON EACH PAGE. THEN CUT THE PAGES IN THE MIDDLE AND TRY TO FIND SOME INTERESTING COMBINATIONS.

LEVELS OF EMOTIONS

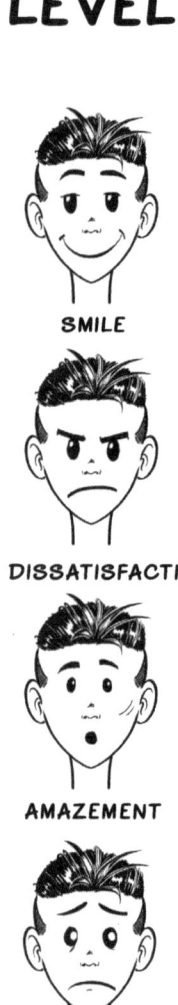
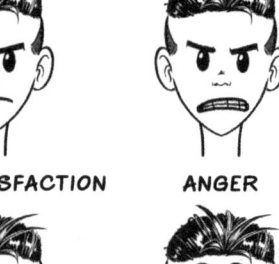
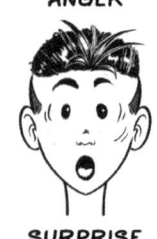
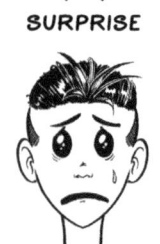
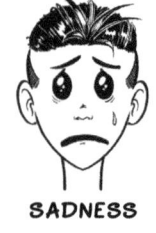
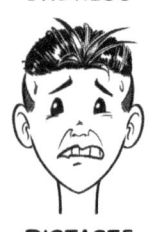
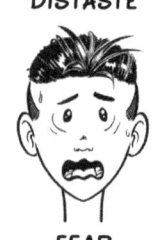
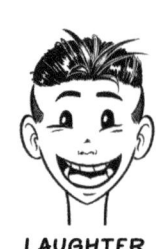
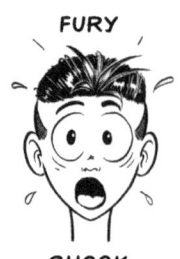
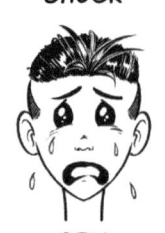
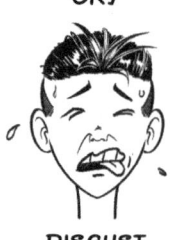
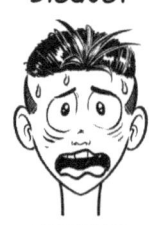
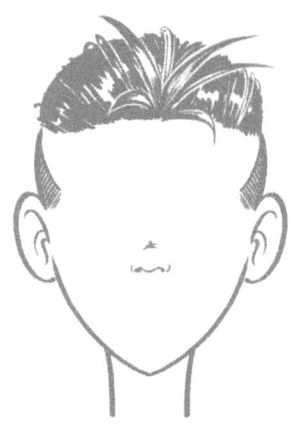

SMILE — AMUSEMENT — LAUGHTER
DISSATISFACTION — ANGER — FURY
AMAZEMENT — SURPRISE — SHOCK
SORROW — SADNESS — CRY
AVERSION — DISTASTE — DISGUST
WORRY — FEAR — HORROR

AS YOU MIGHT HAVE SUSPECTED IT IS NOT THAT SIMPLE. IF YOU HAVE THOROUGHLY STUDIED PREVIOUS PAGES, YOU CAME ACROSS A TINY PROBLEM. SOME EMOTIONS ARE NOT IN AGREEMENT WITH YOUR INTENTION. HOW COME?

IT IS BECAUSE EACH EMOTION HAS CERTAIN LEVELS OF INTENSITY. WHAT IS THAT? I DID NOT SAY IT WAS EASY. I SAID IT COULD BE SORTED.

DO NOT FORGET THAT NOTHING CHANGES IN THIS EXERCISE. JUST THE FACE MOOD. DO NOT HESITATE TO TRY SUPPORT THE EMOTION OF YOUR CHARACTER BY HEAD SHAPE DEFORMATION. FOR EXAMPLE, IN FEAR, LENGHTEN IT OR MAKE THE EYES BIGGER. BE EXPRESSIVE!

ALSO TRY DIFFERENT ANGLES OF THE VIEW ON THE FACE IN DIFFERENT EMOTIONS. WHEN FROWNING, IT HELPS WHEN YOU BEND THE HEAD FORWARD. ON THE OTHER HAND, WHILE LAUGHING, TRY A BACKWARD BEND.

EVERYTHING THAT WE HAVE LEARNT HERE IS **NOT** REALITY. NEVER FORGET THAT THIS IS JUST AN *ILLUSTRATION OF REALITY*. LEONARDO DA VINCI WROTE THAT HE COULD NOT DRAW A CRYING WOMAN AS SHE REALLY LOOKED. SHE WOULD HAVE EVOKED THE SHE LAUGHTER.

YOU JUST NEED TO CONSIDER THIS.

TASK
- DRAW THESE LEVELS OF EMOTIONS AND MOREOVER, LEVEL IT UP.
- MOVE THESE FACES INTO YOUR CUT NOTEBOOK. JUST RIGHT NOW YOU WILL HAVE THE COMBINATIONS YOU NEED!

BODY LANGUAGE

HANDLING EMOJI LANGUAGE IS AN IMPORTANT THING. HOWEVER, IT GOES HAND IN HAND WITH BODY LANGUAGE. THE BODY HAS A SIGNIFICANT IMPACT ON THE GENERAL EMOTION IMPRESSION. JUST FROM THE MERE POSTURE, WALKING STYLE OR WAY OF SITTING, WE CAN READ EMOTIONS THAT CAN BE READ ON THE FACE. AS WE WILL GO THROUGH THE ISSUE ON THE NEXT PAGE, THESE EXPRESSIONAL MEANS DO NOT HAVE TO BE IN AGREEMENT. IF YOU MANAGE THESE TWO DISCIPLINES, WHICH ARE RELATED TO EACH OTHER, YOU WIN!

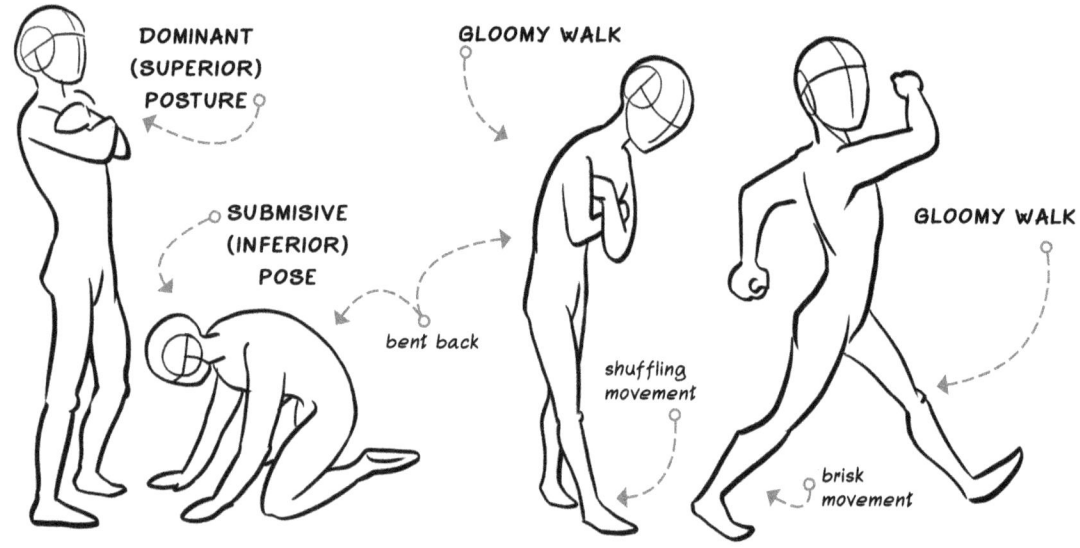

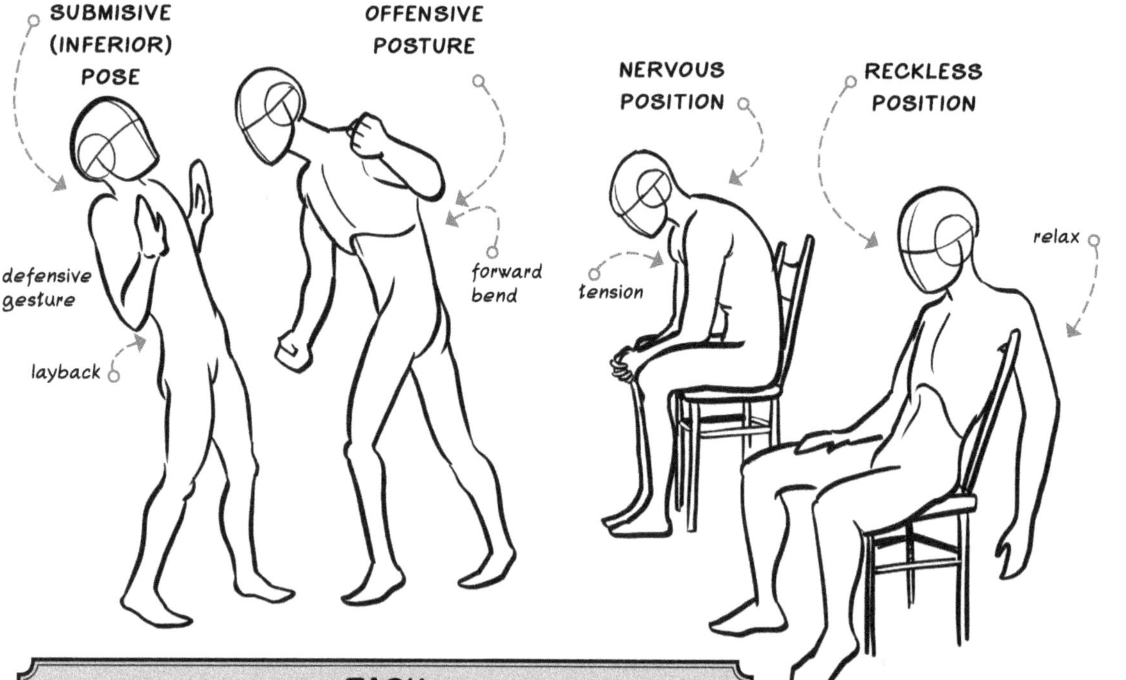

TASK
- TRY THESE POSES OF YOUR HERO FROM DIFFERENT ANGLES.
- WATCH THEATRE ACTORS IN ACTION. THEY USE IDENTICAL EXPRESSIONAL MEANS.

Board 58

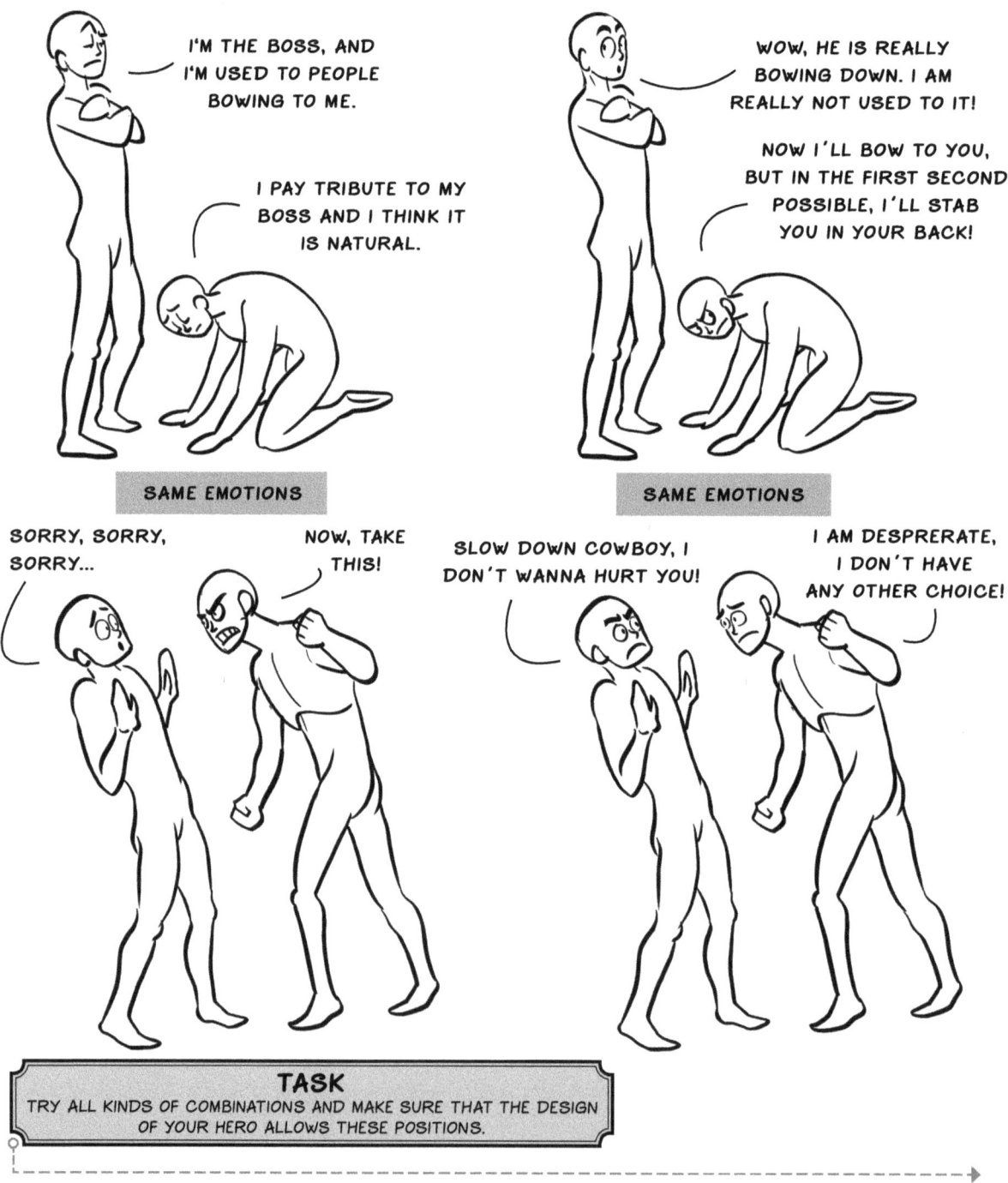

POLARISE YOUR HERO

THERE IS ONE LAST TASK FOR YOU TO MAKE SURE THAT YOUR HERO IS REALLY NEUTRAL. IMAGINE THAT HE OR SHE IS UNDER SOME SPELL OR EVIL TOUCH. IT WILL SPLIT THEM UP INTO TWO. ONE IS GOOD AND ONE IS EVIL. WHAT WILL THEY LOOK LIKE? PEOPLE AROUND YOUR HERO WILL NOT NOTICE A DIFFERENCE BUT THE READER WILL HAVE NO DOUBT.

THE ATTRIBUTES, EVEN POSITIVE OR NEGATIVE, WILL RADIATE FROM THEM. POSTURE, APPEARANCE, FACIAL ATTRIBUTES AND GRIMACE WILL BE SUBORDINATE TO THEIR CHARACTER.

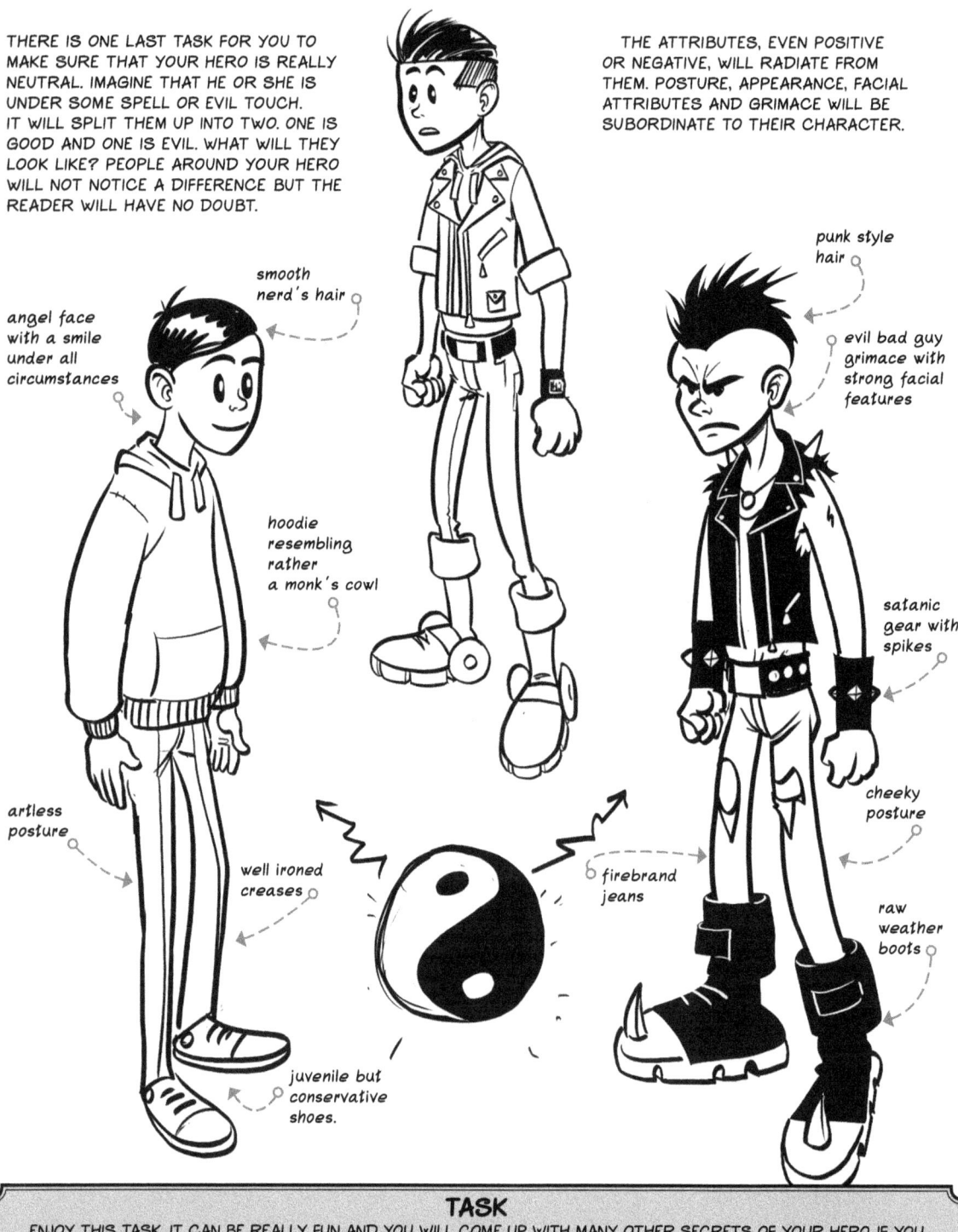

- smooth nerd's hair
- angel face with a smile under all circumstances
- hoodie resembling rather a monk's cowl
- artless posture
- well ironed creases
- juvenile but conservative shoes.
- punk style hair
- evil bad guy grimace with strong facial features
- satanic gear with spikes
- firebrand jeans
- cheeky posture
- raw weather boots

TASK
ENJOY THIS TASK. IT CAN BE REALLY FUN AND YOU WILL COME UP WITH MANY OTHER SECRETS OF YOUR HERO. IF YOU CREATED THEM CORRECTLY, CONGRATULATIONS. YOU CAME UP WITH A PERFECT HERO WHO CAN EXPERIENCE ANY ADVENTURE AND YOUR READERS WILL NOT HAVE ANY PROBLEMS TO INDENTIFY WITH THEM.

IT NEVER RAINS IN A HERO'S FACE

IT SOUNDS LIKE TOTAL NONSENSE BUT THERE IS MORE THAN ONE MESSAGE ABOUT WEATHER HIDDEN BEHIND THIS RULE. THE THING IS THAT ALTHOUGH THINGS GO DIFFERENT IN REAL LIFE, IN A COMIC, EACH MESSAGE MUST BE UNSHAKEABLY CLEAR. THERE MUST NOT BE A CHANCE OF AMBIGUITY IF NOT INTENDED BY THE AUTHOR.

IF A READER, OF AMBIGUITY EACH SQUARE, THINKS OVER HOW YOU WANTED TO INTERPRET THE STORY, THE PLOT CRASHES AND SOMETHING LIKE AN AUTHOR'S, WHICH ALSO MEANS YOURS NIGHTMARE HAPPENS.

IN A COMIC BOOK, YOU CAN BOMB A READER WITH EITHER GOOD OR BAD EMOTIONS, BESIDES ONE. IT IS CALLED **FRUSTRATION**. THANKS TO THIS FEELING, YOUR READER CAN PUT YOUR PIECE OF ART AWAY JUST BECAUSE YOU ARE NOT BEING HONEST WITH THEM.

LET'S TRY IT OUT ON THIS EXAMPLE. WE HAVE GOT THREE SCENARIOS AND ONE OF THEM SAYS:
"THE DEMON'S EYE FIXES ON ROBIN. HE GETS SCARED TO DEATH BUT HE DOES NOT SHOW IT TO THE DEMON."

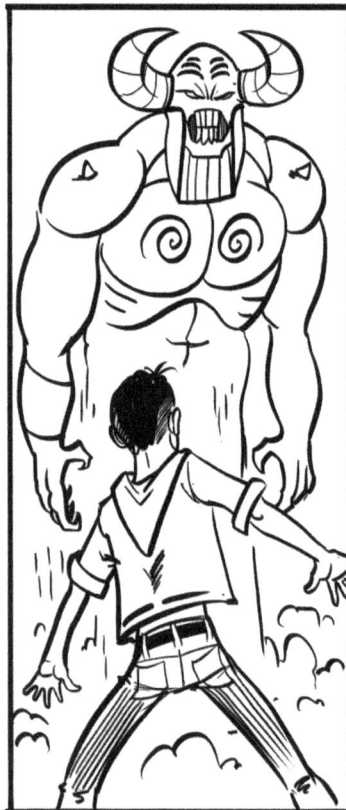

NICE SOLUTION, WE CAN CLEARLY SEE THE DEMON'S AND ROBIN'S SURPRISE. THE DEMON'S BOTTOM VIEW SHOT GINGERS UP THE PICTURE AT THE SAME TIME. ON THE OTHER HAND, WE CANNOT SEE THE FACT THAT ROBIN IS TRYING TO HIDE HIS SURPRISE.

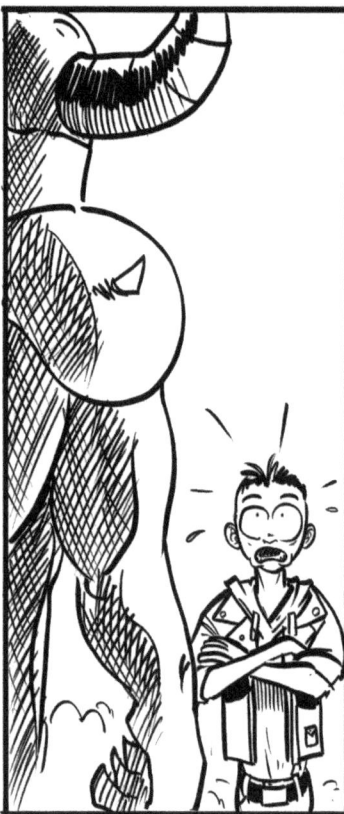

A REALLY TEMPTING OPTION. WE CAN SEE THAT ROBIN'S BODY IS LYING TO US AND HIS FACE PROVES HIM GUILTY. IN A COMIC BOOK, THE READER IDENTIFIES WITH THE CHARACTER, WHOSE POINT OF VIEW IT IS. IN THIS MOMENT, WE ARE THE DEMON SO THE DEMON SEES THE SAME AS WE DO. ALSO, WE CAN SEE THE FACT THAT ROBIN IS TRYING TO DECEIVE HIM. WE CONVEY THIS INFORMATION, WHICH WE DO NOT WANT.

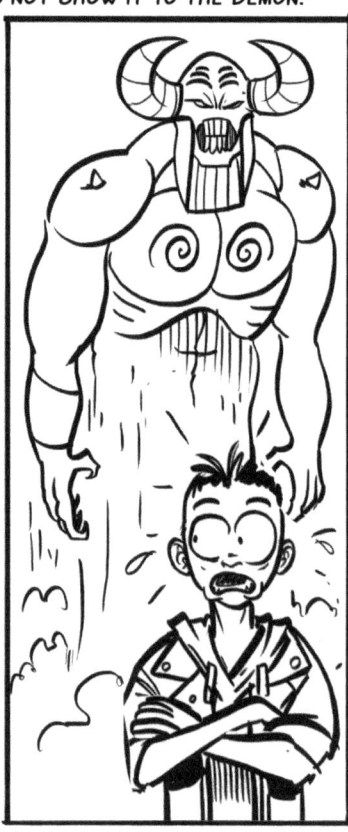

THIS IS IT. OF COURSE, THIS IS HOW IT NEVER IS IN REAL LIFE. THE DEMON IS NOT IN ROBIN'S FIELD OF VISION SO WE CANNOT SEE HIM. HOWEVER, THIS IS THE LICENCE WHICH IS EASILY ACCEPTED BY THE READER. WE ARE STILL IN ROBIN'S SHOES AND WE CAN SEE THE SAME AS HIM. THIS PICTURE PRECISELY ILLUSTRATES THE SENTENCE ABOUT THE SCENARIO AND THAT IS EXACTLY WHAT WE WANT.

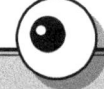

TASK
SOLVE: YOUR HERO IS STANDING IN FRONT OF A MIRROR LOOKING AT HIS OWN REFLECTION. THE REFLECTION IS HIS ENEMY AND WHILE IT HAS SPITEFUL SMILE AND DOMINANT POSTURE, OUR HERO IS HOLDING A BRICK AND WANTS TO BREAK THE MIRROR. HE IS DETERMINED HOWEVER, HE HAS A DESPERATE FACE. ALL OF THIS IS BEEN WATCHED BY A FLUFFY TEDDY AND HE IS MALICIOUSLY HAPPY FROM THIS SITUATION.

IT SOMETIMES RAINS IN HERO'S FACE

NOW, I GUESS, YOU HATE ME. BUT IT'S TRUE. ON THE PREVIOUS PAGE I EXPLAINED HOW AND WHY THE EMOTIONS OF YOUR CHARACTERS MUST BE CLEARLY READABLE. YOU ARE MAKING A COMICK BOOK. YOU ARE EVERYONE YOU NEED TO BE. A WRITER, A DIRECTOR, AN EDITOR. MOST IMPORTANTLY YOU ARE A STORYTELLER INVOLVING THE READER IN THE PLOT SOUNDS REALLY ATTRACTIVE, BUT IF IT IS NOT THE WHOLE STORY'S INTENTION, IT WILL BE DISRUPTING, AND UNCLEAR SCNEENES WILL CONFUSE YOUR READER AND LEAVE THEM OUT OF THE PLOT. TAKE IT AS A GAME. YOU ARE THE AUTHOR AND YOUR READER IS THE LISTENER. DO NO LEAVE STORYTELLING TO YOUR AUDIENCE. YOU GET PAID FOR IT!

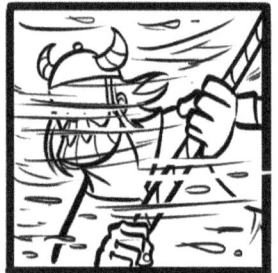

LET'S EXPLAIN THE ISSUE ON THIS VIKING, WHO WAS CAUGHT BY A STORM DURING HIS SAIL. IF IT HEAVILY RAINED IN HIS FACE, WHICH WOULD ACTUALLY HAPPEN IN REAL LIFE, THE PICTURE WOULD LOOK SOMEHING LIKE THIS.

I NEED TO SAY AGAIN THAT WE DO NOT COPY REAL LIFE. NOT IN CARTOONING! **WE ILLUSTRATE IT!** FOR ONE REASON. IF YOU HIDE THE VIKING'S EMOTIONS, EACH READER WOULD IMAGINE SOMETHING REALLY DIFFERENT (SEE PICS BELOW). AND THAT IS YOUR FAULT. YOU HAVE JUST LOST HAVING YOUR READER'S PICTURE UNDER CONTROL AND IF YOU DO IT AGAIN FURTHER IN THE PLOT, YOU BEGIN TO LOSE YOUR AUDIENCE.

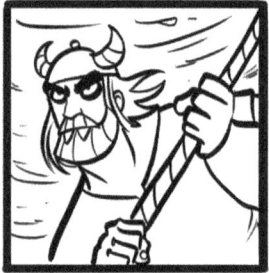 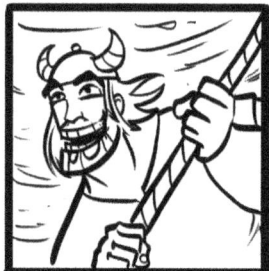 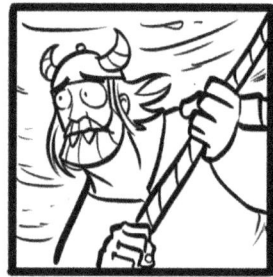 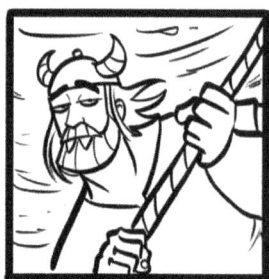

Storm, come on and fight!   *Hell yeah, I love sailing. Give me more!*   *That is a storm, so scary!*   *Piece of cake.*

"DO NOT LEAVE STORYTELLING TO YOUR READERS. YOU GET PAID FOR IT!"

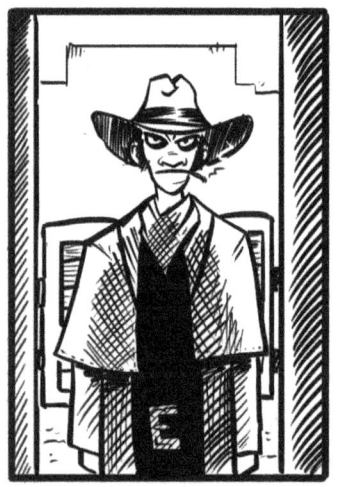 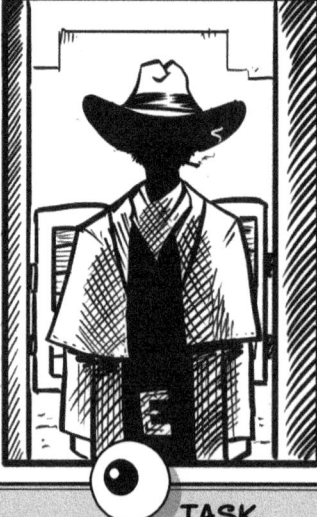

AS THE PAGE HEADLINE REVEALS, IT SOMETIMES RAINS IN THE HERO'S FACE. IT IS SOMETIMES (RARELY) BETTER TO HIDE THE CHARACTER'S FACE.

LET'S SAY THAT WE HAVE THIS DESCRIPTION IN THE SCNEARIO:
A MYSTERIOUS GUNMAN IN A LONG COAT HAS JUST COME IN TO A SALOON. NOBODY KNOWS WHAT TO THINK OF HIM.

WHICH PICTURE ILLUSTRATES THE DESCRIPTION BETTER?

THE EDITOR WANTS TO RAISE SUSPENSE AND ATTRACT THE READER'S CURIOSITY. IT IS BETTER TO SHROUD THE CHARACTER'S FACE.

IT MIGHT BE EVEN MORE IMPRESSIVE TO SEE THE HERO FROM THE BACK AND LOOKING AT THE FACES OF THE SALOON REGULARS. HOWEVER, THE READER WOULD IDENTIFY WITH THE ROLE OF THE GUNMAN. WE WANT TO FEEL THE EMOTIONS OF AN OBSERVER.

TASK
ILLUSTRATE THE FOLLOWING SCENARIO: THERE IS A SANDSTORM AT A FOOT OF A MOUNTAIN YOUR HERO IS RIDING ON A CAMEL PRETENDING TO REALLY ENJOY THE SURROUNDINGS, UNLIKE THE CAMEL. THE RIDER GETS UPSET WITH THE CAMEL'S POSITIVE MOOD. THERE IS A MYSTERIOUS CHARACTER FIGURE IN A TURBAN, WITH A LONG SABRE, WHO STARTS WALKING TOWARDS THE HERO, AND HE KNOWS ABOUT THAT. THE MOTIVATION AND INTENTIONS OF THE MYSTERIOUS STRANGER ARE UNKNOWN TO US. ALL OF THIS IN ONE PICTURE!

ANIMAL PERSONIFICATION

ANIMALS ARE A POPULAR TOPIC FOR COMIC BOOKS AND CARTOONS. WE CAN APPLY VARIOUS APPROCHES TO DRAWING THEM. WE WILL BE DEALING WITH THAT AS WELL. HOWEVER, YOU SHOULD ESTABLISH YOUR OWN RULES FOR THEIR ANATOMY IN ORDER NOT TO CONFUSE YOUR READER.

LEVEL OF BEHAVIOUR HUMANISATION:

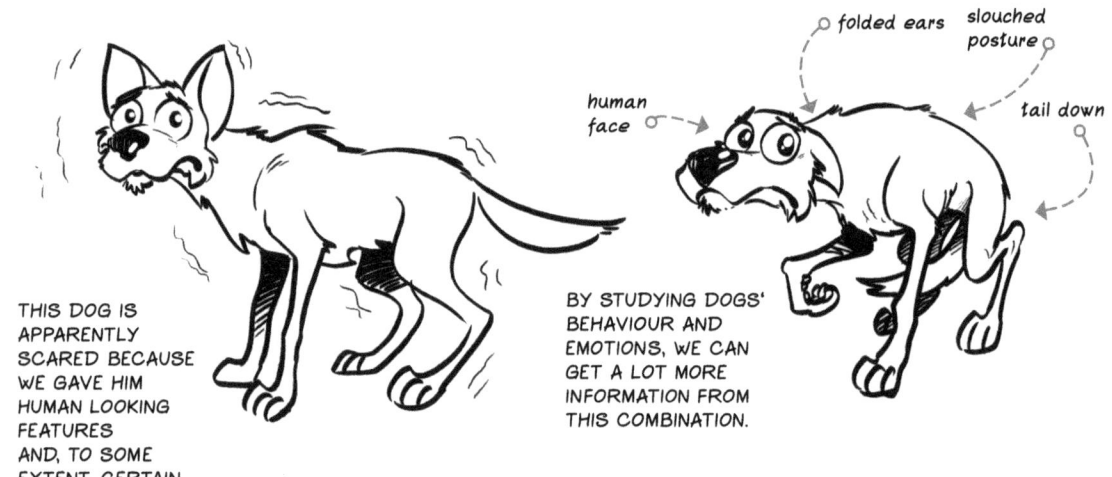

THIS DOG IS APPARENTLY SCARED BECAUSE WE GAVE HIM HUMAN LOOKING FEATURES AND, TO SOME EXTENT, CERTAIN DIMENSIONS.

BY STUDYING DOGS' BEHAVIOUR AND EMOTIONS, WE CAN GET A LOT MORE INFORMATION FROM THIS COMBINATION.

LEVEL OF PHYSIOGNOMY HUMANISING:

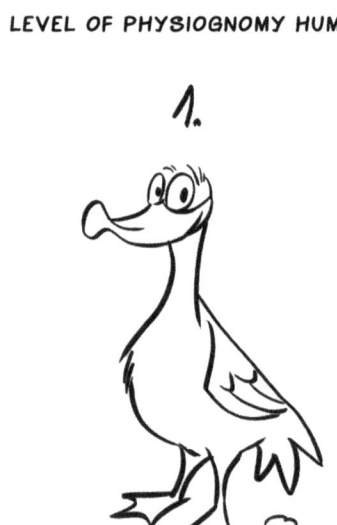
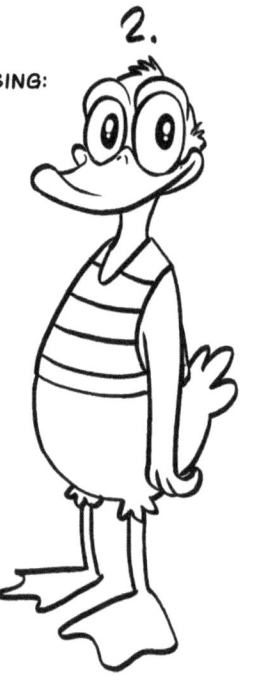
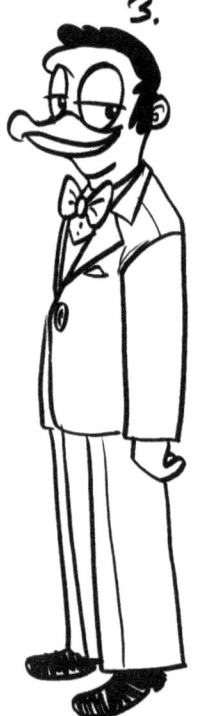

IT IS A QUESTION TO WHAT EXTENT YOU NEED TO HUMANISE YOUR ANIMAL FOR STORY PURPOSE. IN MY OPINION, JUST TO THIS EXTENT, FOR THE PURPOSES OF THE STORY, THE ANIMALS SHOULD BE PHYSICALLY CHANGED ONLY IF REALLY NECESSARY.

THE GOLDILOCKS ZONE... YOU CERTAINLY KNOW THIS GUY. ANY SIMILARITIES ARE COMPLETELY COINCIDENTAL.

THIS DUCK HAS AN ENTIRE HUMAN BODY. JUST HIS BEEK REMAINED. IT IS A QUESTIONS OF WHETHER WE WANT HIM TO BE AN ANIMAL AT ALL.

TASK
DRAW PUPPIES, KITTENS AND OTHER ANIMALS AND PRACTISE DIFFERENT PERSONIFICATION COMBINATIONS.

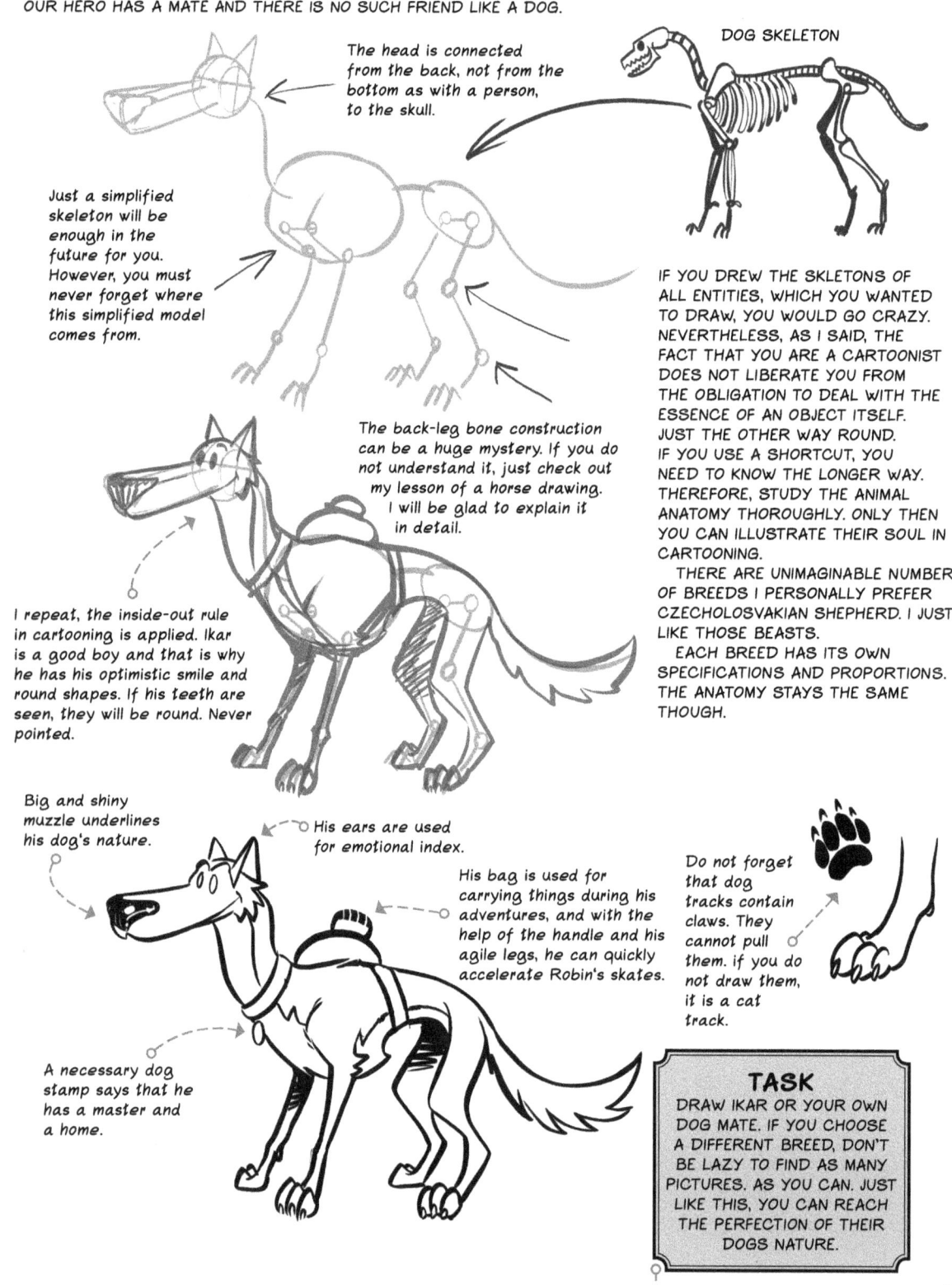

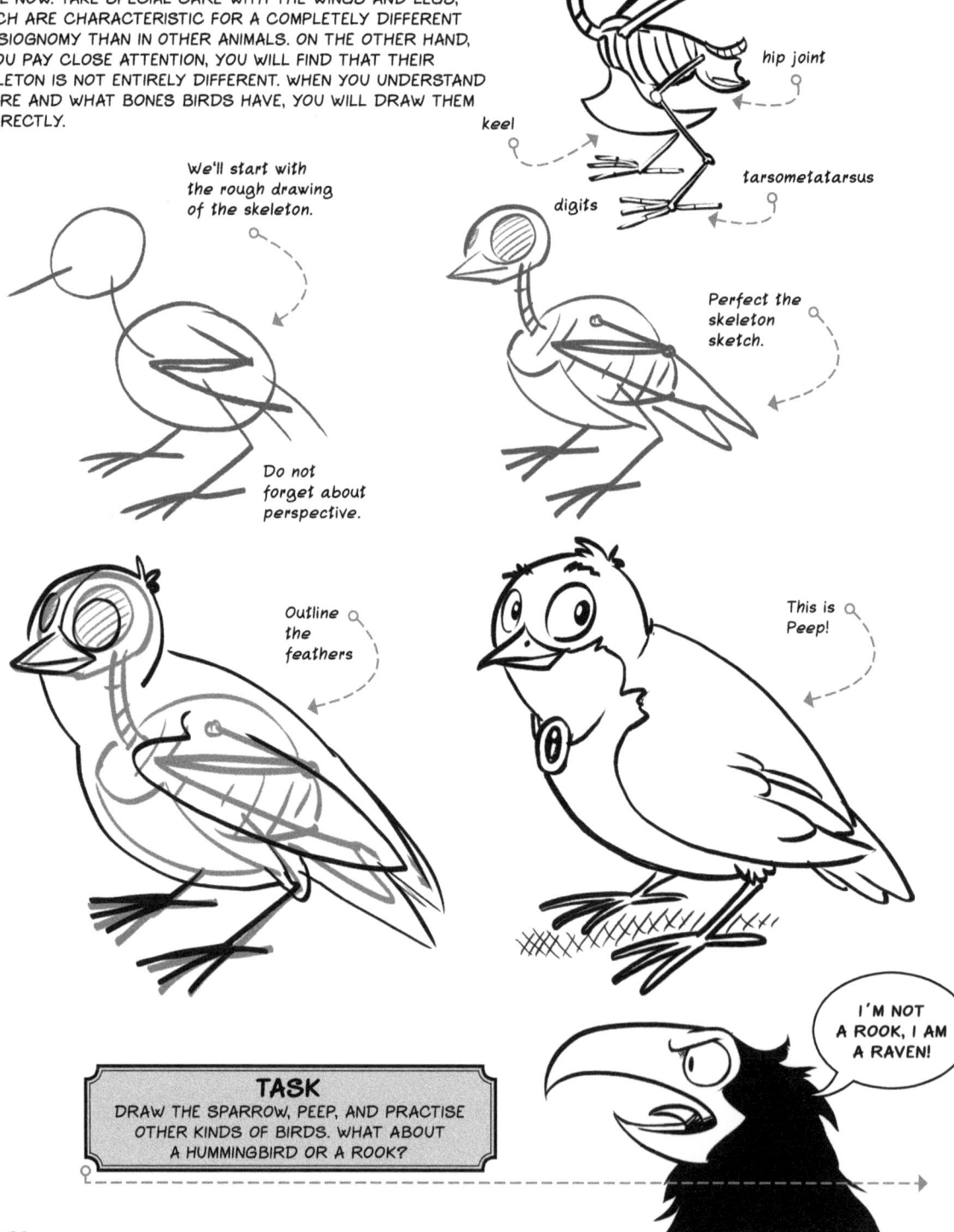

SPARROW PEEP

THIS LITTLE BIRD WILL HELP OUR HERO DURING HIS ADVENTURES. IT IS TRAINED, SKILLED AND SMART. HE ALSO HAS A MINICAMCODER ON HIS NECK, SO THAT ROBIN CAN WATCH PEEP FLY ON HIS CELLPHONE, SINCE PEEP CAN GET INTO PLACES THAT ROBIN CANNOT.

THE BIRD'S SKELETON IS SOMETHING SLIGHTLY DIFFERENT FROM OTHER MAMMALS WHICH WE HAVE DEALT WITH UP UNTIL NOW. TAKE SPECIAL CARE WITH THE WINGS AND LEGS, WHICH ARE CHARACTERISTIC FOR A COMPLETELY DIFFERENT PHYSIOGNOMY THAN IN OTHER ANIMALS. ON THE OTHER HAND, IF YOU PAY CLOSE ATTENTION, YOU WILL FIND THAT THEIR SKELETON IS NOT ENTIRELY DIFFERENT. WHEN YOU UNDERSTAND WHERE AND WHAT BONES BIRDS HAVE, YOU WILL DRAW THEM CORRECTLY.

We'll start with the rough drawing of the skeleton.

Do not forget about perspective.

Perfect the skeleton sketch.

Outline the feathers

This is Peep!

I'M NOT A ROOK, I AM A RAVEN!

TASK
DRAW THE SPARROW, PEEP, AND PRACTISE OTHER KINDS OF BIRDS. WHAT ABOUT A HUMMINGBIRD OR A ROOK?

Board 72

NEUTRAL HORSE

A HORSE IS ONE OF THE BIGGEST CHALLENGES. YOU NEED IT IN YOUR COMIC BOOKS SO OFTEN AND AT THE SAME TIME, IT IS SO DIFFICULT TO DRAW. MAINLY THE LEGS ARE COMPLICATED. HOWEVER, JUST UNTIL THE MOMENT YOU REALISE THAT IT HAS THE SAME NUMBER OF BIG BONES IN THE LEGS AS A HUMAN BEING. A HUMAN BEING JUST HAS THEM IN DIFFERENT LENGTHS WHILE HUMAN BEING BONES ARE ADAPTED TO A STRAIGHTENED WALK, THE HORSE ONES ARE CREATED TO RUN ON ALL FOURS NOTICE THAT THEIR LIMBS ARE CREATED OF EXACTLY THE SAME NUMBER OF JOINTS AND BONES. WHERE THE HECK IS THE PROBLEM!?

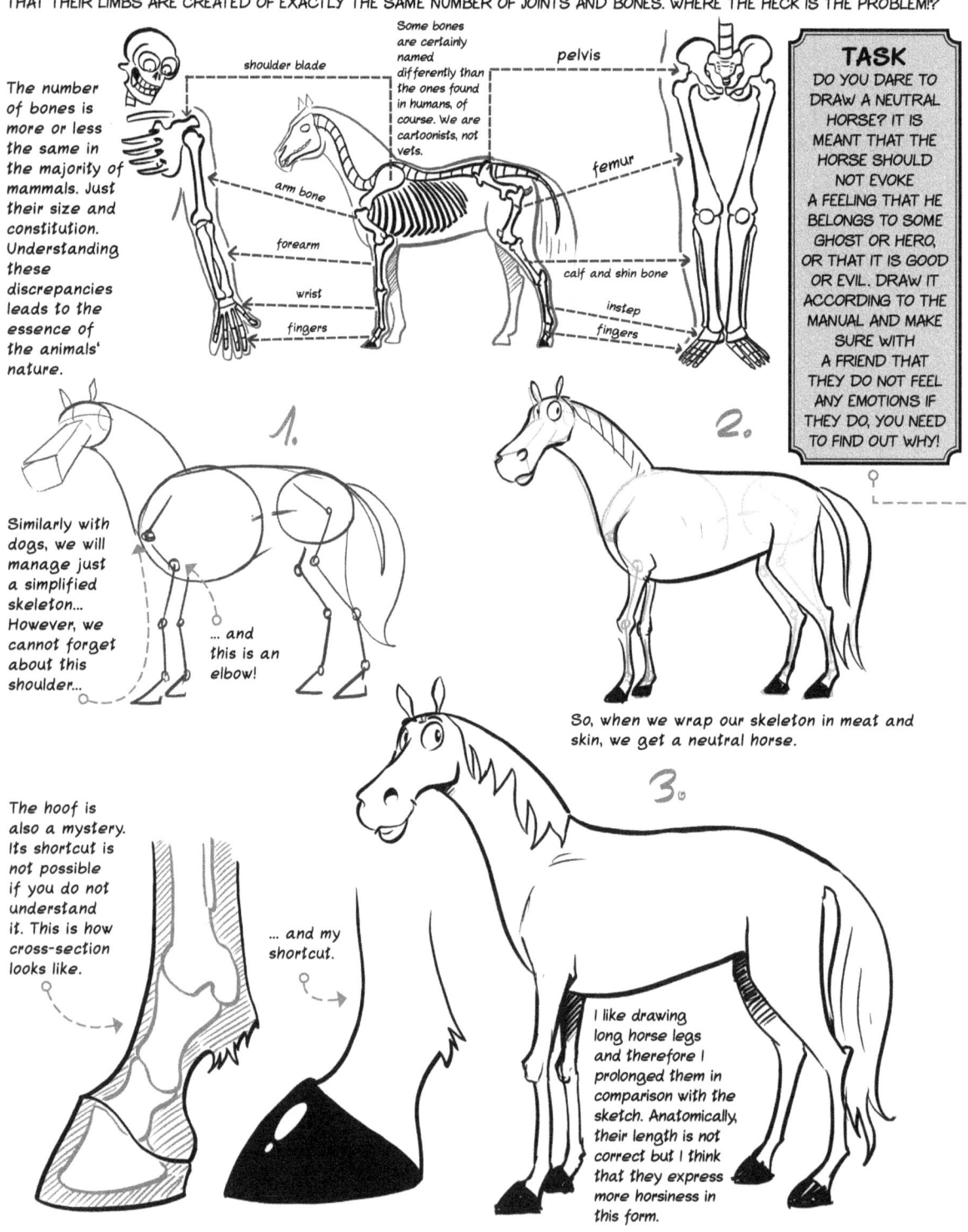

Board 74

POLARITY OF A HORSE

I AM GOING TO SAY IT TO YOU ONCE AGAIN. IT IS IMPORTANT. CARTOONING = WHAT IS INSIDE, IT IS ALSO VISIBLE FROM THE OUTSIDE. THEREFORE, A VILLAIN'S HORSE WILL LOOK DIFFERENTLY THAN A HORSE OF A GOOD KNIGHT. ALTHOUGH, IT IS NONSENSE, CARTOONING WORKS IN THIS MANNER. HOW SHOULD WE EXPRESS THESE DIFFERENCES?

> **TASK**
> DRAW BOTH A GOOD AND EVIL HORSE. THEN ASK YOUR FRIEND FOR THEIR APPROVAL THAT THE CHARACTERS REALLY WORK.

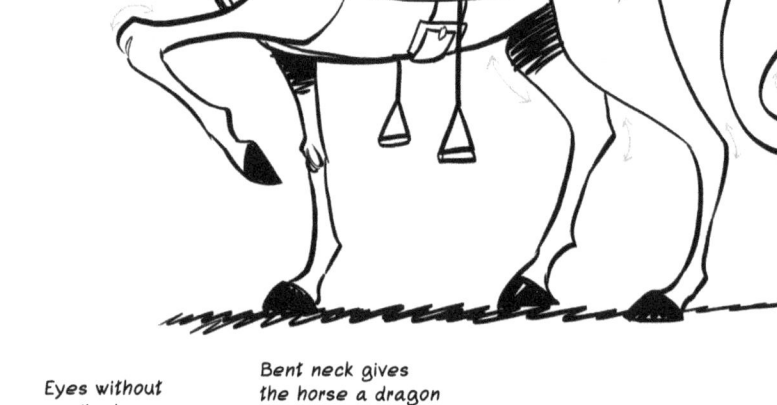

Proud and brave posture, ready anytime to set out on the master's beckon... but this is just its current mood. The real secret is in its shape.

GOOD KNIGHT'S HORSE

THERE ARE AS MANY ROUND AND CIRCULAR CURVES AS POSSIBLE. HE MUST RADIATE POWER. IF WE WANT TO ENHANCE HIS CHARACTER WITH A COLOUR, YOU BET THAT WE SHOULD. IN CARTOONING YOU MUST EMPTY THE MAGAZINE. HE WOULD BE WHITE AND IF HE IS IN THE SHADE, HE SHOULD HAVE A BLUISH TOUCH. SEE COLOUR SYMBOLISM.

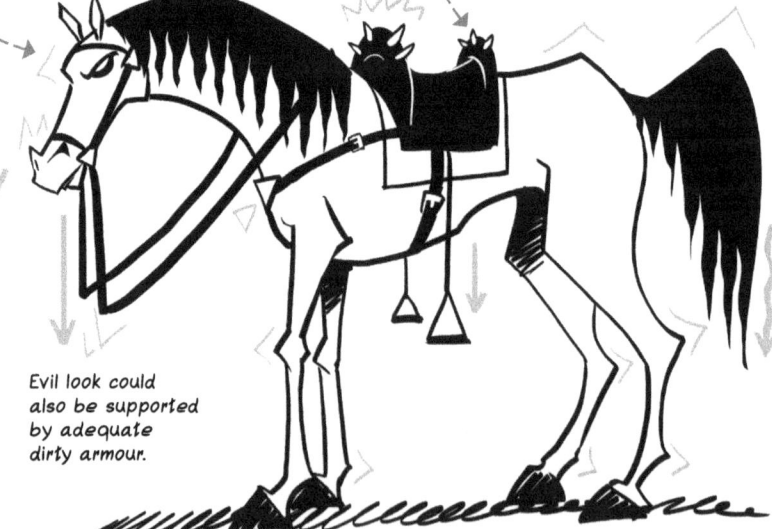

Eyes without pupils deepen the demonic look.

Bent neck gives the horse a dragon look.

Uncomfortable saddle is not a problem just for the villain.

Evil look could also be supported by adequate dirty armour.

VILLAIN'S HORSE

SHARP ANGLES, ANGULARITY AND POINTEDNESS GUARANTEE A DANGEROUS LOOK OF THIS HERBIVORE. HIS LINES SHOULD RATHER POINT TO THE GROUND. HE LOOKS LIKE HE HAS JUST COME OUT OF A SWAMP. HOWEVER, HE MUST NOT LOOK LANKY OR SICK. HE IS SLIM BUT NOT TOO SLIM. HE SHOULD RADIATE SPEED AND DANGER. HE IS A REAL ANTIHERO'S HELPER. HE SHOULD BE BLACK, OF COURSE. DARK GREY OR BROWN OR BLACK WITH BLUISH GLEAM.

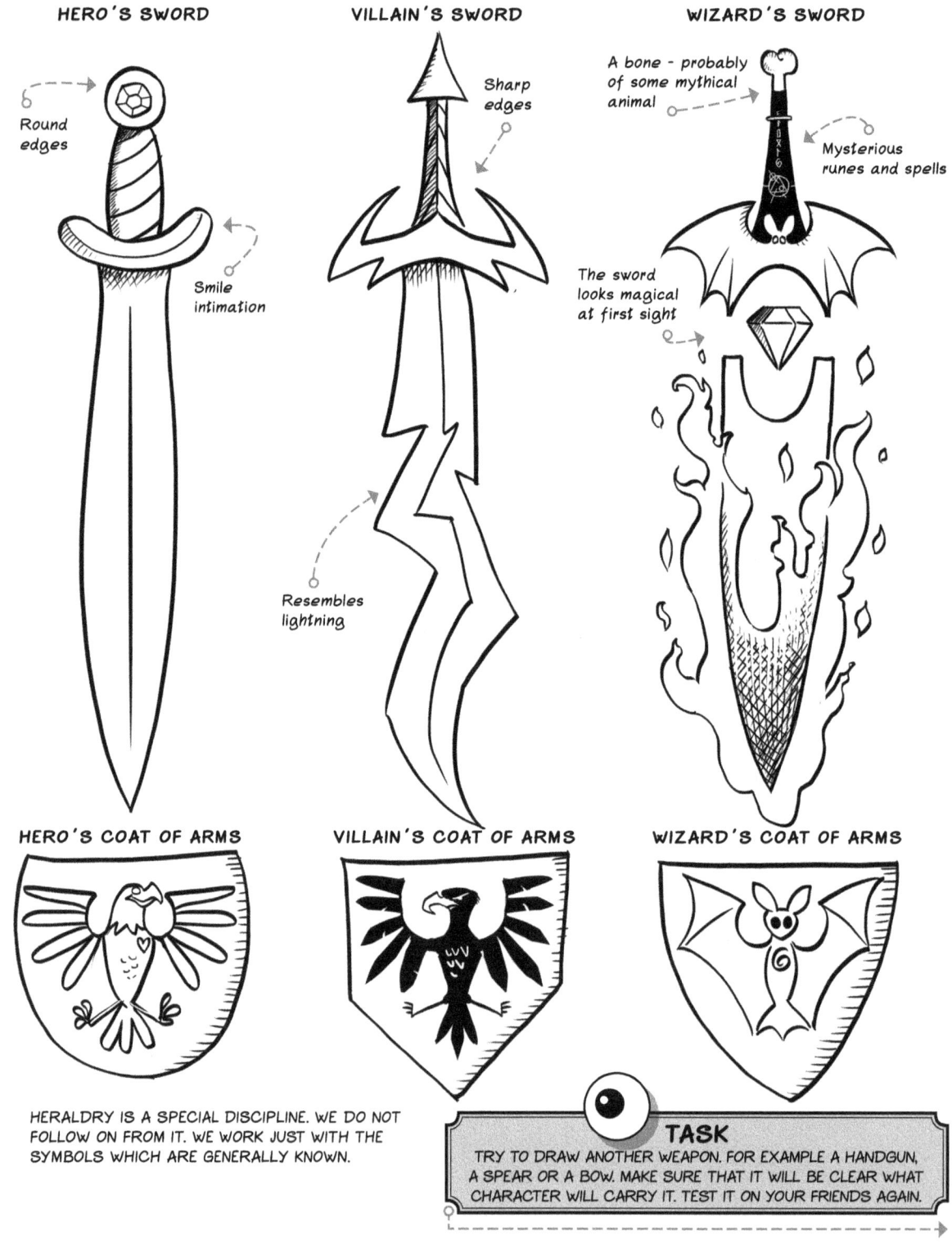

SYMBOLS

SYMBOLS AND ATTRIBUTES ARE OFTEN MISTAKEN. I FEEL A NEED TO EXPLAIN WHAT THE DIFFERENCE BETWEEN THEM IS, AND HOW THEY CAN HELP US EXPRESS OUR IDEAS AND GIVE OUR PICTURES THE RIGHT TONE, POLARITY AND MEANING.
SYMBOLS IN A DRAWING SERVES FOR AN EASY IDENTIFICATION OF A PARTICULAR ITEM OR PERSON. IN A COMIC BOOK, YOU WILL ALWAYS BE DEALING WITH HOW TO EXPRESS A SITUATION OR A CHARACTER, AND NOT TO USE A DESCRIPTIVE TEXT. THERE ARE EVEN COMIC BOOKS, WHICH REPLACED TEXT IN BUBBLES WITH SYMBOLS AND THEY SURPRISINGLY WORK VERY WELL. LET'S NOT UNDERESTIMATE THE POWER OF SYMBOLS. LET'S NOT FORGET THAT THE HUMAN MIND UNDERSTANDS A PICTURE FASTER THAN TEXT.

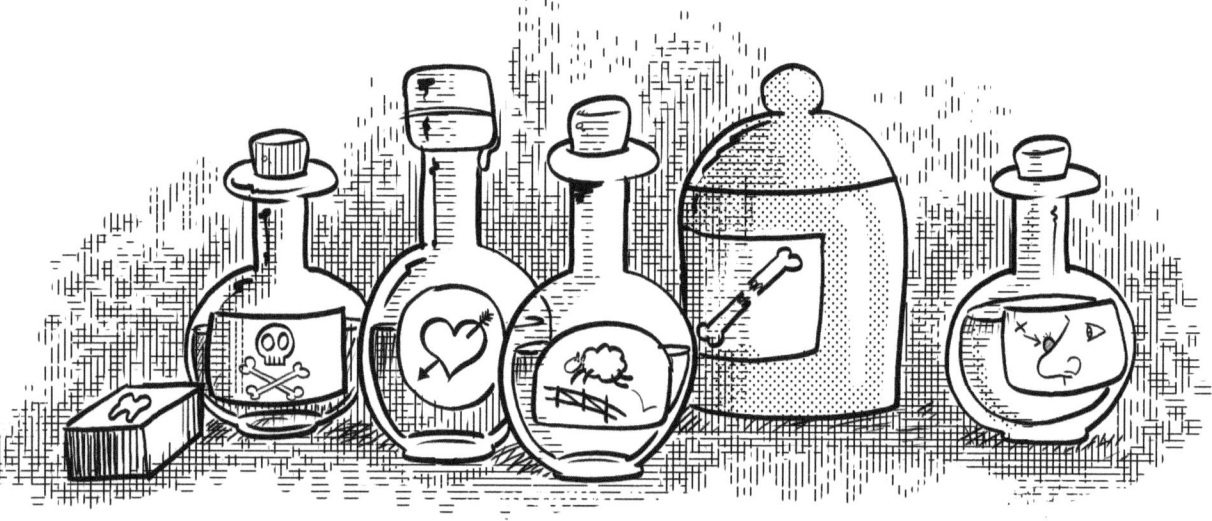

THE WITCH MORGAVSA HAS A LOT OF POTIONS IN STOCK. NONE OF THEM HAS TO BE LABELLED WITH WORDS. A SYMBOL THAT IS EASILY UNDERSTANDABLE FOR EVERYONE IS ENOUGH. CHECK IT OUT.

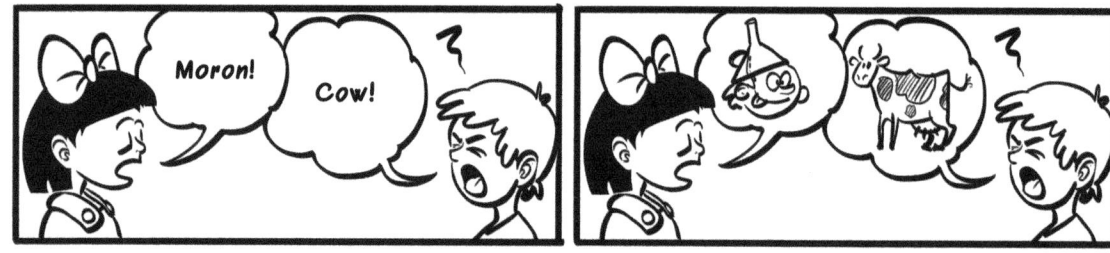

SYMBOLS CAN ALSO BE USED INSTEAD OF DIALOGUES. IT MOSTLY EMPHASISES THE JOKE AND YOU, AT THE SAME TIME, AVOID INAPPROPRIATE OR RUDE WORDS.

HERALDRY WORKS WITH SYMBOLS BUT BE CAREFUL. THE MEANING OF THESE ICONS IS USUALLY SURROUNDED BY SECRETS. THEY DO NOT STICK TO THE INTUITIVE HUMAN EXPERIENCE BUT THEY USUALLY FOLLOW A GROUP OF SOLID RULES AND MEANING INTERPRETATIONS THAT DO NOT HAVE TO BE IN AGREEMENT WITH THE GENERAL UNDERSTANDING OF SYMBOLS.

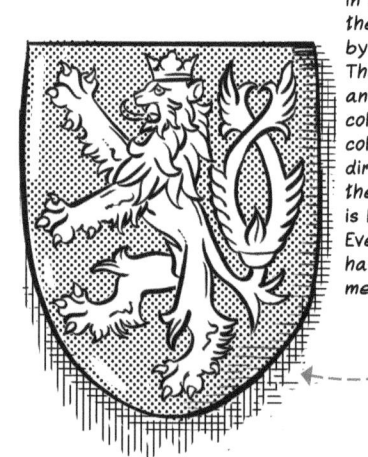

In heraldry, there is nothing by coincidence. The kind of animal and its colour, the field colour, and the direction that the animal is looking. Everything has its own meaning.

TASK
DRAW A CRAZY SCIENTIST WHO IS TRYING HIS NEW GADGET ON AN UNFORTUNATE MAN. THE GADGET WILL HAVE A BIG KEYBOARD WHERE THERE WILL BE SYMBOLS INSTEAD OF LETTERS. AFTER PRESSING A SPECIFIC BUTTON, THE LABORATORY GUINEA PIG SHOULD EXPERIENCE A PARTICULAR EMOTION. BE CAREFUL AND DRAW THE SYMBOLS EASILY UNDERSTANDABLE.

ATTRIBUTES

UNLIKE SYMBOLS, ATTRIBUTES ARE NOT JUST GRAPHICAL MARKS, BUT THEY ARE ITEMS THAT BELONG TO A PARTICULAR CHARACTER, WHO IS EASILY IDENTIFIABLE THANKS TO THESE THINGS. SO, IF YOU DO NOT WANT TO ADD A DESCRIPTION BELOW SUCH AS "THIS IS A WIZARD", GIVE HIM A POINTED HAT A MAGIC WAND AND A LONG WHITE FULL BEARD. YOU WILL NOT NEED TEXT ANY LONGER.

CERTAINLY, YOU WILL NOT HAVE ANY PROBLEM TO MATCH THESE ATTRIBUTES.

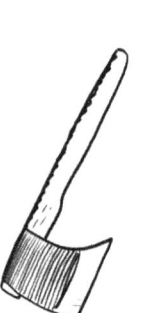
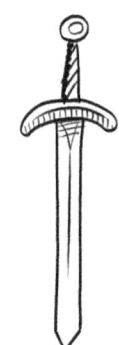

WHEN DOES A THING BECOME A SYMBOL? IN THE MOMENT WHEN IT IS INSTITUTIONALISED OR IT IS SHOWN ENOUGH TO THE COMIC BOOK READER. SUCH A SYMBOL REMAINS A SYMBOL JUST IN A PARTICULAR BOOK. CAN A SYMBOL BECOME AN ATTRIBUTE? LET'S CHECK OUT THIS EXAMPLE:

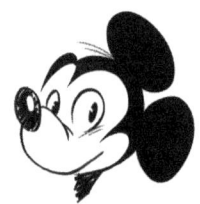
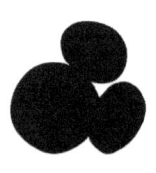
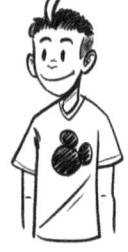
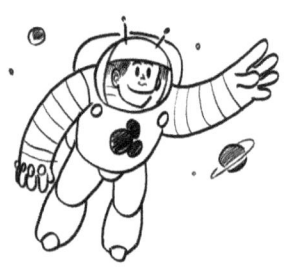

MICKEY IS JUST AN EXAMPLE OF A UNIVERSAL HERO AND IS SO FAMOUS THAT IT HAS BECOME DISNEY STUDIOS' SYMBOL.

HIS SIMPLIFIED SILHOUETTE MAKES AN ICON AS WELL AS DISNEY'S SIGNATURE.

LET'S IMAGINE THAT OUR HERO WILL ALWAYS BE WEARING A T-SHIRT WITH SUCH SYMBOL.

THAT SYMBOL WILL BECOME HIS ATTRIBUTE AND WILL BE SEEN ON OTHER PIECES OF HIS CLOTHING. ANYWAY, IT STILL STAYS A MICKEY'S SYMBOL.

AS IN HERALDRY, THERE IS AN ATTRIBUTE SYMBOLIC IN SAINTS AND EMPERORS PORTRAYALS. THE SAME WORKS FOR THESE ATTRIBUTES AS WELL AS SYMBOLS IN COATS OF ARMS. THEY ARE CONDITIONED BY DEPTH OF EDUCATION OF THE BRANCH AND THERE ARE UNKNOWN TO COMMON PEOPLE. IN CARTOONING, WE CANNOT COUNT ON THEM THEN.

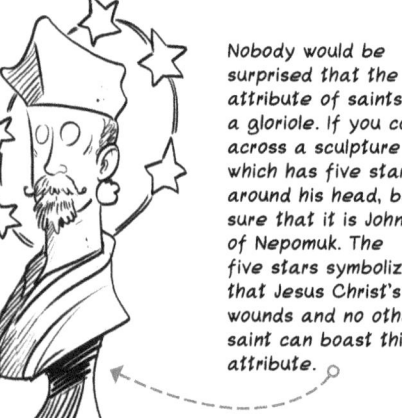

Nobody would be surprised that the attribute of saints is a gloriole. If you come across a sculpture which has five stars around his head, be sure that it is John of Nepomuk. The five stars symbolize that Jesus Christ's wounds and no other saint can boast this attribute.

TASK
A CERTAIN BUILDER IS SITTING ON A HORSE WHICH APPARENTLY COMES FROM THE ROYAL STABLES. THEY ARE PASSING BY A BUTCHER'S. A LUMBERJACK ON A WILD BOAR, WHICH BELONGS TO THE GOD OF SEAS - POSEIDON, IS CHASING THEM. ALL THE SCENERY IS BEING WATCHED BY ALADDIN AND A GOOD KNIGHT FROM THE HEART KINGDOM. THEY ARE LAUGHING AND ALADDIN IS TELLING THE KNIGHT THAT THE LUMBERJACK IS CRAZY. DRAW THIS PICTURE WITHOUT USING A SINGLE LETTER. MAKE USE OF SYMBOLS AND ATTRIBUTES.

CHILDREN

DRAWING CHILDREN IS ONE OF THE DISCIPLINES THAT IS HATED BY A LOT OF CARTOONISTS. IT IS BECAUSE CHILDREN ARE, UNTIL CERTAIN AGE, THE SAME AND IT IS REALLY DIFFICULT TO DIFFER ONE FROM ANOTHER. HOWEVER, FROM THEIR THIRD YEAR, THEY START LOOK DIFFERENT FROM EACH OTHER AND IT ALL STARTS TO BE REAL FUN.

WE NEED A LITTLE GIRL WHO IS APPROXIMATELY SIX YEARS OLD. SHE IS CUTE BUT NOT TOO MUCH. SHE SHOULD BE NICE. SHE WILL BE KIDNAPPED. SHE IS NOT DEFENCELESS BECAUSE TOO MUCH SORROW IS NOT AN EMOTION THAT WE WANT IN A COMIC BOOK.

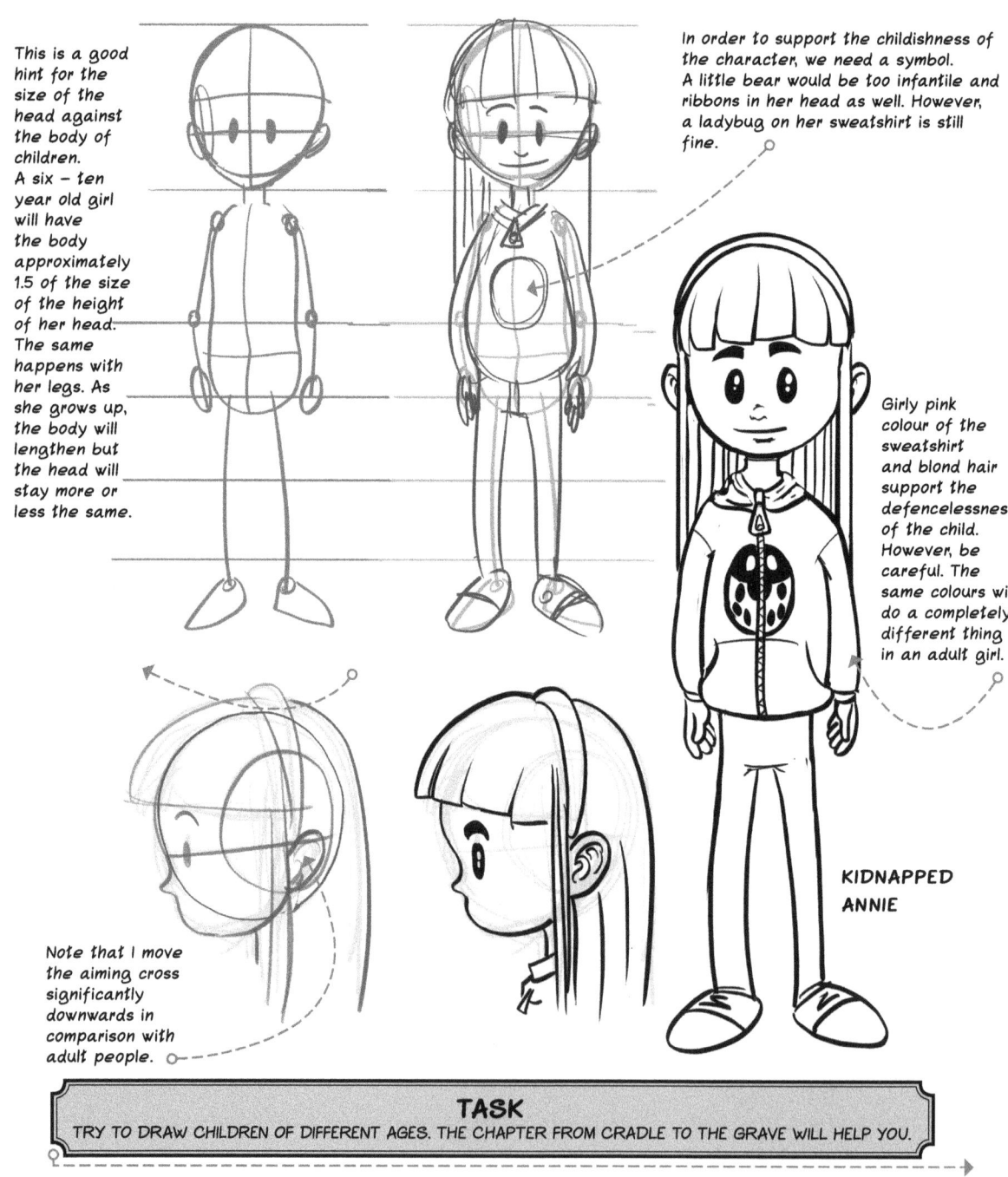

KIDNAPPED ANNIE

TASK
TRY TO DRAW CHILDREN OF DIFFERENT AGES. THE CHAPTER FROM CRADLE TO THE GRAVE WILL HELP YOU.

MODERN VILLAIN

PEOPLE SAY THAT A HERO IS AS GOOD AS THE VILLAIN WHO THEY ARE FIGHTING. IT IS TRUE. UNTIL NOW, WE HAVE BEEN CREATING OUR HERO IN A WAY THAT THEY WOULD NOT BE BURDENED WITH ANY FLAW, THEIR PAST OR EXTRAVAGANTNESS. IT WAS BECAUSE WE WANTED OUR READERS TO IDENTIFY WITH THEM WE CAN SAY THAT A HERO DOES NOT HAVE TO BE INTERESTING BECAUSE THE READER TRANSPOSES THEMSELVES TO THEM. SO, THE VILLAIN SHOULD LOGICALLY BE HIS OPPOSITE VERSION. THE VILLAIN IS BURDENED WITH HIS PAST. WE KNOW EXACTLY WHO HE IS. HE CAN BE AFFECTED BY A BODY FLAW AND HAVE A CHARACTER AS STRONG AS STONE. THE MORE, THE BETTER.

BARON OF LAUTERNITZ IS TYPICAL NAPOLEON. HE WILL RESEMBLE A PENGUIN A BIT. THIS IS WHAT HAPPENS WHEN YOU WORK WITH ARCHETYPES. THEY WILL ALWAYS RESEMBLE SOMEBODY AND THAT'S FINE. YOU WILL NOT HAVE TO SPEND TOO MUCH TIME INTRODUCING THE CHARACTER TO THE READER. HE OR SHE KNOWS THAT HE IS EVIL. JUST LOOK AT HIM. HE A PSYCHO.

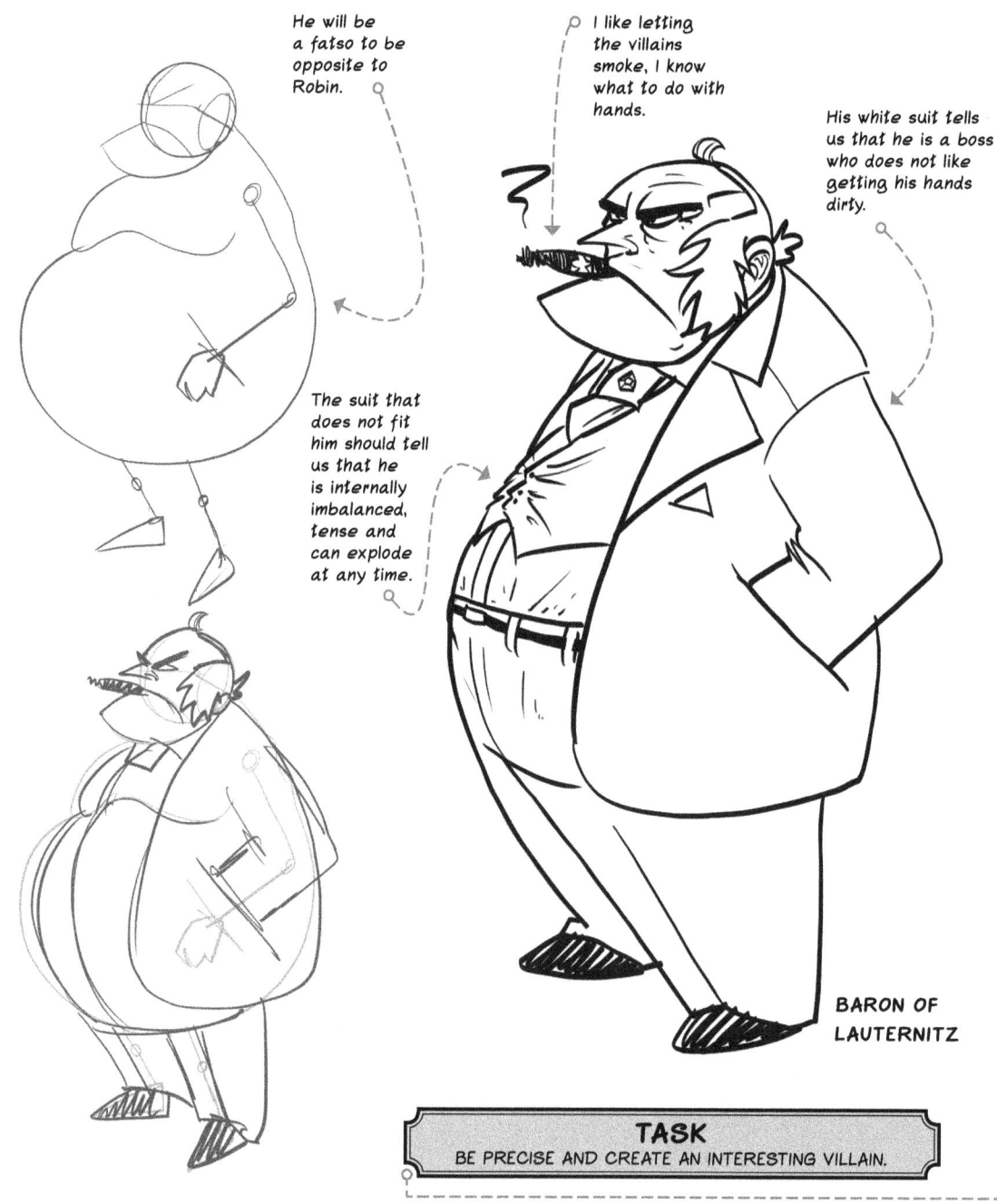

He will be a fatso to be opposite to Robin.

I like letting the villains smoke, I know what to do with hands.

His white suit tells us that he is a boss who does not like getting his hands dirty.

The suit that does not fit him should tell us that he is internally imbalanced, tense and can explode at any time.

BARON OF LAUTERNITZ

TASK
BE PRECISE AND CREATE AN INTERESTING VILLAIN.

PAIR OF HENCHMEN

FOR OUR COMIC BOOK, WE NEED A COMIC PAIR OF HENCHMEN OF A BIG VILLAIN. THEY WILL BALANCE HIS EVIL. THEY WILL NOT LOOK EVIL AT FIRST SIGHT BUT RATHER CLUMSY. LIKE FUNNY CHARACTERS. THEY ARE NOT SO SMART, THEY ARE RATHER STUPID, OTHERWISE, THEY WOULD NOT END UP AS HENCHMEN OF A SECOND CLASS BOSS, RIGHT?

I COULD WRITE A LOT ABOUT PAIRS OF HEROES AND ANTIHEROES BUT THERE IS NOT ENOUGH SPACE. MAYBE NEXT TIME. WE SHOULD KNOW THAT THERE ARE THAT ARE PHYSICALLY OR SPIRITUALLY IN EITHER SHARP CONTRAST (ASTERIX AND OBELIX, PIF AND HERCULES) OR THEY ARE LIKE TWINS (ROSCO AND DESOTO, MILLIE AND MELODY MOUSE, BRUTUS AND NERO). IF THEY ARE SOMETHING BETWEEN THESE TWO GROUPS, IT DOES NOT USUALLY END UP WELL. ON THE OTHER HAND, THE RELATIONSHIP BETWEEN THE TWO PROTAGONISTS MUST WORK. YOU CAN BEST ILLUSTRATE THE DIFFERENCE BETWEEN THEIR NATURES BY THEIR PHYSICAL LOOK. THEY ARE EITHER IN CONTRAST, THEREFORE CONFLICTIVE, OR IN CONFORMITY WITH EACH OTHER.

I HAVE CHOSEN THE FIRST OPTION. A SHORT, THICKSET AND SMARTER CHOLERIC HENCHMAN IS IN CONTRAST WITH A STUPID, TALL, SLIM AND PHLEGMATIC ONE. THIS ARCHETYPE CAN BE FOUND IN A LOT OF MOVIES.

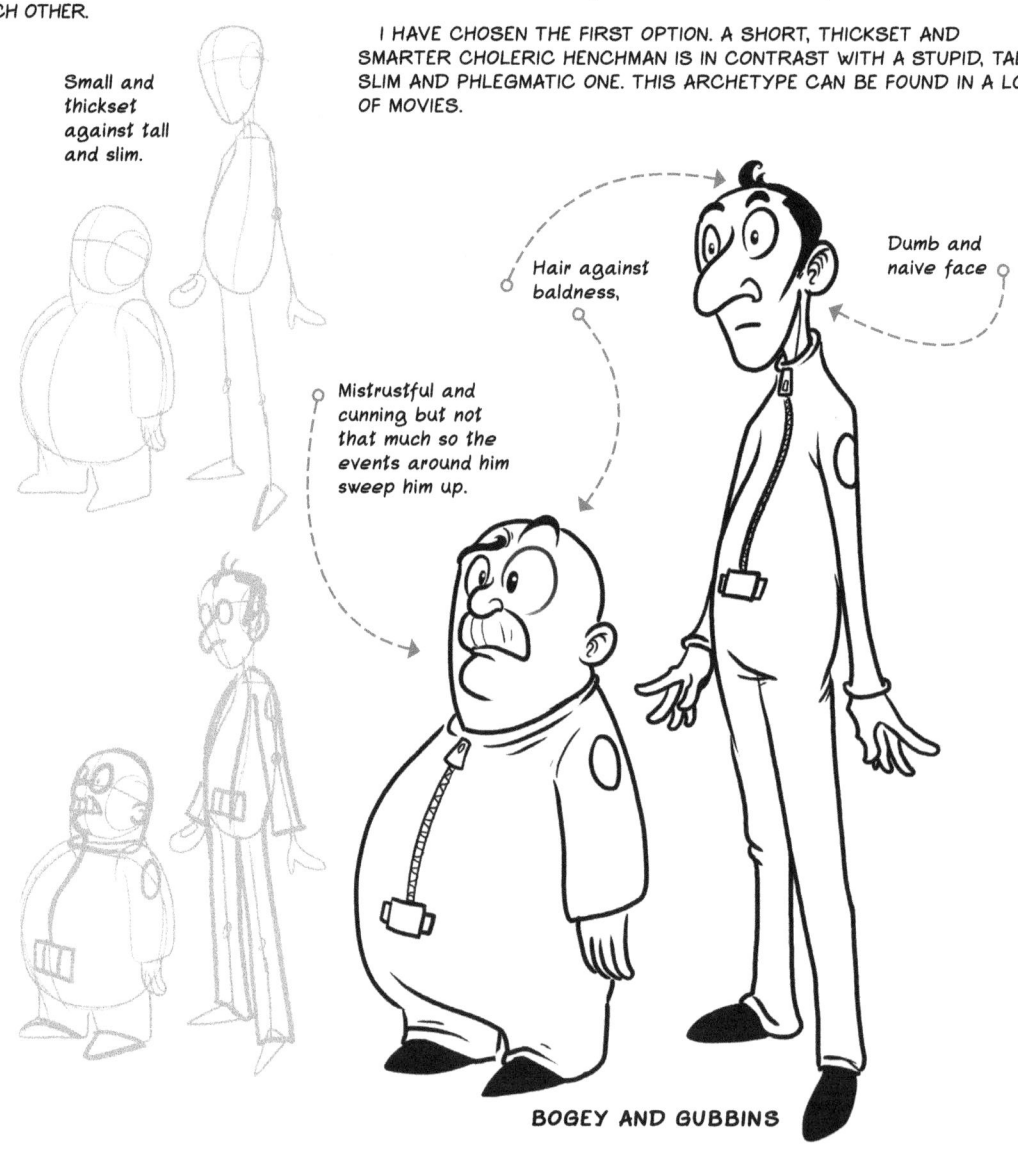

Small and thickset against tall and slim.

Hair against baldness,

Dumb and naive face

Mistrustful and cunning but not that much so the events around him sweep him up.

BOGEY AND GUBBINS

TASK
TRY TO DRAW VARIOUS PAIRS OF HENCHMEN AND GIVE THEM EITHER SAME OR CONTRADICTORY CHARACTERS. TRY TO LIGHT A SPARK BETWEEN THEM.

SCIENTIST

WE DO NOT NEED MORE CHARACTERS TO OUR SAMPLE ANY LONGER. WE ARE GOING TO WORK WITH THEM IN THE FUTURE THOUGH. FOR ILLUSTRATION, I HAVE CHOSEN A COUPLE OF ARCHETYPES. BEAR IN MIND THAT ALMOST ALL ARCHETYPES CAN BE POLARIZED ON THE GOOD OR BAD SIDE. THINK IT OVER IN ADVANCE WHERE YOUR CHARACTER WILL BELONG AND THROUGH THEIR APPEARANCE JUST SIMPLY TELL THIS TO YOUR READERS.

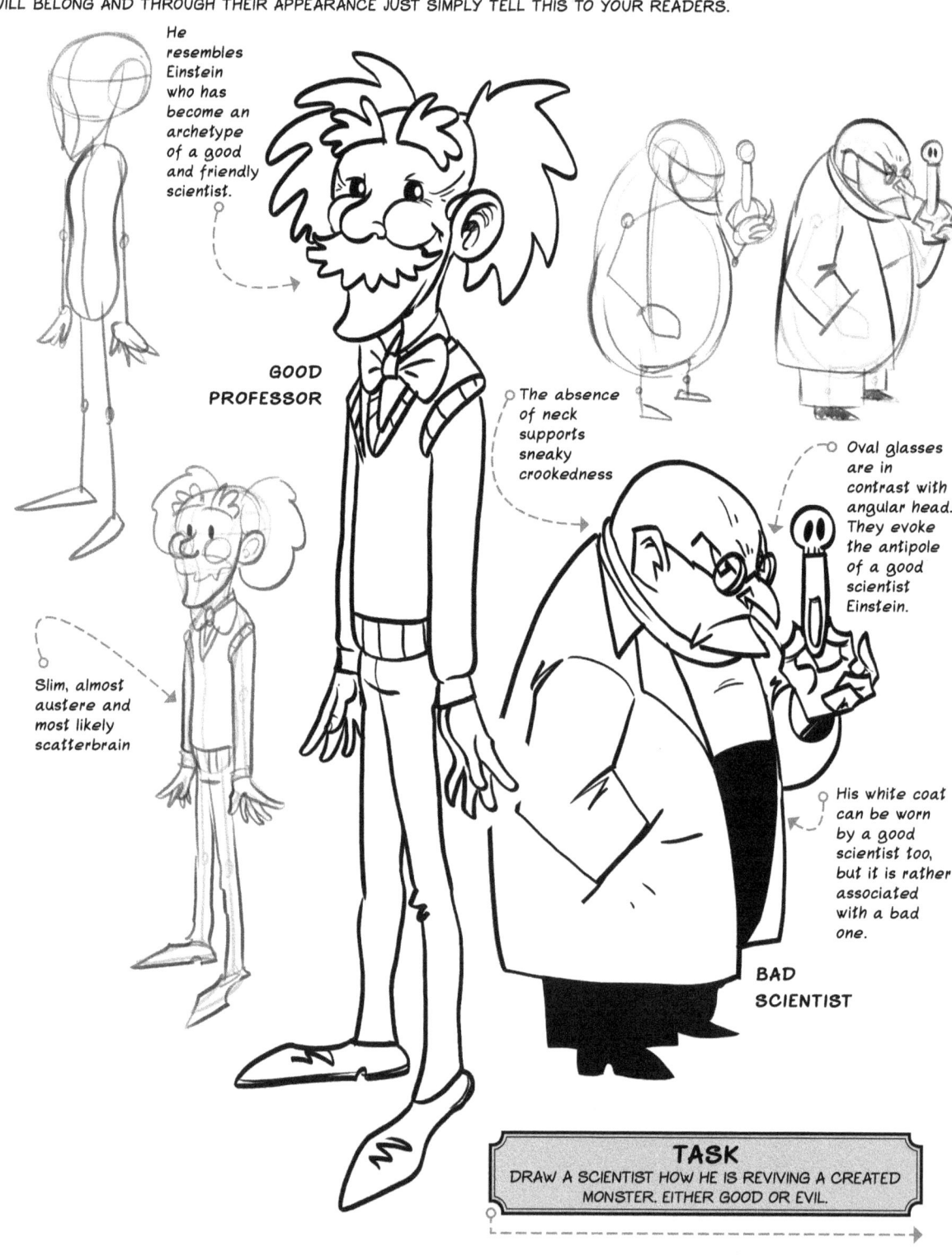

He resembles Einstein who has become an archetype of a good and friendly scientist.

GOOD PROFESSOR

The absence of neck supports sneaky crookedness

Oval glasses are in contrast with angular head. They evoke the antipole of a good scientist Einstein.

Slim, almost austere and most likely scatterbrain

His white coat can be worn by a good scientist too, but it is rather associated with a bad one.

BAD SCIENTIST

TASK
DRAW A SCIENTIST HOW HE IS REVIVING A CREATED MONSTER. EITHER GOOD OR EVIL.

WITCH AND SORCERESS

THE APPEARANCES OF WITCHES AND SORCERESSES ARE CULTURALLY CONDITIONED. HOWEVER, WE CAN FIND THESE BEINGS EVERYWHERE. IN ENGLAND, AMERICA, RUSSIA, CHINA, JAPAN... THEIR APPEARANCE AND BELONGINGS, HOWEVER, DYNAMICALLY CHANGE. IN THE CZECH REPUBLIC, A WITCH IS DESCRIBED AS AN OLD BAT LIVING IN A VERY NON-STANDARD HOUSE ON A CHICKEN LEG WITH NO CONNECTION TO ENGINEERING NETWORKS. IN MOST CASES, SHE IS EVIL AND SHE EATS CHILDREN. MOSTLY FROM THE WEST, SORCERESSES RESEMBLING HERBALISTS AND HEALERS ARE COMING TO US. IN GREAT STORIES, WE CAN FIND MIGHTY WITCHES, ON HALFWAY TO BEING DEMIGODS. NEVERTHELESS, EVEN WITCHES HAVE DIFFERENT CHARACTERS.

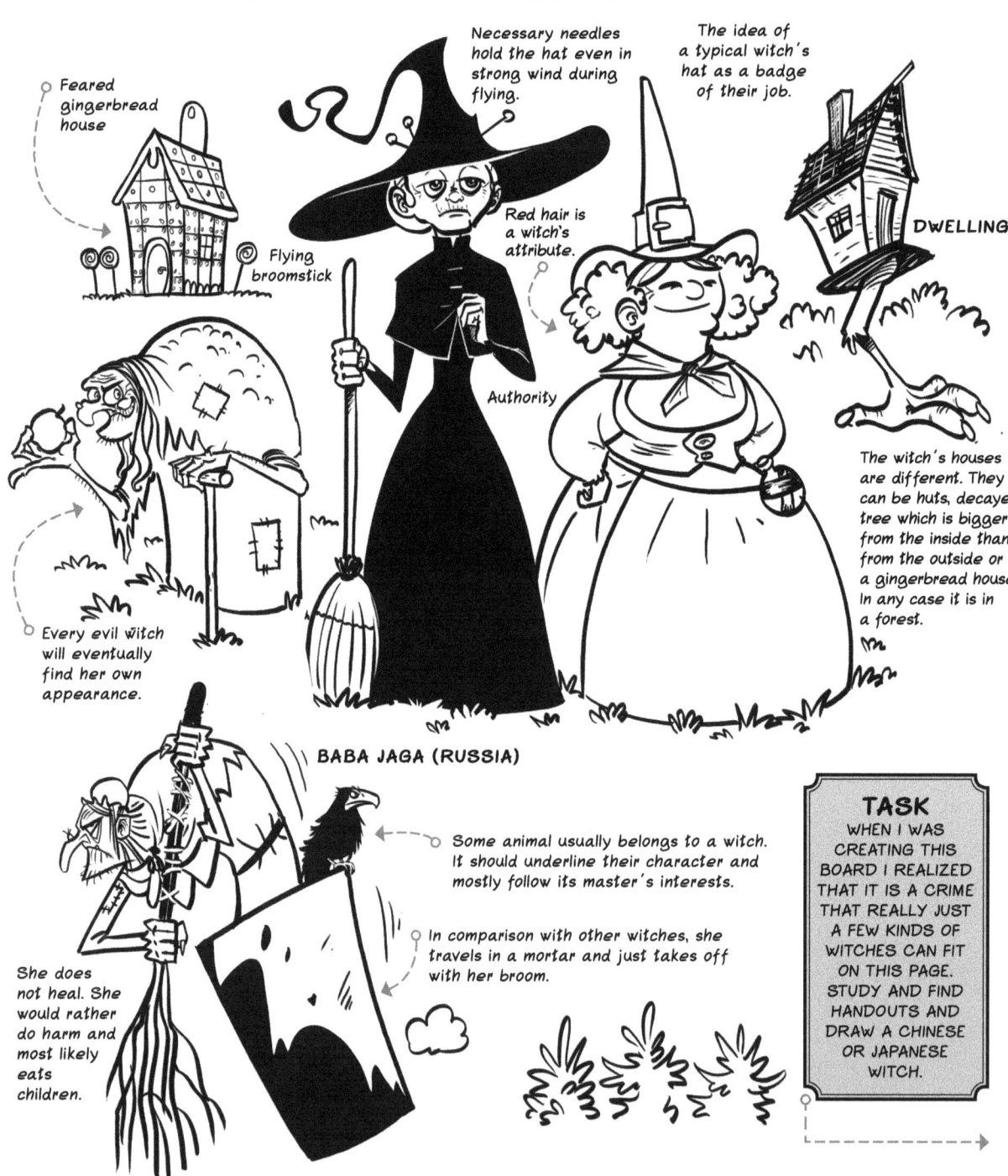

- Feared gingerbread house
- Necessary needles hold the hat even in strong wind during flying.
- The idea of a typical witch's hat as a badge of their job.
- Flying broomstick
- Red hair is a witch's attribute.
- DWELLING
- Authority
- Every evil witch will eventually find her own appearance.
- The witch's houses are different. They can be huts, decayed tree which is bigger from the inside than from the outside or a gingerbread house. In any case it is in a forest.

BABA JAGA (RUSSIA)

- Some animal usually belongs to a witch. It should underline their character and mostly follow its master's interests.
- In comparison with other witches, she travels in a mortar and just takes off with her broom.
- She does not heal. She would rather do harm and most likely eats children.

TASK
WHEN I WAS CREATING THIS BOARD I REALIZED THAT IT IS A CRIME THAT REALLY JUST A FEW KINDS OF WITCHES CAN FIT ON THIS PAGE. STUDY AND FIND HANDOUTS AND DRAW A CHINESE OR JAPANESE WITCH.

BARBARIANS AND BANDITS

WHEN PEOPLE SAY BARBARIAN, YOU AUTOMATICALLY IMAGINE CONAN THE BARBARIAN. WHAT CAN WE DO WHEN IT IS ALREADY A USUAL COLLOCATION. CONAN THE BARBARIAN HAS BECOME AN ARCHETYPE. JUST HAVE A LOOK AT HOW YOU CAN SORT OUT HIS FORM IN CARTOONING.

CONAN WAS NOT A FOOL BUT WAS CHARACTERIZED BY SIMPLE (I REPEAT: NOT STUPID) THINKING. WE CAN SAY HE WAS A PRIMITIVE. I REPEAT AGAIN. A PRIMITIVE DOES NOT EQUAL FOOL.

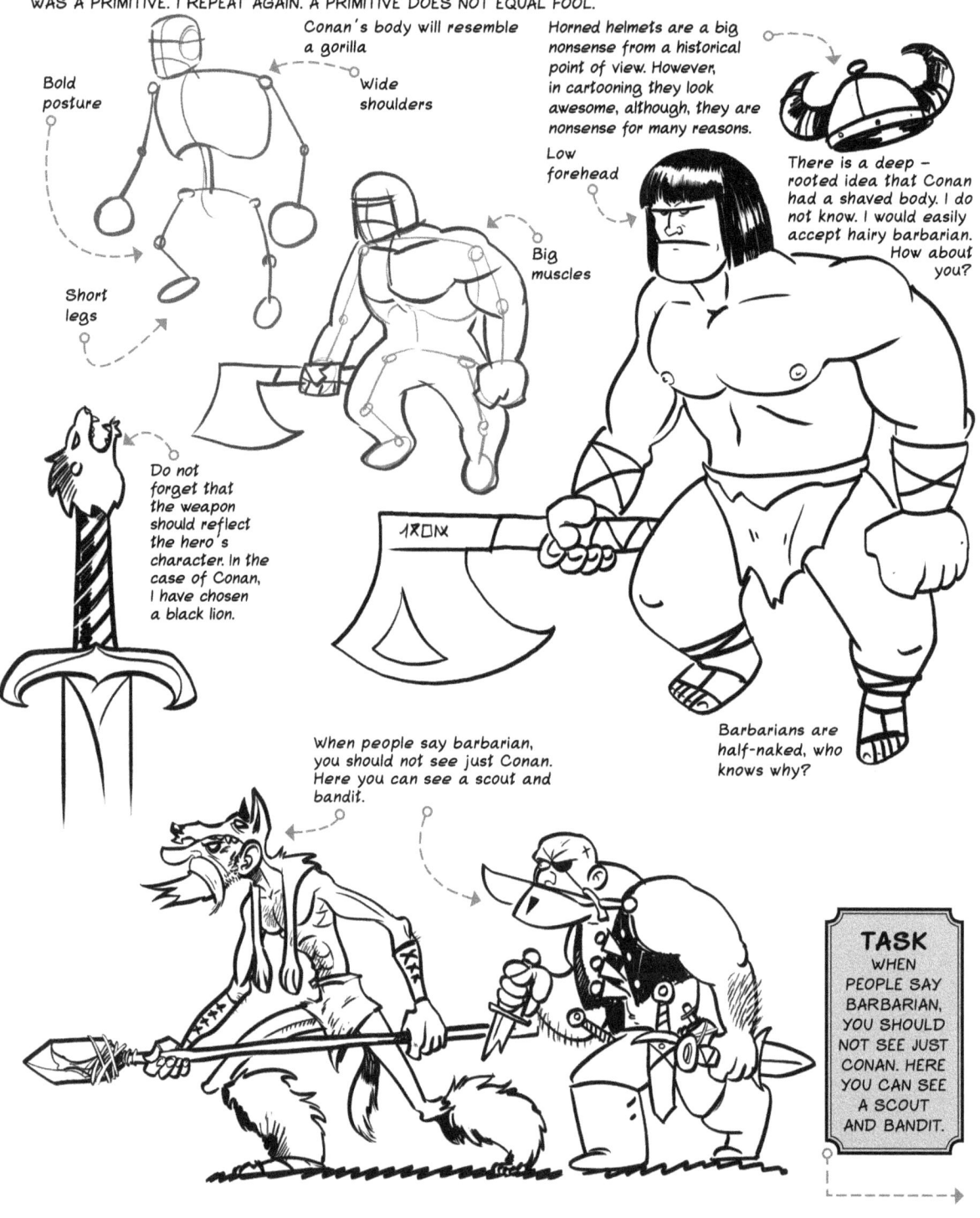

Bold posture

Conan's body will resemble a gorilla

Wide shoulders

Short legs

Horned helmets are a big nonsense from a historical point of view. However, in cartooning they look awesome, although, they are nonsense for many reasons.

Low forehead

Big muscles

There is a deep-rooted idea that Conan had a shaved body. I do not know. I would easily accept hairy barbarian. How about you?

Do not forget that the weapon should reflect the hero's character. In the case of Conan, I have chosen a black lion.

Barbarians are half-naked, who knows why?

When people say barbarian, you should not see just Conan. Here you can see a scout and bandit.

TASK
WHEN PEOPLE SAY BARBARIAN, YOU SHOULD NOT SEE JUST CONAN. HERE YOU CAN SEE A SCOUT AND BANDIT.

SUPERHERO

I AM SORRY BUT WE DO NOT HAVE ENOUGH SPACE TO DISCUSS THE SUPERHERO TOPIC. WHAT KIND OF A COMIC BOOK WOULD IT BE IF THIS TOPIC WASN'T EVEN MENTIONED. WHEN PEOPLE SAY SUPERHERO, MOST PEOPLE IMAGINE SUPERMAN. IT IS NO WONDER; HE IS AN ICON OF A SUPERHERO. HE HAS BECOME AN ARCHETYPE AND THE OTHER ONES SUPERHEROES PROCEED HIM. AS WE HAVE DISCUSSED MANY TIMES, IN CARTOONING, ANYTHING THAT HIDDEN INSIDE IS VISIBLE FROM THE OUTSIDE. IT MEANS THAT AT FIRST SIGHT, A HERO'S ABILITIES THAT ARE HIDDEN FROM THE READER WILL STILL BE REFLECTED IN THEIR APPEARANCE. WHEN YOU HAVE A LOOK AT THE CHARACTER BELOW, IT IS CLEAR THAT THIS HERO IS GOOD. HE IS TREMENDOUSLY STRONG AND CAN FLY. MOST HEROES WITH CAPES CAN FLY; HOWEVER, IF WE ARE INTERESTED IN ARCHETYPES, CLASSIC HEROES WHO WEAR UNDERPANTS OVER THEIR TROUSERS WILL RULE FOR A LONG TIME.

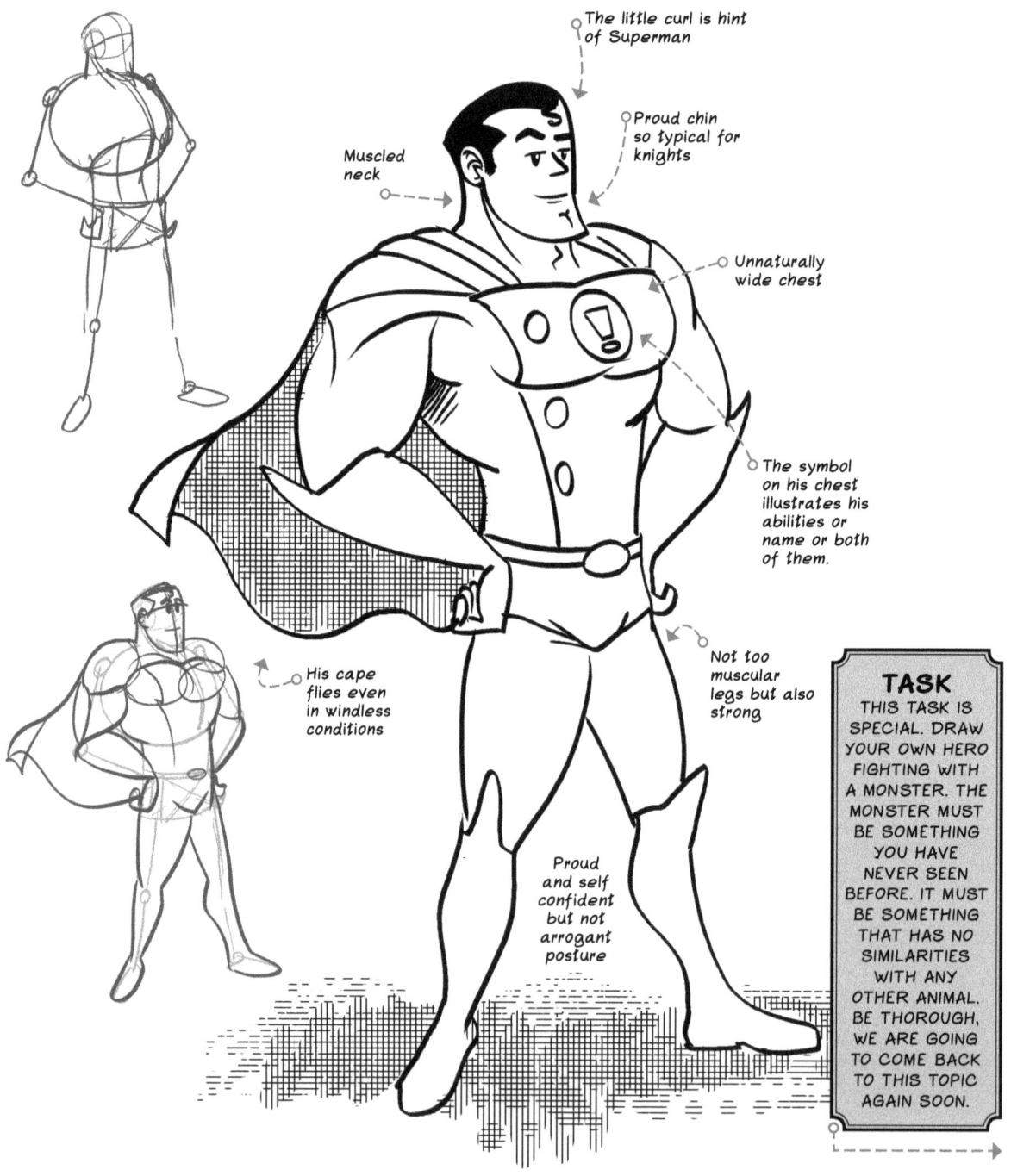

- The little curl is hint of Superman
- Proud chin so typical for knights
- Muscled neck
- Unnaturally wide chest
- The symbol on his chest illustrates his abilities or name or both of them.
- His cape flies even in windless conditions
- Not too muscular legs but also strong
- Proud and self confident but not arrogant posture

TASK

THIS TASK IS SPECIAL. DRAW YOUR OWN HERO FIGHTING WITH A MONSTER. THE MONSTER MUST BE SOMETHING YOU HAVE NEVER SEEN BEFORE. IT MUST BE SOMETHING THAT HAS NO SIMILARITIES WITH ANY OTHER ANIMAL. BE THOROUGH, WE ARE GOING TO COME BACK TO THIS TOPIC AGAIN SOON.

INTRODUCTION TO COMIC BOOKS

WHAT IS A COMIC BOOK?
IN THIS SKETCH BOOK, WE ARE JUST SCRATCHING THE SURFACE, SO I LEAVE A PRECISE COMIC BOOK DEFINITION, WHICH WILL EXCLUDE ALL OTHER MEDIA, TO THE PROFESSIONALS IF YOU WANT TO GET TO THE BOTTOM OF THIS QUESTION, I RECOMMEND "UNDERSTANDING COMICS: THE INVISIBLE ART" BY SCOTT MCCLOUD (BB ART).
  HERE WE JUST DEFINE A COMIC BOOK FOR OUR OWN PURPOSES IN ORDER TO CAPTURE ITS SPIRIT, AND WE WILL NOT BE BOTHERED IF THE RESULT INCLUDES OTHER MEDIA AS WELL.
  IF YOU THINK YOU FULLY UNDERSTAND AND YOU DO NOT NEED THIS INTRODUCTION, YOU CAN DO A TEST STRAIGHT AWAY ON THE OPPOSITE PAGE. IT IS A TEST WHICH SHOULD CHECK IF YOU, WITH NO HESITATION, KNOW HOW TO DIFFER THIS MEDIUM FROM OTHER SIMILAR ONES. IF YOU SUCCEED IN PASSING ALL QUESTIONS, YOU ARE READY TO MOVE TWO PAGES FORWARD (YOU CAN FIND OUT THE TEST RESULTS WHEN YOU LOOK AGAINST THE LIGHT). IF NOT, I WILL TRY TO RECTIFY SOME MISTAKES WHICH MAKE IT IMPOSSIBLE TO DIFFER FROM A COMIC.

WHAT DOES A COMIC BOOK CONSIST OF?
  WE WILL BE TALKING ABOUT CLASSIC COMIC BOOKS, COMMON FORMATS AND MOST COMMON COMIC BOOK SHAPES. THERE ARE EXCEPTIONS BUT WE ARE NOT GOING TO DISCUSS THEM.
  A COMIC BOOK USUALLY CONTAINS PANELS, PICTURES, BUBBLES, LETTERING AND SFX (TERM EXPLANATION IS AT PAGE 101). BUT BE CAREFUL. THE ABSENCE OF ANY OF THESE PARTS DOES NOT MEAN THAT IT IS NOT A COMIC BOOK. THERE ARE COMIC BOOKS WITHOUT BUBBLES, LETTERING OR EVEN PICTURES. THE KEY THING WHICH IS CRUCIAL TO DIFFERENTIATE COMIC BOOKS FROM OTHER MEDIA IS CALLED JUXTAPOSITION. WHAT IS IT? SIMPLY SAID, IT IS A NAME GIVEN FOR WHEN PICTURES FOLLOW EACH OTHER IN LINEAR SPACES. THE SPACE, IN A COMIC BOOK, BECOMES TIME. YOU CANNOT SEE SUCH A THING IN OTHER MEDIA AND FROM THIS FEATURE; THE EXCEPTIONALITY COMES OUT OF THIS FORM OF EXPRESSION.

CAN I ALREADY COME TO KNOW THE DEFINITION?
  IF YOU WANT TO THINK OVER ART, YOU WILL FIND A DEFINITION THAT ART IS A MANIFESTATION OF YOUR INNER FEELINGS AND EXPERIENCE.

ART IS
A MANIFESTATION THEN.

IF ART IS A MANIFESTATION, CAN A SINGLE SPECIFIC PICTURE BE DEFINED?

A PICTURE IS
A MESSAGE.

NOW IT IS PRETTY CLEAR WHAT A COMIC BOOK IS.

A COMIC BOOK IS
A NARRATION.

  AT THIS MOMENT, THIS SHOULD BE A PIECE OF CAKE FOR YOU. I JUST POINT OUT ONE TRICKY QUESTION. A COMIC BOOK DOES NOT HAVE TO CONTAIN MORE PICTURES. ONE PICTURE COULD BE ENOUGH. HOWEVER, THE TIME FLOW MUST BE OBVIOUS FROM IT. IN MY SEMINARS, I GIVE A VERY SIMPLE HINT. IMAGINE THAT A PHOTOGRAPHER COULD CAPTURE THE SCENERY BY A SINGLE SHUTTER RELEASE PRESS. HOWEVER, IF TIME FLOWS IN IT AND THE ARTIST MUST JOIN MORE PHOTOS TOGETHER IN ORDER TO ACHIEVE THIS RESULT, THIS IS A COMIC BOOK.

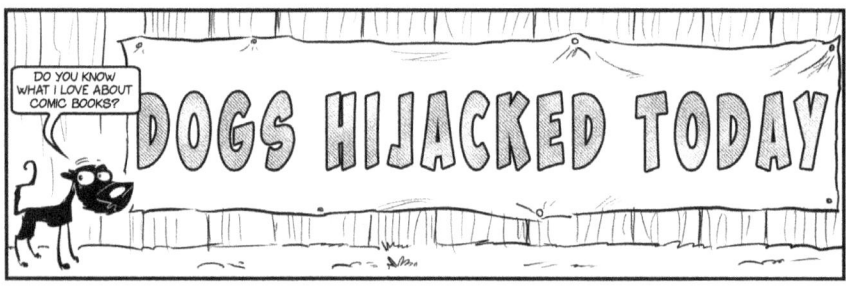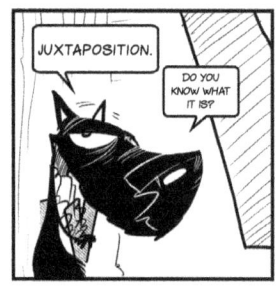
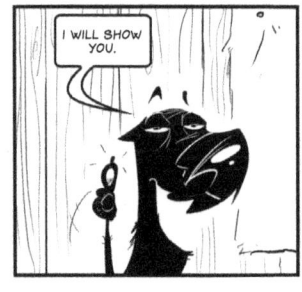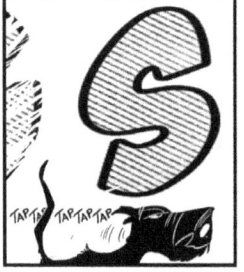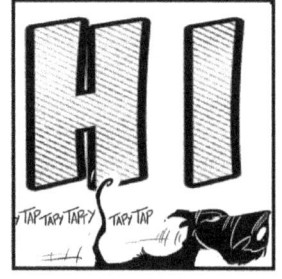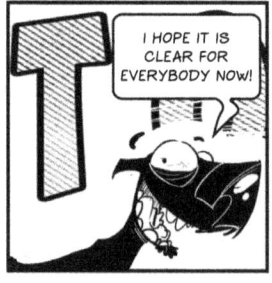

COMIC BOOK TEST – QUESTIONS

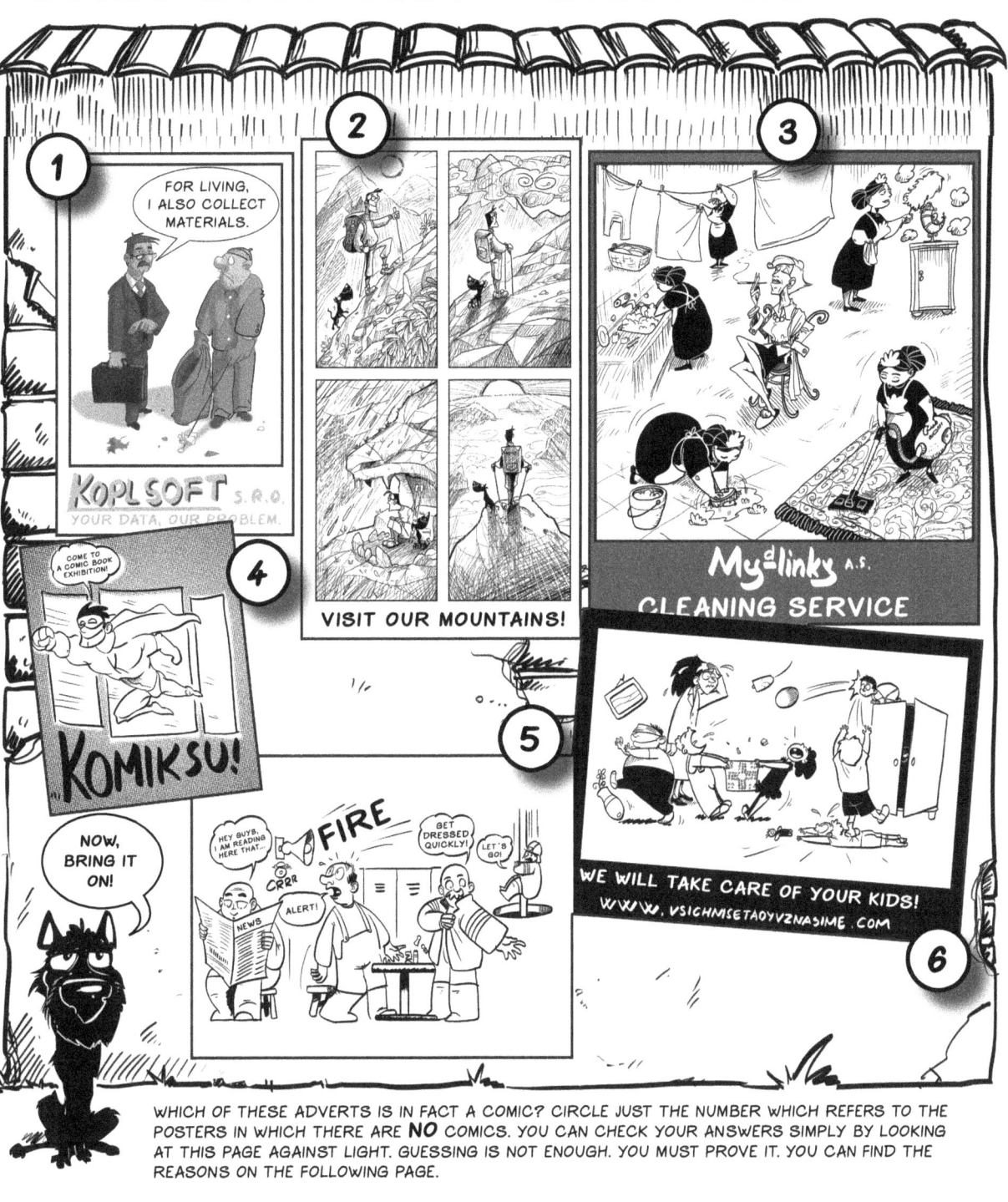

WHICH OF THESE ADVERTS IS IN FACT A COMIC? CIRCLE JUST THE NUMBER WHICH REFERS TO THE POSTERS IN WHICH THERE ARE **NO** COMICS. YOU CAN CHECK YOUR ANSWERS SIMPLY BY LOOKING AT THIS PAGE AGAINST LIGHT. GUESSING IS NOT ENOUGH. YOU MUST PROVE IT. YOU CAN FIND THE REASONS ON THE FOLLOWING PAGE.

1   2   3   4   5   6

COMIC TEST - ANSWERS

1. JUST A PICTURE. ALTHOUGH IT CONTAINS A BUBBLE – ONE OF COMICS ATTRIBUTES BUT WE CANNOT SEE ANY SEQUENCE AND THAT IS THE MOST IMPORTANT THING IN COMICS.

2. THE SEQUENCE OF FOLLOW-UP PICTURES IS CLEAR. ALTHOUGH THERE IS NO BUBBLE, THAT IS IRRELEVANT. IT IS A COMIC.

3. THIS IS A TRICKY ONE. CAN ONLY A SINGLE PICTURE BE A SEQUENCE? OF COURSE IT CAN. IF YOU LOOK AT IT CLOSELY, IT IS CLEAR THAT THIS IS NOT A SNAPSHOT. THE CLEANER IS OBVIOUSLY MOVING THROUGH TIME. IT IS A COMIC STRIP.

4. THE FACT THAT THIS IS ABOUT COMICS, OR A MOVIE ABOUT COMICS OR A PLAY ACCORDING TO A COMIC BOOK, DOES NOT MAKE IT A COMIC BOOK. THIS IS NOT A COMIC STRIP.

5. SAME CASE AS WITH THE CLEANER. IN ONE PICTURE, YOU HAVE GOT THE WHOLE STORY ABOUT HOW THE FIRE FIGHTERS MOVING FROM POINT ZERO TO ACTION. IF THERE WAS A PHOTOGRAPHER, THEY WOULD TAKE 4 OR 5 PHOTOS TO PUT THIS SCENE TOGETHER. THIS IS THE MAGIC OF COMICS.

6. IT IS A CRAZY AND WILD SCENE... BUT IS JUST A PIECE OF INFORMATION. YOU COULD MAKE SUCH PICTURE WITH ONE SHOT IF YOU EVER WERE IN SUCH HELL.

I HAVE INTENTIONALLY CHOSEN NON-TYPICAL COMICS TO NOT MAKE IT TOO EASY FOR YOU. IF I PUT BATMAN HERE, I BELIEVE YOU WOULD NOT HESITATE HERE. HOWEVER, I WANTED YOU TO KNOW THAT UNDERSTANDING A COMIC BOOK IS NOT EASY IF YOU DO NOT UNDERSTAND ITS ESSENCE.

BASIC COMIC BOOK TERMS

BUBBLES - THE AREA WHERE DIALOG TEXTS ARE PLACED. THEIR SHAPE MAY VARY A LOT BUT THEY ALWAYS SHOW WHICH CHARACTER IS SPEAKING.

LETTERING - THE TEXT WHICH IS NOT CONTAINED IN BUBBLES, DESCRIPTIVE PANELS OR SFX, IN A COMIC BOOK.

PICTURES - THE PANEL CONTENT WHICH DOES NOT HAVE TO SEQUENTIALLY FOLLOW EACH OTHER, HOWEVER, THEY MAKE TOGETHER ONE UNIT.

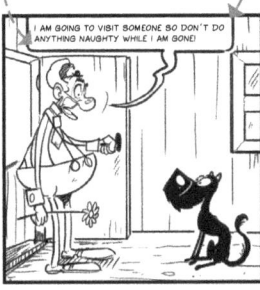
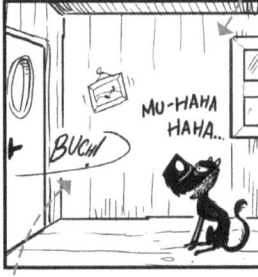
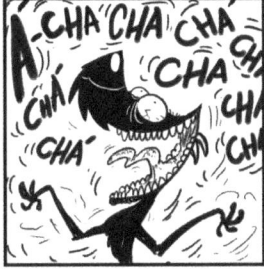
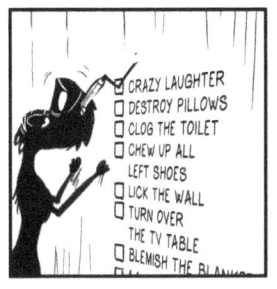

PANEL - SINGLE PICTURES OF COMIC BOOKS, AS A RULE IS BORDERED BY A FRAME.

SFX - AN ABBREVIATION FOR SOUND EFFECTS

COMIC STRIP - IS A COMIC THAT IS LINEARLY AND CLASSICALLY ARRANGED, USUALLY INTO ONE OR TWO LINES. NEWSPAPERS HAVE GOOD EXAMPLES OF THIS.

COMICS MAINSTREAM - WHAT MAINSTREAM COMICS ARE, IS A REALLY SUBJECTIVE MATTER. FROM MY POINT OF VIEW, IT CAN BE DIVIDED INTO TWO WAYS OF THINKING:

1. MAINSTREAM ART - MAINSTREAM IN ANY BRANCH REQUIRES A BIGGER NUMBER OF INTERCHANGEABLE ARTISTS. IN SPITE THE FACT THAT THEIR STYLE IS RECOGNIZABLE, A READER WOULD NOT MIND IF, EACH YEAR, BOTH THE CARTOONIST AND SCENARIST CHANGE BECAUSE THEY WILL CONTINUE WITH THE SAME THING. ON THE OTHER HAND, IF ALBERT UDERZO, THE CARTOONIST OF ASTERIX, TOOK UP ON THAT, IT WOULD PROBABLY NOT BE THE BEST NO MATTER HOW INTERESTING IT WOULD BE. MAINSTREAM MEANS SOMETHING DIFFERENT IN EVERY SINGLE COUNTRY BECAUSE IF UDERZO DREW ONE VOLUME OF SPIROU OR LEONARDO THE SCIENTIST, WE WOULD PROBABLY NOT HAVE ANYTHING AGAINST IT.

2. MAINSTREAM COMIC BOOK - MAINSTREAM, IN ANY BRANCH, AFFECTS THE BIGGEST NUMBER OF FANS POSSIBLE, IN OUR CASE, THEY ARE READERS. THE MORE FANS OF A PARTICULAR COMIC BOOK THERE ARE, THE MORE MAINSTREAM THE COMIC BOOK IS. THE MORE POPULAR THE PIECE OF ART IS, THE MORE THE MARKET COMES WITH SOMETHING SIMILAR AND INTERCHANGEABLE. SO JUST LIKE THAT, A BRAND NEW PIECE OF ART BECOMES A MAINSTREAM ONE PRETTY QUICKLY IF THE AUDIENCE EXPRESSES THEIR FAVOR.

THIS MEANS THAT THE MAINSTREAM CREATES THE MARKET AND MARKET CREATES THE MAINSTREAM.

WE CAN CLAIM THAT ANY PIECE OF ART, OF ANY ARTISTIC NATURE, BECOMES COMMERCIAL UNDER THE FAVOR OF ITS AUDIENCE. A COMMERCIAL PIECE OF ART DOES NOT HAVE TO BE ARTISTICALLY REALLY BAD.

THE FACT THAT A COMIC BOOK IS APPRECIATED BY THE MAJORITY OF THE AUDIENCE IS NOT ITS WEAKNESS BUT THE OTHER WAY ROUND. IT MEANS THAT THE COMIC BOOK IS CREATED FOR A CONTEMPORARY READER, THE READERS UNDERSTAND IT AND THE ARTIST WHO CREATED IT UNDERSTANDS THE READERS. AFTER ALL, SHAKESPEARE WAS AMONG THE FIRST MAINSTREAM ARTISTS. DO YOU THINK THAT IF HE CREATED PIECES OF ART FOR A SMALL GROUP OF INTELLECTUALS, WHO WERE NOT UNDERSTOOD BY THEIR CONTEMPORARIES, CROWDS OF PEOPLE WOULD GO TO SEE HIS PLAYS? MOREOVER, IF THE CROWDS DIDN'T GO TO SEE HIS PLAYS, DO YOU THINK THAT HE WOULD WORK AT THE THEATRE? MOST LIKELY NOT.

HOWEVER, DO NOT GET MISTAKEN. I DO NOT DESPISE HIGH ART. THE OTHER WAY ROUND. IT IS NECESSARY BECAUSE IT MOVES THE BORDERS OF PERCEPTION FURTHER AND HIGHER. HOWEVER, EVERY THEATRE DIRECTOR KNOWS THAT THEY CAN AFFORD JUST ONE PLAY OUT OF TEN OF THOSE WHICH THE AUDIENCE WOULD WANT TO SEE. IN OTHER WORDS, COMMERCIALISM NEEDS TO EARN FOR HIGH ART. HIGH ART AND COMMERCIALISM NEED EACH OTHER. IT WOULD BE FINE IF BOTH SIDES ALWAYS REMEMBERED THAT.

> "HIGH ART AND COMMERCIALISM NEED EACH OTHER."

PANELS

AT THE MOMENT, TRY TO IMAGINE THAT YOU ARE A COMPOSER AND YOU DECIDED TO COMPOSE AN OPERA BUT WITH THE CURTAINS DOWN. YES, THE ESSENCE STAYS THE SAME. MUSIC AND ACTORS... BUT IT IS NOT THE RIGHT EXPERIENCE WITHOUT THE VISUALS. YOU VOLUNTARY GAVE UP ONE OF THE MAIN EXPRESSIONAL TOOLS OF ITS KIND.

THE SAME HAPPENS IF YOU DO NOT SET THE WHOLE COMIC BOOK LAYOUT. THE GAPS BETWEEN EACH PANEL, COLOUR, OUTLINE THICKNESS, STYLE, PANEL OVERLAPS, THEIR SHAPE AND THEIR LAYOUT ON THE BOARD. YOU SHOULD PLAN AND DETERMINE ALL OF THAT IN ADVANCE. YOU DO NOT HAVE TO. YOU CAN DRAW A WILD COMIC BOOK WITHOUT ANY RULES OF PANELLING. HOWEVER, YOU ARE GIVING UP ON SUCH A SIGNIFICANT EXPRESSIONAL TOOL IN COMICS THAT IS PART OF ITS ESSENCE.

HOW TO DO IT? IF YOU SET A CLASSIC PAGE, USUALLY FOR EXAMPLE: 3 X 3 (WATCHMEN) OR CLASSIC 4-LINE (ASTERIX) PAGE, AND BY DIVIDING AND JOINING YOU ACHIEVE HORIZONTAL OR VERTICAL SHAPE – ANY DEVIATION FROM THIS ORDER WILL HAVE ITS OWN NARRATIVE REASON AND YOU CAN ACHIEVE EMPHASISED EFFECTS THAT WILL SUPPORT THE PLOT OR WILL JUST MAKE THE READING MORE INTERESTING, FOR EXAMPLE IN A BORING BUT NECESSARY PART OF THE STORY.

FIRST OF ALL, LET'S SAY THAT IF YOU CHOOSE ANY STYLE, TAKE INTO ACCOUNT THE READER'S AGE FOR WHOM THE COMIC BOOK IS INTENDED. FOR CHILDREN FROM 6 TO 12, IT IS BETTER TO STICK TO CLASSIC RULES AND MAKE ONLY FEW EXCEPTIONS. YOU CAN APPROACH OLDER READERS MORE EXPRESSIVELY BUT DO NOT EXPERIMENT. THE PAGE LAYOUT SHOULD REALLY HAVE SOME ORDER. OTHERWISE, IT WOULD BE CHAOS. YOUR INTENTION IS NOT TO CONFUSE OR FRUSTRATE YOUR READER. YOU MUST REALLY EMBRACE THIS RULE.

THIS BOOK HAS ALSO ITS LAYOUT. NOTE THAT THE FONT FOR PICTURE DESCRIPTIONS AND THE FONT FOR CONTINUOUS TEXT ARE DISTINGUISHED. THEIR SIZE, THICKNESS OF COLUMNS, TASK BOXES ALWAYS HAVE THE SAME SHAPE AND COLOUR, AND I ALWAYS STICK TO THESE RULES. ALL OF THOSE MAKE IT EASIER FOR YOU TO UNDERSTAND THE PAGE. I PLAY FAIR WITH YOU.

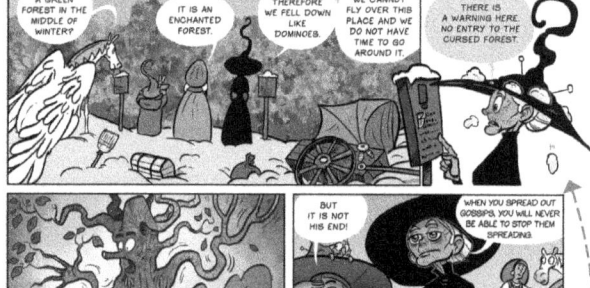

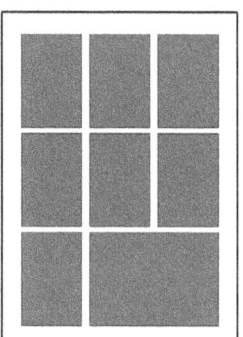

3 X 3 – Watchmen model

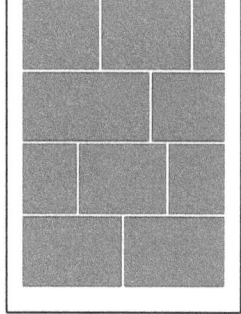

4 lines – Asterix model

IF YOU INSIST ON THE FACT THAT, EACH TIME, THE PANELS WILL HAVE A DIFFERENT SHAPE, AND YOU BREAK THE PAGE INTO HETEROGENEOUS FRAGMENTS, YOU MIGHT ACHIEVE GREAT DYNAMICS, WHICH, ON THE OTHER HAND, CAN BE BORING AND EVEN CONFUSING. THEREFORE, IF YOU STUDY THOROUGHLY THE ARTWORK OF PROFESSIONAL CARTOONISTS (IN THIS CASE I RECOMMEND JIM LEE), YOU WILL FIND OUT THAT, AT FIRST SIGHT, THE BOARD DOES NOT HAVE ANY RULES. HOWEVER, IT HAS A BASIC LAYOUT AND THE POSITION OF THE PANELS ON THE PAGE HAS ITS OWN MEANING.

If you do not strictly stick to given layout of the panels, the monotonous impression can be broken by the absence of edges of one picture and by that you liven up the story style. This can be done just in case that a comic book follows clear rules. Otherwise this effect fades in a chaotic sea of heterogeneous storytelling elements.

 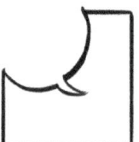

Will there be bubbles in the panels in your comic book or are you going to cut them out? Or will they just overlap the picture borders? It is up to you.

TASK

DETERMINE RULES OF THE PAGE STRUCTURE THE GAPS BETWEEN PANELS, THE OUTLINE THICKNESS, PAGE MIRROR (SEE TERMS EXPLANATION AT THE BEGINNING OF THIS BOOK). DETERMINE IF AND HOW THE BUBBLES WILL OVERLAP THE PANELS. AT THE END, JUST ALLOW YOURSELF SOME EXCEPTIONS AND DRAW THEM IN THE PLAN. FOR EXAMPLE, IF THERE WAS A TWIST IN THE STORY, THICKEN THE FRAME LINE TO 1 CM (0, 39 INCH) SO YOU SUPPORT ITS IMPORTANCE. THINK ABOUT WHEN AND AT WHAT OPPORTUNITY WILL THE CHARACTERS COME OUT THE FRAMES AND STEP IN OTHER PANELS. THIS SHOULD HAPPEN JUST RARELY AND THERE SHOULD BE A REASON FOR IT. THE REASON IS USUALLY TO MAKE A PARTICULAR SCENE MORE INTERESTING.

BUBBLES

BUBBLES HAVE BEEN AN INTEGRAL PART OF A COMIC BOOK FOR MORE THAN 100 YEARS. NEVERTHELESS, YOU CAN INVENT OTHER METHODS OF HOW TO CONNECT TEXT WITH PICTURES. IT IS UP TO YOU, WHAT WILL FIT YOUR COMIC BOOK BEST. WE WILL DISCUSS JUST A COUPLE OF THE MOST FREQUENTLY USED ONES, AND THE ONES THAT ARE PREFERRED BY THE READERS. DO NOT LET THIS TIE YOU DOWN. IT IS JUST AN OVERVIEW. HOWEVER, THE BUBBLES SHOULD HAVE THEIR OWN RULES. THEY ARE A PART OF THE STORY TELLING AND IF THEY ARE NOT CLEAR, THEY WILL CONFUSE THE READER.

A BUBBLE CAN EVEN LOOK LIKE THIS.

DIALOGUE BUBBLES

THIS IS THE MOST CLASSIC ONE. YOU WILL SEE IT IN 90% OF COMIC BOOKS. IF YOU WANT TO APPROACH YOUR READER, THIS IS A CLEAR CHOICE.

ANOTHER KIND THAT COPIES THE TEXT CHARACTER BUT PRESERVE ITS ROUNDNESS...

... IT IS DIFFICULT TO INSERT A PIECE OF TEXT INTO A BUBBLE SO THAT IT WOULD LOOK GOOD ...

TEXT LOOKS A BIT BETTER IN A RECTANGLE BUBBLE, BUT THEY MAY SEEM TO LOOK A BIT BORING THEN.

The little beak does not have to show which person is speaking. It is a part of the expressive tone, mood and emphasises what the speaker says.

MIND BUBBLES

THINKING BUBBLES TELL US THE THOUGHTS OF THE COMIC BOOKS CHARACTERS ...

... ADJUST THESE BUBBLES TO YOUR STYLE AND THINK ABOUT THEIR USAGE THOROUGHLY. YOUR READER SHOULD ORIENTATE IN THEM INTUITIVELY.

CHOOSE THE RIGHT SIZE. THE TEXT SHOULD NOT TOUCH THE FRAME; IT SHOULD NOT OVERFILL THE BUBBLE. IT IS OBVIOUS IN THIS EXAMPLE WHAT I AM TRYING TO TELL YOU.

YOU KNOW THESE BUBBLES FROM CARTOONS. THEY ARE FOR ANIMALS WHICH DO NOT TALK.

SPECIAL BUBBLES

WHISPERING BUBBLES ARE USUALLY INSIDE DOTTED LINES OR BLURRED EDGES.

SHOUTING BUBBLE!

OTHER SHOUTING BUBBLE

VOICE OF A ROBOT, MACHINE OR RADIO.

SETTING THE RULES OF YOUR COMIC BOOK, IS LIKE FURNISHING A FLAT. EVERYTHING YOU CHOOSE SHOULD BE PRACTICAL AND SHOULD LOOK NICE. YOU SHOULD FEEL ITS COSINESS AND SAFETY.

TASK
DEVELOP YOUR OWN SYSTEM OF BUBBLES AND FIND OUT WHICH BUBBLES WILL WORK WITH YOUR STYLE OF DRAWING. EXAMINE VARIOUS THICKNESSES OF EDGES, AND WAYS OF THE BEAK. TRY TO RESIST THE TEMPTATION OF ENDING ALL DIALOGUES WITH AN EXCLAMATION MARK. SOMETIMES DRAW A FULL STOP.

LETTERING

THERE IS A GENERAL OPINION THAT AN AUTHOR'S HANDWRITING MATCHES BEST WITH THEIR OWN DRAWING STYLE. LET ME ADD IT TO THOSE COUPLE OF DEEP-SEATED MISTAKES WHICH ARE RELEVANT TO COMIC BOOKS. THE FACT THAT YOU ARE AN AWESOME CARTOONIST DOES NOT MEAN THAT YOU KNOW SOMETHING ABOUT PAINTING OR CALLIGRAPHY. CALLIGRAPHISTS AND CARTOONISTS ARE NOT THE SAME. IT IS AS DIFFERENT AS COMPARING A BRICKLAYER AND CARPENTER. THEY WORK WITH SIMILAR TOOLS AND MATERIALS A LOT OF THEM MASTER THE CRAFT OF THE OTHER ONE, BUT THEY ARE TWO DIFFERENT PROFESSIONS. FOR EXAMPLE, I AM AWARE THAT MY WRITING IS POOR. I AM NOT PATIENT ENOUGH FOR IT. I ACTUALLY DO NOT ENJOY IT. HOWEVER, I NEED WRITING FOR MY COMIC BOOKS. THEREFORE, I HAD A COMPUTER MAKE A CUSTOM FONT OUT OF MY OWN HANDWRITING, WHICH I THEN INSERT INTO MY COMIC BOOKS. I AM NOT TOTALLY CONVINCED THAT IT ACTUALLY FITS MY DRAWINGS. HOWEVER, IT HAS BEEN THE BEST SOLUTION THAT I HAVE COME UP WITH SO FAR.

THIS MEANS THAT YOUR HANDWRITING DOES NOT HAVE TO FIT YOUR DRAWINGS BUT IT IS NECESSARY TO CHOOSE A FONT THAT FITS. HERE, YOU WILL HAVE TO BELIEVE IN YOUR FLAIR. THERE ARE NO RULES FOR THAT.

HOWEVER, THERE ARE TYPOGRAPHIC RULES WHICH HAVE TO BE FOLLOWED. I AM NOT TALKING ABOUT GRAMMAR, WHICH IS A MATTER OF COURSE. THE SAME CONDITIONS FOR TEXT INSERTING IN BOOKS ALSO APPLY HERE, AND I ADMIT THAT IT IS A BIT BORING, BUT IT IS AN ABSOLUTELY NECESSARY PART OF A COMIC BOOK MAKING. GET A TYPOGRAPHIC MANUAL AND STUDY THE RULES OF QUOTATION MARKS, DASHES, UPPER AND LOWER CASE LETTERS, PARAGRAPHS AND SO ON. HAVE YOU NOTICED THAT NO LINE IN THIS BOOK ENDS WITH A ONE-LETTER WORD? IT IS ONE OF THE RULES THAT WE NEED TO FOLLOW. HERE, WE ARE DISCUSSING JUST A COUPLE OF BASIC RULES BUT DO NOT GET SATISFIED WITH THAT. IF YOU ARE WORKING ON A COMMERCIAL COMIC BOOK, DRAW IT UP WITHOUT TEXT. INSERT IT ELECTRONICALLY SO THAT IT COULD BE EDITED IN ANY CASE IN 100 % BLACK (SEE PAGE 146 FOR EXPLANATION).

DIVIDING OF WORDS - FOR THE PURPOSES OF FLUENT READING, WE ARE TRYING NOT TO DIVIDE WORDS, BUT BECAUSE WE ARE TRYING TO GET PIECES OF TEXT IN A REALLY SMALL SPACE, IT CAN SOMETIMES LOOKS STRANGE. IN THAT CASE, I WOULD RATHER DIVIDE THE WORD.

UNIFIED SIZE - WRITING IS A REALLY IMPORTANT EXPRESSIONAL TOOL, SO ITS SIZE SHOULD BE UNIFIED AND ONLY DIFFER IN CASES WHEN IT MAKES SENSE. FOR EXAMPLE, WHEN A SPEAKER SHOUTS.

BOLD LETTERS - IN SOME COMIC BOOKS I HAVE SEEN THE WORDS IN BOLD WHICH THE AUTHOR WANTED THE READER TO REMEMBER. NAMES, DATES AND SO ON. HOWEVER, WE ARE NOT IN A TEXTBOOK! IN A COMIC BOOK WE USE BOLD JUST FOR THINGS THAT ARE EMPHASISED BY THE SPEAKER. CONSIDER THE FOLLOWING PANELS. A SECRET AGENT IS SAYING THE SAME SENTENCE BUT DIFFERENT WORDS ARE STRESSED IN EACH CASE. SURPRISINGLY, WE RECEIVE DIFFERENT INFORMATION EACH TIME.

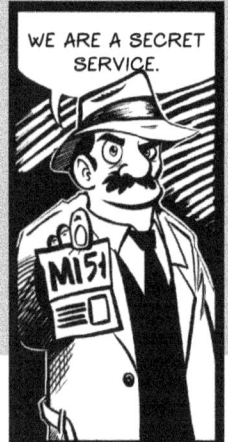 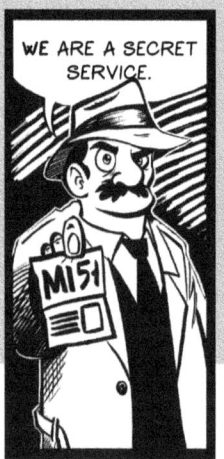 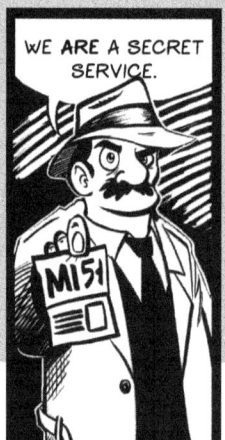 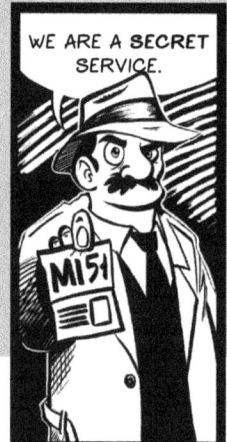 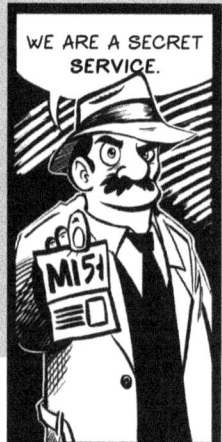

THE SPEAKER JUST PURELY INFORMS WHAT HE DOES.

NEITHER YOU NOR ANYBODY ELSE, BUT WE! SOMEBODY WAS PRETENDING BEING A SECRET SERVICE?

SOMEBODY THOUGHT WE ARE NOT A SECRET SERVICE? THEY ARE MISTAKEN BECAUSE THAT IS WHO WE ARE!

WE ARE NO BLABBERMOUTHS. NOT THAT ANYONE WOULD SAY A WORD! WE ARE THE SECRET SERVICE!

WE DO NOT WORK JUST FOR OURSELVES. WE ARE NEITHER A COMPANY NOR A SERVICE, AND WE ARE HERE FOR YOU.

TASK
FIND OUT HOW YOUR WRITING WILL CORRESPOND WITH YOUR DRAWING. EVEN THOUGH YOU DECIDE TO HANDWRITE OR USE OTHER OPTIONS, DETERMINE THE SIZE OF NORMAL DIALOGUES, THEIR STYLE, RULES OF THICKNESS, WRITING FOR SHOUTING AND WHISPERING AND ALSO PAY ATTENTION TO THE LINE SPACING.

SOUNDS AND SCREAMS

SOUNDS AND SCREAMS SFX IN SLANG ARE AN INTEGRAL PART OF A COMIC BOOK IMAGE. IT IS ACTUALLY STRANGE BUT THE TEXT SHOULD NOT LOOK DISTURBING IN THE PICTURE. HOWEVER, IF IT IS USED CORRECTLY AND SENSITIVELY, IT INTENSIFIES THE ATMOSPHERE AND ADEQUATELY SUBSTITUTES THE SFX WHICH ARE MADE BY SOUNDS IN FILMS. SFX ARE USED TO EXPRESSIVELY EXAGGERATE, BECAUSE THE CREATOR WANTS THE READER TO FEEL THE SOUND.

YOU REALLY WILL NOT AVOID GETTING INVOLVED IN CALLIGRAPHY. YOU CANNOT AVOID IT BECAUSE EVEN IF YOU INSERT TEXT ELECTRONICALLY, YOU STILL NEED TO KNOW THE ELEMENTARY RULES.

YOU HAVE A COUPLE OF WAYS HOW TO CREATE SOUNDS AND EACH OF THEM HAS THEIR OWN PROS AND CONS.

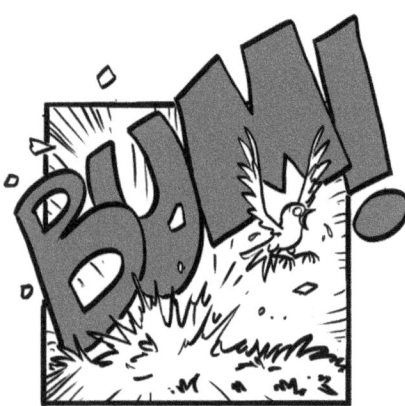
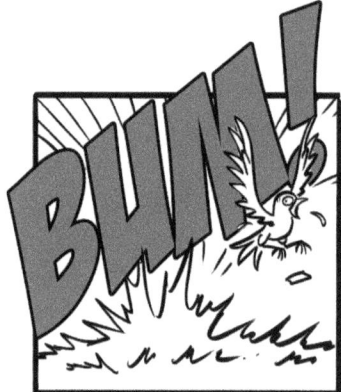
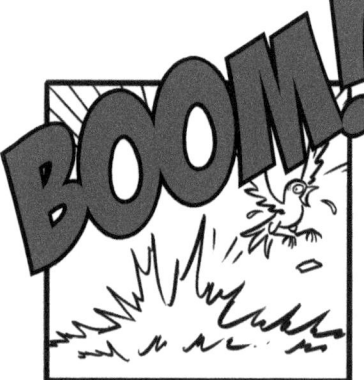

I PERSONALLY PREFER MANUAL SFX CREATION ALTHOUGH IT HAS ITS CONS. IF YOU TRANSLATE SOMETHING INTO A DIFFERENT LANGUAGE, A CARTOONIST WHO WILL TRANSFER THESE SFX WILL BE NEEDED AND THEREFORE THE CREATION OF A COMIC BOOK BECOMES MORE EXPENSIVE. HOWEVER, I STILL INSIST ON THE FACT THAT THIS IS THE BEST SOLUTION.

THE EXPLOSION WAS PLACED HERE IN BADABOOM FONT. IT IS INSERTED SO SENSITIVELY THAT IT RESPECTS THE LAYERS OF THE PICTURE. ON THE OTHER HAND IT IS NOT SUITABLE FOR CO-EDITION AND EXPENSES WILL INCREASE BECAUSE OF RE-DRAWING AND AND TRANSLATING INTO A FOREIGN LANGUAGE.

THE WORD BOOM! WAS INSERTED HERE IN A PROGRAMME FOR TEXT INSERTING. IT IS THE MOST FREQUENTLY USED METHOD EVEN IF THE CO-EDITION IS NOT AN ISSUE HERE; IT IS EASY TO TRANSLATE SOUNDS AND RE-WRITE THEM FOR AN AVERAGE GRAPHIC DESIGNER. HOWEVER, YOU CAN SEE THAT THIS OPTION CANNOT RESPECT THE LAYERS OF THE PICTURE AND COVERS THE WINGS OF THE BIRDS IN FRONT. THE MAGIC OF THIS COMIC BOOK FADES AWAY A BIT.

TASK
DRAW VARIOUS SCREAMS AND SOUNDS. ALSO, TAKE INTO ACCOUNT THE SOUND DIRECTION, AND TRY TO EXPRESS THE EFFECT NOT ONLY BY TEXT WORDING BUT ALSO ITS LOOK AND COLOUR.

CO EDITION: COMIC BOOK PLAGUE AND SALVATION

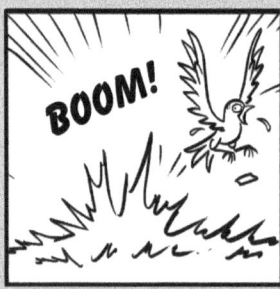

IN THE CZECH REPUBLIC WHERE A COMIC BOOK READER IS REALLY DEMANDING (WHICH IS GOOD) THERE IS A FREQUENTLY ASKED QUESTION WHY SFX IN DISNEY'S COMIC BOOKS ARE SO...SLOPPY EVEN IF THE ORIGINALS ARE SO BEAUTIFUL. DURING THEIR TRANSLATION IT HAPPENS THAT THAT ORIGINAL SFX ARE ERASED AND SUBSTITUTED BY AVERAGE FONT OF AN INADEQUATE SIZE. MOREOVER, WE ABSOLUTELY CANNOT TALK ABOUT EXPRESSIVENESS HERE. THE ANSWER IS CO-EDITION. WHAT IS IT? YOU CERTAINLY KNOW THAT THE MORE NUMBERS OF COPIES ARE ORDERED AT A PRINTING COMPANY, THE CHEAPER THE PRINTING WILL BE. HOWEVER, IF YOU PRINT FOR SUCH A SMALL MARKET LIKE THE CZECH, IT IS NEARLY NOT WORTH IT. WHAT TO DO ABOUT IT? WE CREATE THE SAME BOOK FOR PUBLISHING IN A COUPLE OF COUNTRIES. LET'S SAY POLAND, SLOVAKIA, THE CZECH REPUBLIC AND HUNGARY. THE NUMBER OF COPIES FOR THE CZECH REPUBLIC WOULD BE AROUND 10 000 COPIES BUT WITH THE OTHER COUNTRIES IT WOULD BE SOME HUNDREDS OF THOUSANDS! THIS WILL LOWER THE PRICE OF ONE ISSUE TO LITERALLY A COUPLE OF PENNIES. AS THE TEXT WILL BE JUST 100 % BLACK. CHANGING THE CARTRIDGE WITH BLACK COLOUR IS JUST ENOUGH, AND PRINTING WILL GO ON IN OTHER LANGUAGE MUTATIONS BUT WILL BE COUNTED AS THE SAME BOOK.

THEREFORE, YOU CAN BUY SUPER-COMICS, TINTIN OR ASTERIX FOR AROUND 100 CZK (APPROX. £3.50), OTHERWISE THESE BOOKS WOULD BE AROUND £10.

THE TAX FOR CO-EDITION AT A LOWER PRICE IS DEVASTATING HOWEVER. FOR THE CREATORS IT MEANS REALLY RESTRICTIVE MEASURES. THE TEXT MUST BE JUST BLACK, NO PICTURE SHOULD OVERLAP IT, 100 % BLACK IS TRANSPARENT AND THE RE-PRINT NEVER COVERS COMPLETELY. (SEE THEORY OF COLOURS AT PAGE 146). YET, FOR EXAMPLE, THE CREATORS OF ASTERIX AND TINTIN COUNT ON THIS LIMITATION AND ARE ABLE TO WORK WITH IT VERY WELL IN A WAY THAT THE READER DOES NOT EVEN NOTICE. ON THE OTHER HAND, DISNEY'S PUBLICATIONS PROVE THAT COMIC BOOKS ARE JUST MERCHANDISING AND ADVERTISING ITEMS FOR THEM. PUBLISHERS FROM DIFFERENT COUNTRIES RECEIVE A PRE-WRITTEN PATTERN, WHICH THEY MUST FOLLOW, EVEN IF THEY DO NOT AGREE.

EXPRESSIVE LOOK OF SOUND

IT IS ONE OF THE MOST BEAUTIFUL CHARMS OF A COMIC BOOK, AND AT THE SAME TIME AN ASPECT WHICH DEFINES IT. YOU CAN HARDLY FIND SUCH AN OPTION IN ANY OTHER MEDIA. DO NOT OVERLOOK THE EXPRESSIVE POTENTIAL OF THIS NARRATIVE WEAPON. JUST TAKE A LOOK AT COUPLE OF OPTIONS OF AND USAGE. THERE ARE MUCH MORE OF THEM. I DO NOT DOUBT THAT YOU WILL COME UP WITH MILLIONS OF OTHER EXAMPLE OF HOW TO MAKE YOUR COMIC BOOK EXTRAORDINARY AND SUPPORT THE STORYTELLING WITH INVENTIVE SFX.

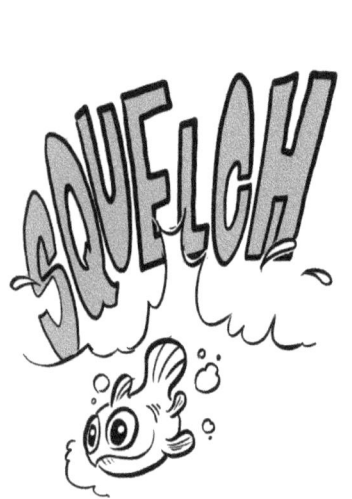
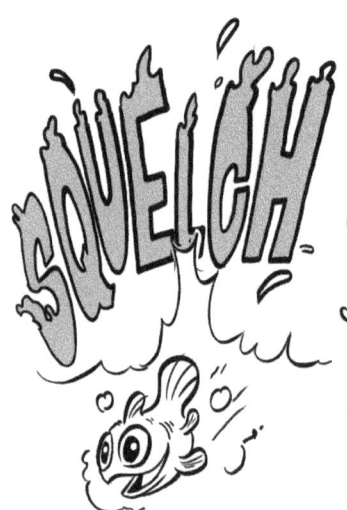
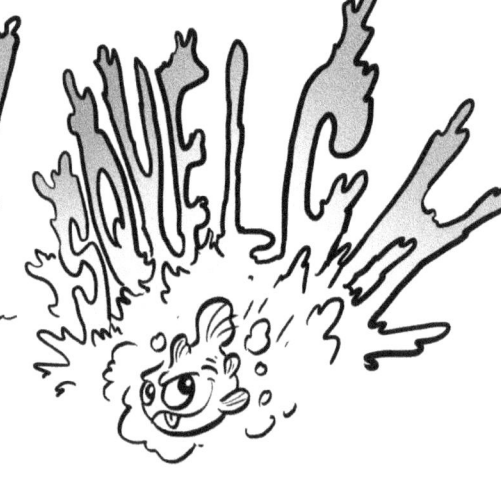

CLASSIC SOUND PLACEMENT COPIES THE MOVEMENT SHAPE. CAN IT BE DONE MORE EXPRESSIVELY?

YES! WHY NOT MAKE THE WORD OUT OF THE ELEMENT WHICH IS REPRESENTED BY THE SOUND. IT THIS CASE IT IS WATER ...

... AND WHAT IF THE NAME WAS THE ORIGIN OF THE SOUND? ISN'T IT GREAT HOW MANY OPTIONS WE HAVE?

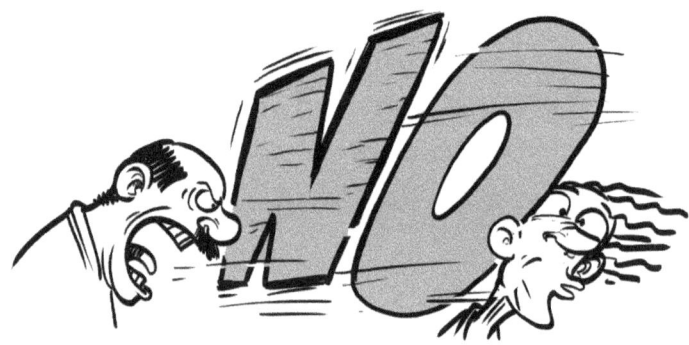

YOU CAN PLACE THE SCREAM IN A BUBBLE AND EXPRESS THE SOUND WITH FLYING HAIR ...

BUT ISN'T THIS A BIT MORE ...UMM ...STRIKING?

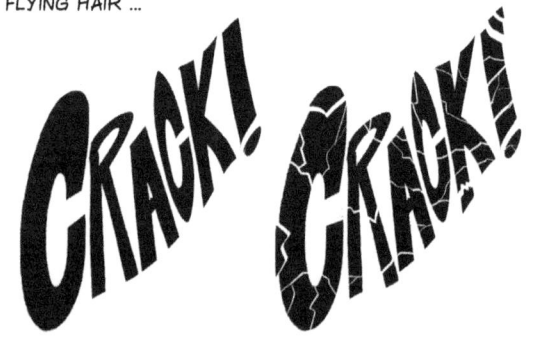

WHICH OF THESE SOUND EFFECTS IS CRUNCHIER?

TASK
TRY OUT VARIOUS SFX AND GIVE THEM THE MOST EXPRESSIVE LOOK POSSIBLE. THEY SHOULD EXPRESS THE DIRECTION OF THE SOUND, EMPHASISE ITS SOURCE AND INVENTIVELY COMPLEMENT THE STORYTELLING. TRY TO DRAW, FOR EXAMPLE, A PASSING BY VEHICLE – VROOOM AND TRY TO SIMULATE DOPPLER EFFECT ON IT. OR A HELICOPTER CHOP CHOP, A SHOT FROM A HANDGUN – BANG! OR SLIPPING OVER A BANANA SKIN. – ZLOPP! BE CREATIVE!

INSPIRATION

IF YOU PUBLISH YOUR BOOK OR GIVE AN INTERVIEW, YOU WILL FIND OUT THAT LAYMEN OFTEN ASK SAME QUESTIONS. THEY ARE QUESTIONS WHICH DO NOT HAVE RIGHT ANSWERS. DO NOT GET UPSET. TELL THEM WHAT THEY WANT TO HEAR. MAKE UP STORIES, KEEP THE MYTHS ABOUT CARTOONING ALIVE. IT IS PART OF YOUR JOB.

ONE OF THE QUESTIONS IS: "MISTER, WHERE DO YOU TAKE YOUR INSPIRATION FROM?". TELL ME, HONESTLY, CAN I POSSIBLY SAY I STEAL? IT IS ACTUALLY NOT POSSIBLE (AND SORRY TO HURT YOUR FEELINGS) TO COME UP WITH SOMETHING NEW WITHOUT USING WHAT HAS BEEN USED BEFORE.

YOU DO NOT BELIEVE ME? OK. GO BACK TO PAGE 97. YOUR TASK WAS TO CREATE AN ORIGINAL MONSTER. YOU MIGHT HAVE CREATED IT, BUT ITS PARTS WERE MADE FROM PARTS WHICH YOU HAVE ALREADY SEEN SOMEWHERE, RIGHT? SOMETHING WHICH CAN BE IDENTIFIED IN ITS SINGULARITY, RIGHT?

ONLY GOD CAN DO SOMETHING FROM NOTHING AND WE WERE NOT GIVEN THIS ABILITY BUT IT DOESN'T MATTER. WE ARE VERY GOOD AT COMBINING. THE MORE SURPRISING COMBINATION THE BETTER RESULT WE GET.

A PROBLEM HAPPENS WHEN WE FIND OUT THAT OUR BRAIN MOVES IN A CIRCLE OF ASSOCIATIONS. IT IS PARTLY CAUSED BY OUR PARENTS' UPBRINGING AND PARTLY BY THE IMPACT OF CULTURE IN WHICH WE LIVE. IN OTHER WORDS, WE STRUGGLE WITH COMING UP WITH NEW COMBINATIONS BECAUSE OUR BRAIN RECORDS ASSOCIATIONS AUTOMATICALLY ON THE BASIS OF ALREADY CREATED SYNOPTIC CONNECTIONS. YOUR THINKING HAS A CLEAR PATH TO FOLLOW AND AVOIDING THIS PATH IS REALLY HARD. SO, WHEN SOMEBODY SAYS BLUE, YOU START TO THINK ABOUT SKY. WHEN YOU HEAR GREEN, YOU THINK OF GRASS AND WHEN YOU HEAR STRIPES YOU THINK ABOUT A TIGER OR ZEBRA.

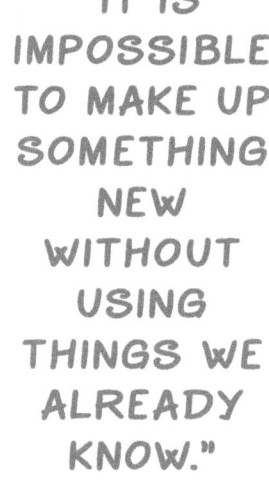

"IT IS IMPOSSIBLE TO MAKE UP SOMETHING NEW WITHOUT USING THINGS WE ALREADY KNOW."

IT IS JUST NORMAL AND IF YOU WERE NOT AFFECTED BY THAT YOU WOULD NOT BE ABLE TO COMMUNICATE CORRECTLY. WHAT CAN YOU DO ABOUT IT? HOW TO COME UP WITH AN ORIGINAL COMBINATION? HOW CAN I ACHIEVE THINKING ABOUT, FOR EXAMPLE, AN EARTHWORM WHEN SOMEONE SAYS BLUE.

THERE ARE EXERCISES FOR THAT. THE BASIS IS TO TEAR DOWN BORDERS OF THOSE CLEAR PATHS AND, AS STEPHEN KING WRITES, LET OUR BRAIN DO NUISANCES.

FIRST OF ALL, I CAN ADVISE YOU A TRICK, WHICH IS CRUCIAL FOR MY VERY SUCCESSFUL SERIES MORGAVSA AND MORGANA. BUT PSSSSSST. IT'S A SECRET!

DO YOU HAVE AN ENGLISH GRAMMAR BOOK? NO? HOW DO YOU WANT TO WRITE COMIC BOOKS WITHOUT RULES? SO, DO YOU HAVE THEM IN YOUR HEAD? O.K. WHO DOES NOT PHYSICALLY HAVE THOSE BOOKS AT HOME, IT IS YOUR RESPONSIBILITY. EVEN THE GREATEST MASTERS LOOK IN THOSE BOOKS IN ORDER TO CHECK THE CORRECTNESS OF THEIR EXPRESSIONS. DO NOT PRETEND YOU ARE SOMETHING MORE THAN THEM!

WELL, FIND RANDOMLY TWO OR THREE WORDS. REALLY SURPRISING COMBINATIONS WILL COME UP. PUT THE WORDS INTO CONNECTIONS AND MAKE A STORYLINE, NEW CREATURE, SITUATION OR AN INVENTION. THESE WORDS WILL BE SUCH AN INSPIRATION AND GREAT ADVENTURE.

WE HAVE DISCUSSED STORYLINES AND PLOT CREATION WHICH DIRECTLY FOLLOWS THE DRAWING. BELIEVE ME, IF YOU TAKE A BLANK PIECE OF PAPER AND CAN'T THINK OF WHAT TO DRAW, YOU ARE NOT A CARTOONIST, I AM AFRAID.

THIS QUESTION IS NOT ASKED BY A CARTOONIST. AFTER ALL, EVERYTHING IS WORTH DRAWING! THE QUESTION IS NOT "WHAT" BUT "HOW". IF YOU REALLY ARE A CARTOONIST, YOU DO NOT ASK YOURSELF "WHAT TO DRAW?" BUT "WHAT TO DRAW FIRST?"

I HAVE FOLLOWED MY PIECES OF ADVICE AND MADE THESE COMBINATIONS.

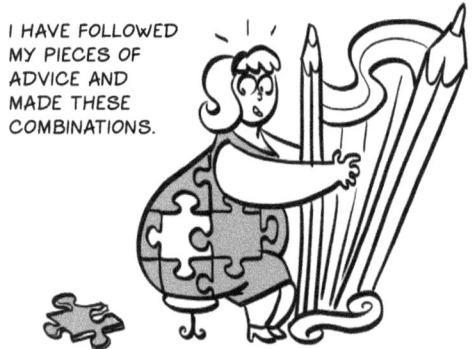

PUZZLED HARPIST

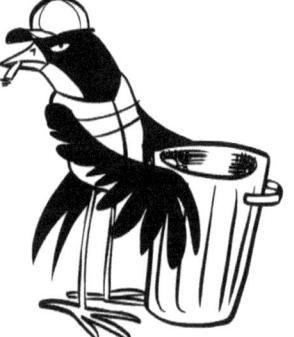

BINMAN SWALLOW

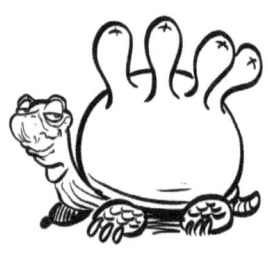

MILKY TORTOISE

IF YOU OFTEN PRACTISE LIKE THIS, YOU WILL FORCE YOUR BRAIN TO DO IMPROPRIETIES AND REALLY SOON, WHEN YOU SEE A MAIN ROAD, WILD GARLIC OR APPLE PUREE, YOU WILL START TO BE INTERESTED IN WHAT A MAIN ROAD HEAD WILD GARLIC OR PIRATE APPLE WILL LOOK LIKE. IT IS JUST MATTER OF TIME WHEN YOUR BRAIN BREAKS THE SHACKLES OF MEDIOCRITY. HOWEVER, YOU MUST PRACTISE.

TASK
TAKE A DICTIONARY AND FIND TWO OR THREE WORDS AND COMBINE THEM. IT DOES NOT MATTER HOW CRAZY THEY WILL SOUND. DRAW THEM LATER ON. IT WILL NOT WORK EVERY TIME BUT IN MOST CASES IT WILL. DO IT! I AM INTERESTED IN THAT SO MUCH!

STORY CONSTRUCTION

AS I HAVE WRITTEN SEVERAL TIMES, THE READER MUST BE DEALT WITH FAIRLY. THIS MEANS THAT IF YOU PROMISE THEM A NARRATION AND YOU DO ANYTHING ELSE, YOU WILL HAVE TO FACE A DECEPTION BECAUSE YOU ARE COMMITTING A FRAUD. HOWEVER, THERE ARE PERMITTED AND FORBIDDEN FRAUDS. WHAT YOU CAN DO IS BEFORE YOU START NARRATE A GANGSTER STORY AND IT THE FIRST THIRD THE PLOT WILL TURN INTO A VAMPIRE FIGHT. IT IS FINE BECAUSE THE TWO GENRES ARE NOT FAR FROM EACH OTHER. HOWEVER, YOU CANNOT START NARRATING A FAIRY TALE WHICH TURNS INTO PORNO. NOT IF THIS IS NOT CLARIFIED IN THE BEGINNING. THERE ARE EXCEPTIONS THOUGH. INDEED. LET US LEARN THE RULES FIRST AND THEN LET US BREAK THEM.

FIRST OF ALL, IT MUST BE MENTIONED THAT COMMON STORIES SHARE THE SAME NARRATIVE ARCS. IT RISES AND DROPS ACCORDING TO THE READER'S INTEREST. WE DISTINGUISH THREE ELEMENTARY NARRATIVE ARCS OF COMMERCIAL STORIES.

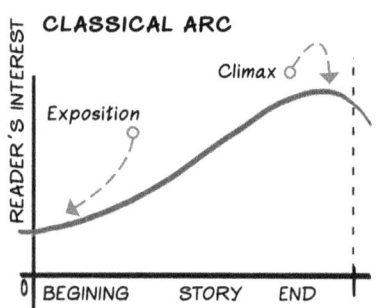
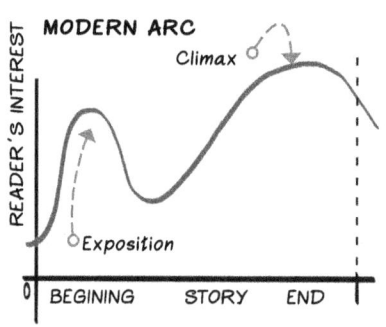
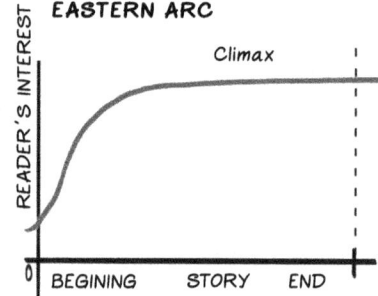

THE MOST COMMONLY USED FORM OF STORY. THE EXCITEMENT AND INTEREST OF THE READER CONSTANTLY GROWS TO THE STORIES CLIMAX AND DENOUEMENT. IN ACTION STORIES, IT IS THE WILDEST SCENE. HOWEVER, AS SOON AS THE HERO DOES THE THING WHICH WAS COMING FROM THE BEGINNING, THE STORY MUST FINISH SOON BECAUSE THE INTEREST OF THE READER QUICKLY DROPS.

OUTLINE:
1. EXPOSITION
2. PLOT
3. CLIMAX
4. CONCLUSION

I CALL THIS ARC MODERN BECAUSE YOU CAN NOTICE IT IN NEWER STORIES. DURING THE EXPOSITION YOU GET A SAMPLE OF THINGS TO COME. THE END, HOWEVER, MUST BE AT A MORE INTENSE LEVEL THAN THE BEGINNING. IT MUST CONVINCE THE READER AS MUCH AS POSSIBLE. YOU CAN FIND THIS ARC IN RAIDERS OF THE LOST ARK OR IN EVERY SERIES OF STAR TREK WHERE THAT SAMPLE HAPPENS JUST BEFORE THE OPENING CREDITS.

OUTLINE:
1. EXPOSITION
2. EXPOSITION CLIMAX
3. PLOT
4. CLIMAX
5. CONCLUSION

I CALL IT EASTERN BECAUSE I HAVE SEEN IT MAINLY IN MANGA. THEY ARE STORIES WHICH DO NOT WANT TO PROVE ANYTHING AND THERE IS NOT ONLY ONE GOAL. THESE STORIES DO NOT END. THEY LIVE ON THEIR OWN. THEY ARE MOSTLY LONG SAGAS POSSIBLY WITH A MULTI GENERATION DEVELOPMENT. YOU CAN FIND SUCH AN ARC FOR EXAMPLE IN GAME OF THRONES.

OUTLINE:
1. EXPOSITION
2. EXPOSITION CLIMAX
3. PLOT WITH VARIOUS INCIDENTS
4. OPEN CONCLUSION

TERMS

EXPOSITION - THE BEGINNING OF THE STORY INTRODUCES MAIN HEROES AND ENVIRONMENT. IT SHOULD LAST AT MOST UNTIL THE FIRST THIRD OF THE STORY. AFTER THAT IT IS NOT DESIRABLE TO INTRODUCE NEW CHARACTERS OR CHANGE THE RULES OF THE WORLD WHERE THEY ACT.

INCIDENT - RAPID STORY CHANGE AND ITS DIRECTION HAVING MOSTLY THE PURPOSE OF SUDDEN ACCELERATION OF THE EVENTS THEIR ENTERTAINMENT LEVEL.

CLIMAX - THE MOMENT WHEN THE MAIN HERO OR PLOT REACHES THE GOAL OF THE STORY.

DENOUEMENT - THE SOLUTION OF A PART OR ALL THE INCIDENTS.

TASK

THINK OVER CAREFULLY TO WHICH GROUP YOUR STORY WILL BELONG. IN THE PAGE HEADWORD, DRAW THE ARC WHICH YOU WILL FOLLOW AND WRITE THE OUTLINE. CERTAINLY, YOU HAVE ALREADY MADE THE PLOT. NOW MATCH ITS THE SINGLE PARTS TO EXPOSITION NAMES, AND BECAUSE YOU KNOW THAT YOU WILL BE CREATING THE MULTIPAGE COMIC BOOK, MATCH THE SINGLE PARTS WITH THE NUMBER OF PAGES WHICH YOU SHOULD NOT EXCEED. COMIC BOOK DRAWING IS NOT JUST FUN BUT IF YOU LOVE IT, YOU LOVE IT WITH EVERYTHING WHAT IS A PART OF IT.

COMIC STRIP

COMIC BOOK STRIP IS A VERY SPECIFIC DISCIPLINE. AS IN LITERATURE, WHERE WE DISTINGUISH BETWEEN GLOSSES, FEUILLETONS, SHORT STORIES, NOVELS AND ETC., A COMIC BOOK HAS ALSO ITS OWN CERTAIN LENGTH RESTRICTIONS. WHILE YOU CAN NARRATE A SPECTACULAR STORY IN USUAL 40 – 50 A4 PAGES, YOU CAN DO IT IN 20 – 30 PAGES WITH SHORT STORY, A DRAMATIC ARC STILL FITS THERE. THEN YOU ARE ABLE TO TELL AN EVENT, A STRIP, IN 10 PAGES. IF THERE IS NO FOLLOW-UP, IT IS JUST AN ANECDOTE. NOTHING MORE. BUT NOTHING LESS EITHER. TO BE HONEST, IT IS THE MOST DIFFICULT DISCIPLINE. PREPARE THAT THE LESS SPACE YOU WILL GET, THE MORE DIFFICULT WILL THE STORY MAKING BE. DO NOT GET MISTAKEN THOUGH. IT IS POSSIBLE TO JAM AN EXTENSIVE NOVEL INTO FIVE COMIC BOOK PAGES. PEOPLE DO IT. YOU CAN EASILY ADAPT VERNE'S AROUND THE WORLD IN 80 DAYS IN FIVE PAGES AND THE PLOT WILL BE COMPREHENSIBLE. I DON'T RECOMMEND DOING THIS. IT DOES NOT END UP WELL AND THE COMIC BOOKS ARE NOT GOOD. HOWEVER, YOU WILL HAVE TO DO SUCH THINGS AS A COMMERCIAL CARTOONIST. YOU WILL NOT BE PLEASED BY THAT BUT REJECTING CONTRACTS IS NOT EASY OR EVEN, IMPOSSIBLE IN THE BEGINNING. AT LEAST HAVE IT PAID ADEQUATELY.

NOW LET US JUST CONCENTRATE ON THE GENRE OF WHICH THE COMIC STRIP WAS CREATED. JOKE!

NOT EVERYBODY CAN MASTER THIS ART. A CERTAIN AMOUNT OF IMPERTINENCE IS NEEDED HERE. THE NARRATOR CAN NOTE IMMEDIATELY IF THE JOKE WORKED OUT, OR NOT. THE MOMENT THE AUDIENCE BURSTS INTO LAUGHTER, OR THE OTHER WAY ROUND, THEY ARE SO SILENT THAT YOU COULD HEAR A PIN DROP, YOU KNOW IF YOU SUCCEEDED. ON THE OTHER HAND, IN A SERIOUS PIECE OF ART YOU CAN MAKE A FOOL OF YOURSELF AND LIE TO YOURSELF WHETHER YOU REACHED THE AUDIENCE OR NOT.

> "THE ART IS WHEN YOU KNOW WHEN TO STOP IN ORDER NOT TO PUT OUT THE ESSENCE BY THE EXCESSIVE CARE."

IT IS MORE DIFFICULT WITH COMIC STRIPS BECAUSE IT RARELY ABOUT AREA. IT IS ABOUT SINGLE SHOTS WHICH MUST BE RESOLUTE, SIMPLE AND COMPREHENSIBLE AT FIRST SIGHT.

I RECOMMEND EXPLORING THE PIECE OF WORK OF JIM DAVIS – GARFIELD AND MAX CANNON – RED MEET. I CONSIDER THESE TWO AUTHORS AS MONDRIAAN'S OF COMIC STRIPS. WHILE MONDRIAAN TOOK BASIC PAINTING TOOLS – COLOURS AND WITH THEIR HELP, HE CLEARLY AND SIMPLY DEFINED THE ESSENCE OF COLOUR COMPOSITION, MAX CANNON TOOK THE BASIC TOOLS AND HE WORKS WITH THEM BRILLIANTLY.

FORGET ABOUT DETAILED AND DIFFICULT DRAWN BACKGROUNDS, NOT IMPORTANT DETAILS AND MESSAGES HIDDEN IN THE PICTURE. DO NOT CHANGE THE CAMERA ANGLES AND DO NOT COME UP WITH SUPER INTERESTING PERSPECTIVES IN ORDER TO SHOW HOW BEAUTIFULLY YOU CAN DRAW... THIS DOES NOT FIT HERE. THE COMIC STRIP HAS JUST ONE PURPOSE – TO MAKE THE READER LAUGH. IT DOES NOT MATTER THAT ALL THE PICTURES IN THE STRIP WILL BE COPIES OF THE FIRST ONE.

I HAVE TWO PIECES OF ADVICE FOR YOU:
1. THE READER SHOULD NOT TRY TO SOLVE ANYTHING. THE EASIER THE PICTURE IS TO UNDERSTAND, THE HARDER THE PUNCHLINE WILL HIT. SEE MAX CANNON'S PIECE OF WORK.
2. THE READER MUST GO TO MEET THE STORY EVEN BEFORE THAN THEY READ THE FIRST BUBBLE. YOU SEE GARFIELD IN THE PICTURE. YOUR BRAIN WILL SUBCONSCIOUSLY SAY: NOW IT WILL BE FUN. AND IT IS. GARFIELD IS THE ICON OF A WELL DONE STRIP.

NOW, YOU MIGHT SAY THAT IT IS NOT ART. NO BACKGROUND, COPYING PICTURES. WHAT IS THAT KOPL FORCING ME TO THINK? THE MASTERY IS NOT TO SPEND TWO DAYS OVER ONE PICTURE AND CREATE A MASTER PIECE. THE ART IS WHEN YOU KNOW WHEN TO STOP IN ORDER NOT TO PUT OUT THE ESSENCE BY THE EXCESSIVE CARE.

IDEAL ARC OF LEVEL OF JOKE EXCITEMENT

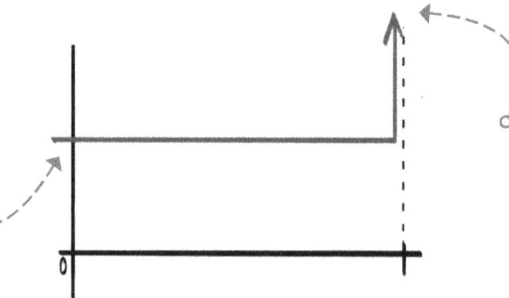

While in normal narrating we can start from scratch, we cannot afford it with a joke. We do not have space for that. Therefore we use a simple at first sight funny picture which informs the reader that now it will be fun. Haha.

This is what I call a Twist. The climax must be unexpected even though logical. Only such jokes will get the audience burst into laughter.

TASK
DO NOT SAY THAT ANY JOKE HAS NOT COME ACROSS YOUR MIND. DRAW IT IN A COMIC STRIP AND DRAW IT TWICE. DRAW ONE THE SIMPLEST, WITH NO BACKGROUND AND WITH CUTE AND FUNNY CHARACTERS, AND THE SECOND ONE WITH REALISTICALLY, DRAWN IN DETAILS. CHANGE THE CAMERA ANGLES AND DRAW THE BACKGROUND IN DETAIL. YOU WILL HAVE TO ADMIT THAT THE FIRST VERSION WILL BE BETTER. TRY IT WITH YOUR FRIENDS. WATCH HOW THEY LAUGH. YOU WILL SEE.

PURPOSEFULLNESS VS LAZINESS

WHETHER YOU WANT IT OR NOT, AT YOUR WORK YOU MEET A LOT OF SELF-PROCLAIMED CRITICS WHO DO NOT UNDERSTAND BUT TALK SMART. THEY PRESENT THEIR OPINIONS AS GENERAL FACTS AND THEY DO NOT TAKE CARE WHETHER THEY TALK BULLSHIT OR NOT. YOU WILL HAVE TO BEAR IT. YOU CANNOT DO ANYTHING WITH THAT. IT WILL HURT. HOWEVER, IN ANY CASE, DO NOT GET CONFUSED OR EVEN STOP! ANY DUMMY CAN TALK BULLSHIT ON THE INTERNET BUT THERE ARE JUST A FEW CRITICS WHO REALLY MASTER THIS CRAFT.

SO YOU WILL HEAR THAT YOU EASED YOUR WORK IN YOUR COMIC BOOK BECAUSE YOU DID NOT DRAW THE BACKGROUND OR THAT YOU COPIED THE BACKGROUND FROM A PREVIOUS PANEL. OR EVEN THAT YOU PICKED A PHOTOGRAPH WHICH YOU OUTLINED. OH! WHAT A SHAME!

LIES! THE MEANS MENTIONED ABOVE ARE TRULY COMMON IN COMMERCIAL AND NON-COMMERCIAL COMIC BOOKS. WHY NOT TO TAKE ADVANTAGE OF A TECHNIQUE WHEN IT SAVES ME HOURS OF WORK? ANCIENT PAINTERS ALREADY USED CAMERA OBSCURA TO PORTRAITURE SO THEY OUTLINED THE PROJECTED IMAGE ON THE CANVAS AS IF IT WERE A PHOTOGRAPH. WHY WERE THEY DOING IT WHEN, WITH A COMMON TECHNIQUE, THEY WOULD ACHIEVE THE SAME RESULT? BECAUSE THEY ACHIEVE IT IN A FRACTION OF THE TIME. YOU CAN BE CREATING HEROES AND WORK INEFFECTIVELY. HOWEVER, YOU WOULD REGRET THAT YOUR COLLEAGUES ACHIEVE BETTER RESULTS WITH A COMBINE HARVESTER WHILE JUST A FEW PEOPLE APPRECIATE YOUR WORK WITH A SCYTHE.

THE TRUTH IS THAT THE DECISION IF THERE WILL BE BACKGROUND IN THE PICTURE OR NOT SHOULD NOT BE A DECISION DEPENDING ON LAZINESS OR FRUGALITY, BUT IT SHOULD DEPEND ON THE THINGS WHICH JUST SUIT US BEST IN OUR NARRATION. TAKE A LOOK AT THESE EXAMPLES.

WHICH OF THESE TWO PICTURES IS MORE DYNAMIC? OF COURSE, THE RIGHT ONE. THIS IS NOT A QUESTION OF LAZINESS. I NEED ROBIN TO FALL DOWN REALLY DANGEROUSLY QUICKLY. THEREFORE, I CHOSE THE SOLUTION IN THE LEFT PICTURE. HOWEVER, IF I WANTED TO UNDERLINE THE EPICNESS OF THE PANEL AND EMPHASISE ITS IMPORTANCE, I WOULD CHOOSE THE SOLUTION ON THE RIGHT. I AM TRYING TO SLOW DOWN THE PLOT AND THE READER STOPS FOR WHILE AT THE PANEL. BY THAT, I AM LOSING A QUICK PACE OF THE STORY. HOWEVER, IF THAT IS THE PURPOSE, THAT IS FINE.

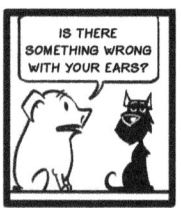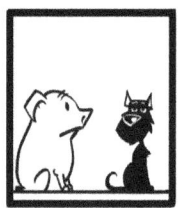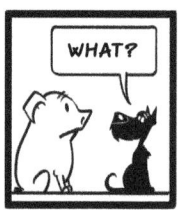

A TYPICAL EXAMPLE OF HOW A COMIC STRIP WORKS. WHILE AT THE TOP I EMPHASIZE THE COMICALITY OF THE SITUATION AND GET RID OF ALL BARRIERS OF THE PACE OF THE ANECDOTE, IN THE BOTTOM SOLUTION I UNDERLINE THE MOOD OF THE MOMENT. I SLOW DOWN THE PLOT AND I OVERSHADOW THE JOKE. THESE ARE PURPOSE-BUILT DECISIONS DEPENDING ON WHAT I WANT TO ACHIEVE IN A COMIC BOOK. THEY DO NOT DEPEND ON MY LAZINESS!

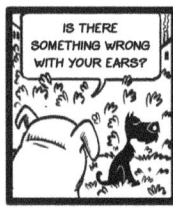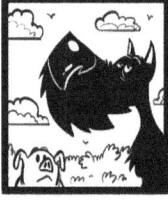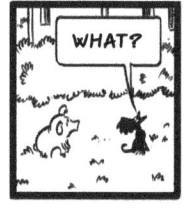

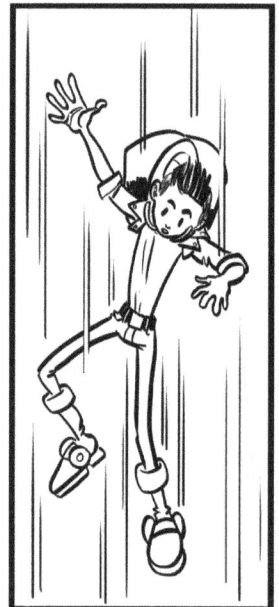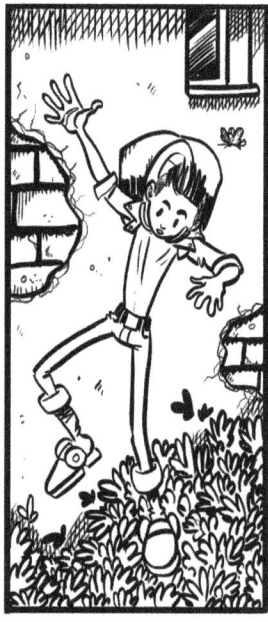

Note that the movement direction is succumbed to the panel shape. If the picture was horizontal, it would not be so dynamic.

TASK
TRY OUT THE PANEL DYNAMICS. DRAW YOUR HEROES IN VARIOUS SITUATIONS AND FIND OUT HOW THE ILLUSTRATED BACKGROUND WILL INFLUENCE THE READING PACE.

DYNAMICS IN COMICS

MOTION IS ONE OF THE MOST EXCITING CHALLENGES THAT YOU WILL BE DEALING WITH IN YOUR COMIC BOOK. LET'S SAY THAT WE WANT TO CREATE DYNAMIC PICTURES, BUT IN ANY CASE, I DO NOT WANT TO SAY THAT STATIC PICTURES ARE ANY BAD. I JUST LOVE MOVEMENT. THERE ARE, TYPICALLY FOR ART, ENDLESS POSSIBLE SOLUTIONS. WHAT CAN YOU DO WITH THAT? IT IS SIMPLE. CHOOSE THE STYLE WHICH SUITS YOU BEST AND STICK WITH IT.

DO NOT FORGET THAT MOTION DYNAMICS IS ENDORSED EVEN BY THE SHAPE OF THE PANEL IN WHICH THE PICTURE IS PLACED.

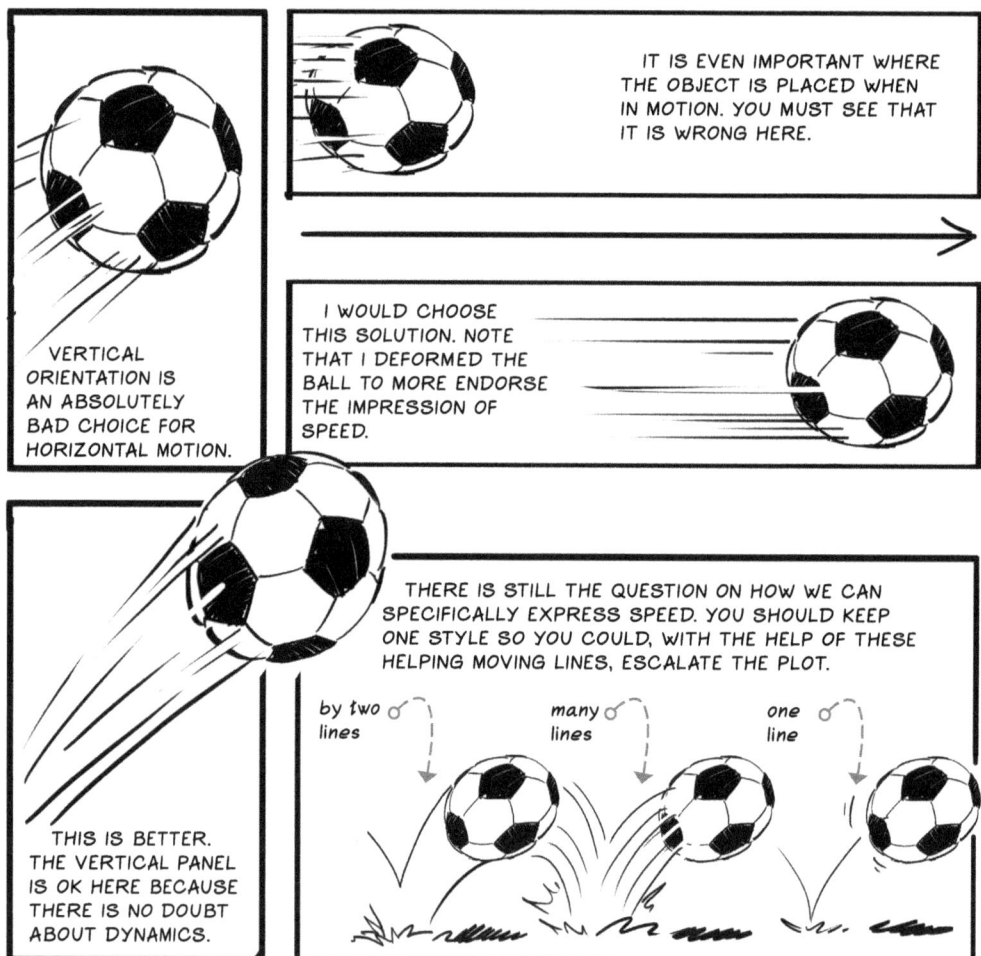

Board 120

MOTION DEPENDING ON THE STORY

SOMEWHERE I HAVE READ THAT MOTION IN A COMIC BOOK IS EXPRESSED BY ITS DIRECTION. IN OTHER WORDS, IF AN ITEM MOVES IN THE DIRECTION IN WHICH WE READ, IT GIVES THE IMPRESSION OF SPEEDING UP. IF IT IN THE OPPOSITE DIRECTION IT GIVES THE IMPRESSION OF SLOWING DOWN. IT MIGHT BE JUST ME, BUT I DO NOT SEE THE CONNECTION THERE. IT WOULD MEAN ALL MANGAS WOULD EVOKE THE EXACT OPPOSITE IMPRESSION IN PEOPLE LIKE YOU AND ME. I CONSIDER IT NONSENSE BECAUSE JUST MANGAS ARE ON THE TOPIC IN DYNAMICS. I HAVE DISCOVERED A MUCH MORE IMPORTANT RULE. PICTURES DEPENDING ON THE STORY. CHECK OUT THE FOLLOWING THREE PANELS BELOW. ALL OF THEM ILLUSTRATE RUNNING IKAR. JUST IN ONE OF THEM HE IS RUNNING CORRECTLY THOUGH. WHICH ONE AND WHY?

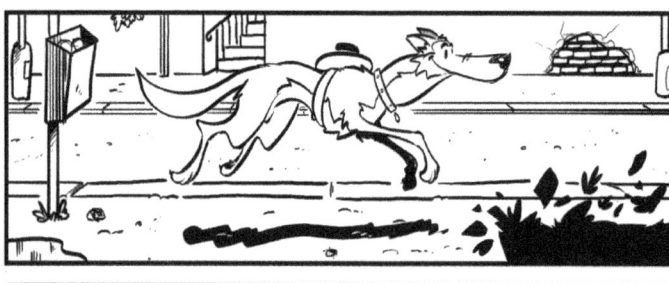

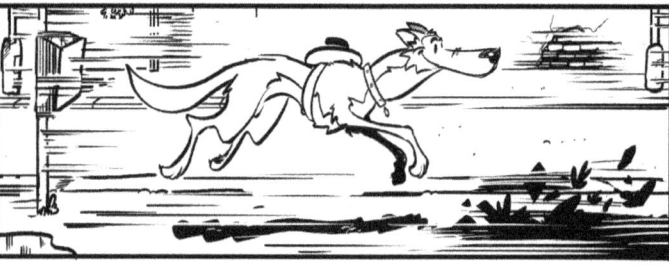

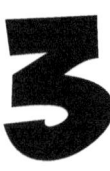

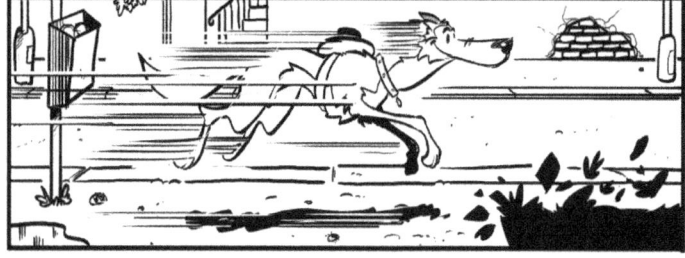

"IN ANY CASE IT REALLY MATTERS WHICH ONE YOU CHOOSE!"

THIS WAS A BIT TRICKY. REGARDING YOUR KNOWLEDGE YOU HAVE, ALL OF THEM ARE CORRECT. HOWEVER, JUST UNDER CERTAIN CIRCUMSTANCES! ALTHOUGH THE FIRST PICTURE IS NOT BADLY DRAWN, DYNAMICS AND SPEED ARE MISSING. THEREFORE WE WILL NOT DEAL WITH IT. WHEN YOU ARE PLANNING A COMIC BOOK, YOU HAVE TO BEAR IN MIND THAT ANGLE FROM WHICH YOU ARE WATCHING THE STORY MATTERS. THE DIFFERENCE IN THE SECOND AND THIRD PICTURES IS NOT ABOUT SPEED BUT THE NARRATION STYLE. SO TELL ME UNDER WHAT CIRCUMSTANCES I SHOULD CHOOSE SOLUTION NUMBER 2 AND WHEN NUMBER 3.

IT IS SIMPLE. YOU WILL CHOOSE ACCORDING TO THE ROLE YOU WANT THE READER EMPATHISE WITH. IN PICTURE 2 I BLURRED THE BACKGROUND AND I DID NOT DRAW DETAILS. IT IS BECAUSE I WANT THE READER EMPATHISE WITH IKAR AND IMAGINING RUNNING WITH HIM AND ENJOYING THE SPEED AND THE PASSING BY LANDSCAPE.
ON THE OTHER HAND, IN PICTURE 3 I BLURRED IKAR AND LET THE SURROUNDINGS STATIC. THAT PUTS THE READER INTO THE ROLE OF AN OBSERVER AND NOT A PROTAGONIST. THE READER SHOULD ADMIRE THE LANDSCAPE AND NOT RUN WITH IKAR.
IT MEANS THAT PICTURE NUMBER 1 LOSES THESE TWO EXCITING PIECES OF INFORMATION THAT ARE CONTAINED IN THE OTHER TWO ONES. ALTHOUGH THIS SCENE WAS THE MOST THE MOST DIFFICULT, FROM THE NARRATION POINT OF VIEW, IT IS ACTUALLY THE ONE, BECAUSE IT SHRUNK JUST IN A PIECE OF INFORMATION WITHOUT EMOTION AND DYNAMICS. IF IT WAS THE INTENTION, OK, THEN.

OK, SO ALL THREE PICTURES ARE FINE BUT IT DOES DEFINITELY NOT MATTER WHICH ONE YOU CHOOSE!

TASK
DRAW A FLYING BALL JUST RIGHT OVER A GOALKEEPER. FIRST OF ALL, DO IT WITH RESPECT TO THE FOOTBALL PLAYER DYNAMICS, THEN FROM THE BALL POINT OF VIEW AND FINALLY FROM THE WATCHER'S POINT OF VIEW. USE THE SAME ANGLE AND DEPICT THE DIFFERENCE IN THE DYNAMICS.

GRAPHIC STORY OUTLINE

IF YOU DO NOT CREATE A STORY OUTLINE, IT WOULD BE THE SAME AS IF YOU DID NOT DRAW A SKETCH TO YOUR DRAWING. I KNOW. THERE ARE STORIES THAT DO NOT HAVE ANY OUTLINE. STORIES IN WHICH THE AUTHOR LET HIMSELF CARRY AWAY AND LET THEM DO WHAT THEY WANTED. AUTHORS THEMSELVES SOMETIMES DO NOT EVEN KNOW HOW THEY WILL FINISH THEIR PIECE OF ART. THESE CAN BE REALLY GOOD STORIES. AT THE MOMENT, WE ARE NOT MAKING SUCH STORIES THOUGH. WE ARE MAKING A COMIC BOOK WHICH HAS A RESTRICTED NUMBER OF PAGES AND THEREFORE, WE MUST THINK ABOUT WHAT IT WILL LOOK LIKE IN ADVANCE.

I WILL NOT LIE TO YOU. THANKS TO THAT RESTRICTION THAT WE SET RIGHT AT THE BEGINNING, A LOT OF YOUR IDEAS WILL FALL UNDER THE TABLE. DO NOT REGRET IT. AT LEAST YOU CAN CHOOSE THE BEST ONES. HOWEVER, DO NOT THROW AWAY THE UNREALISED IDEAS. WRITE THEM DOWN AND KEEP THEM. THEIR TIME WILL COME SOMETIME IN THE FUTURE. TRUST ME!

DUE TO THE FACT THAT I DO NOT KNOW YOUR STORY, AS AN EXAMPLE, I WILL INTRODUCE THE OUTLINE OF MY STORY. TAKE IT AS AN EXAMPLE FOR YOURS.

FOR MY STORY I CHOSE THE MODERN ARC AND ITS WRITTEN FORM IS AS FOLLOWS:
1. EXPOSITION
2. EXPOSITION CLIMAX
3. PLOT
4. CLIMAX
5. CONCLUSION

NOW I CREATE ITS GRAPHIC FORM AND I WILL BE MAKING IT MORE PRECISE ON THE RIGHT-HAND SIDE. ON THE RIGHT HAND SIDE, I WILL PLACE THE EMOTION LINE, WHICH WILL SHOW ME WHETHER THE STORY IS DIVERSE ENOUGH. EVERYTHING YOU NEED TO KNOW ABOUT EMOTIONS IN A STORY CAN BE FOUND AT THE NEXT BOARD. TRY IT IN A ROUGH OUTLINE.

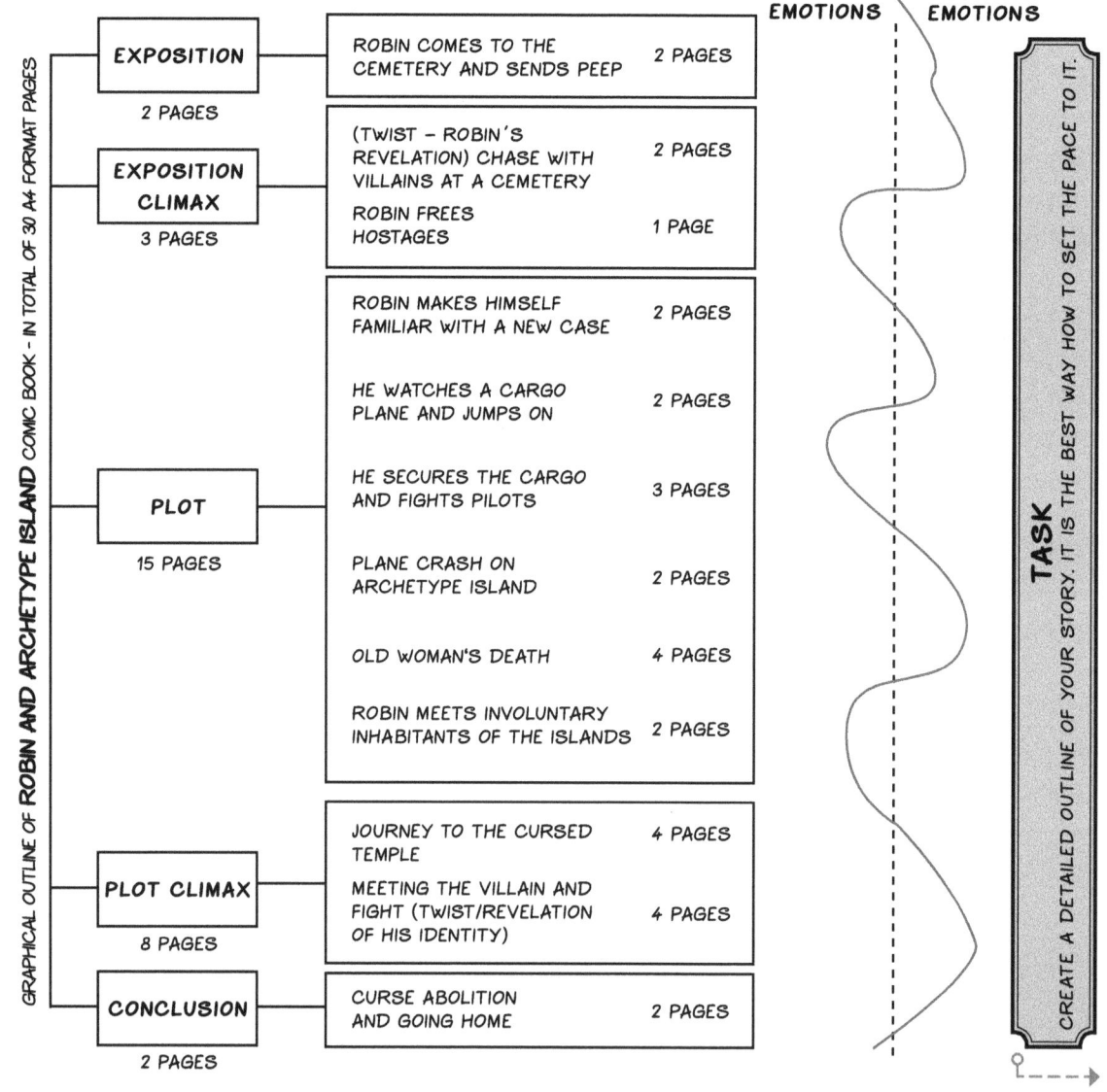

TASK: CREATE A DETAILED OUTLINE OF YOUR STORY. IT IS THE BEST WAY HOW TO SET THE PACE TO IT.

HOW TO WRITE A GOOD STORY

HOW COME THAT ALL SPACE IS TORN INTO PIECES, PLANET DESTROYED, ALL DIMENSIONS COLLAPSE AND WE ARE STILL BORED YAWNING? AND THEN WE TAKE ANOTHER BOOK AND WE ARE NOT ABLE TO PUT IT ASIDE ALTHOUGH IT IS ABOUT TRIVIAL SHORT STORIES WHERE NOTHING SPECIAL HAPPENS. THE UNBELIEVABLE POETICS OF THIS PIECE OF ART IS BASED ON NARRATION FROM A CHILD'S POINT OF VIEW. YOU CAN CLEARLY RECOGNISE WHICH SENTENCE IS FROM HIM, WHICH ONE WAS IMPOSED ON HIM AT SCHOOL AND WHICH ONE WAS HEARD FROM THE ADULTS. BASED ON THIS CONTRADICTION, AN ASTOUNDING FUN AND COMICALITY EMERGE. FROM THIS POINT OF VIEW, WE CAN SAY THAT IT DOES NOT REALLY DEPEND ON THE EVENTS THAT HAPPEN IN THE STORY BUT ON THE MANNER THE STORY IS WRITTEN IN. HOWEVER, IT IS NOT THAT SIMPLE.

HOW CAN WE ACTUALLY RECOGNISE A GOOD STORY? THE ANSWER IS BLATANTLY OBVIOUS. APART FROM SOME EXCEPTIONS, THE STORY SUCCESS IS MEASURED ACCORDING TO HOW STRONG EMOTIONAL FEEDBACK IT CAUSES IN US. IT REALLY MATTERS WHO THE BOOK IS AIMED AT. FOR EXAMPLE, I DO NOT READ ROMANTIC FICTION. IT IS BORING TO ME. HOWEVER, I WOULD NEVER SAY THAT THE BOOKS ARE BAD. THEY WERE JUST NOT WRITTEN FOR ME. WELL, I MIGHT NEVER TOUCH ROMANTIC FICTION IN MY LIFE, BUT MAYBE I WILL WHEN I BECOME WISER.

THE TRUTH IS THAT THE MORE THE STORY EMOTIONALLY TOUCHES US, EITHER POSITIVELY OR NEGATIVELY, THE BETTER WE EVALUATE IT. THE PROBLEM APPEARS WHEN WE, BASED ON OUR EXPERIENCE, REALISE THAT HUMAN MIND IS ABLE TO ADAPT DURING NARRATION, AND IF WE CONSTANTLY GIVE IT THE SAME EMOTIONS, IT WILL STOP PERCEIVING IT. IT IS SIMILAR WITH WHIPPING. IF YOU DO NOT TAKE A BREAK WITH THE WHIPS, THE WHIPPED ONE STOPS FEELING THE PAIN. OR IF YOU FEED SOMEONE WITH SWEETS, THEY WILL SOON GET USED TO IT. WHAT TO DO ABOUT IT? WHAT DO YOU THINK? WELL, IT IS BEST TO CHANGE! LET US DISCUSS WHAT EMOTIONS YOU CAN DOSE TO YOUR READER. WRITE IT DOWN INTO A DIAGRAM. WE WILL DISCOVER A REALLY SURPRISING THING.

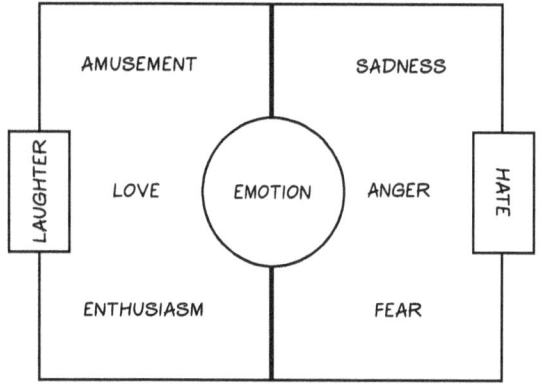

THE ONLY EMOTION WHICH SHOULD NOT BE HERE IS FRUSTRATION. I STRONGLY WARN YOU AGAINST IT. THANKS TO FRUSTRATION, YOU WILL LOSE YOUR READERS.

WELL, DOES THE DIAGRAM REMIND YOU OF SOMETHING? YES. IT IS A FOOTBALL PITCH. NEGATIVE EMOTIONS AGAINST POSITIVE ONES AS THE AWAY TEAM AGAINST THE HOME TEAM. WHILE THE AVERAGE EMOTIONS ARE THERE SUCH AS COMMON PLAYERS ON BOTH SIDES OF THE PITCH,

THE STRONGEST ONES ARE, OF COURSE, IN THE GOAL. EVERYTHING BECOMES EMOTIONAL WITH GOING FROM ONE POLARITY TO ANOTHER.

THE COMPARISON WITH A FOOTBALL PITCH IS NOT ODD AT ALL. IF YOU ASK A RIGHT FOOTBALL FAN TO EVALUATE A MATCH THEY HAVE JUST SEEN (INDEPENDENTLY ON IF THEIR TEAM WON OR LOST), THEY WILL TELL YOU:

1. IT WAS POOR BECAUSE THE BALL WAS KEPT JUST ON ONE SIDE OF THE PITCH, DURING THE GAME THERE WAS NO TWIST, FRUSTRATION CAME AND THERE WAS NO EXCITEMENT.

2. IT WAS GOOD BECAUSE THE TEAMS WERE PLAYING EQUALLY WELL, THE BALL WAS ON BOTH SIDES OF THE PITCH AND THE PLAYERS SCORED SOME GOALS ON BOTH SIDES.

YES, ACCORDING TO THE SIDE THAT THE BALL IS ON, WE EXPERIENCE A CERTAIN EMOTION. JUST WHEN THE SITUATION IS NOT CHANGING IN THE RIGHT MOMENT, WE LOSE INTEREST BECAUSE OUR EMOTION DISAPPEARS IN RELATION WITH THE BALL.

ANYWAY, WHAT CAUSES THAT WE LAP UP THESE SITUATIONS THAT BRING US EMOTIONAL FEEDBACK? WHY DO WE NEED IT? WELL, IT IS BECAUSE THEY ARE THE TRIGGER. THEY GIVE THE BRAIN THE INFORMATION AND IT FLOODS OUR BODY WITH THE CORRESPONDING SUBSTANCE. IN CASE OF POSITIVE EMOTIONS, IT IS ENDORPHIN AND IN CASE OF NEGATIVE ONES, IT IS ADRENALIN. LADIES AND GENTLEMEN, THESE ARE DRUGS! THIS IS ALSO, THE REASON WHY IT IS NECESSARY TO CHANGE THE POLARITY OF EMOTIONS IN A STORY. YOU WILL GET USED TO BOTH OF THESE DRUGS BUT IT IS NECESSARY TO OVERTRUMP THEM WITH EITHER SOMETHING STRONGER OR SOMETHING FROM THE OPPOSITE END OF THE SPECTRUM. IN ANY CASE, THE FASTER THE BALL IS AND THE LONGER DISTANCE IT REACHES, THE GREATER EMOTIONAL FEEDBACK AND IMPACT WILL THE READER FEEL. DUE TO ALL THESE FACTS, MY BASIC RECOMMENDATION FOR CREATIVE WRITING IS:

"DO YOU WANT TO BE A GOOD AUTHOR? BECOME A DRUG DEALER!"

AND, AS A PROPER DRUG DEALER YOU MUST DOSE THE DRUGS TO YOUR CUSTOMER, SO THAT THEY LAST AS LONG AS POSSIBLE BEFORE YOU COMPLETELY BLOW THEM AWAY. IN ANY CASE, OFFER QUALITY AND NOT THIN DOWN STUFF!

P.S.: THE READER WILL FEEL JUST EITHER ONLY POSITIVE OR NEGATIVE EMOTION. IF YOU MIX BOTH ELEMENTS IN ONE STORY SITUATION, BOTH OF THEM WILL GET LOST AND CANCEL OUT EACH OTHER. I KNOW, YOU HAVE A LOT OF IDEAS BUT A GOOD NARRATOR IS DISTINGUISHED BY NOT ONLY THE QUANTITY, BUT ALSO BY WHAT IRRELEVANT CONTENT THEY ARE ABLE TO CROSS OUT.

TASK
DRAW AGAIN THE GRAPHIC OUTLINE OF YOUR STORY IN MORE DETAIL AND TRY TO INDICATE THE STRENGTH OF THE EMOTION YOU WANT TO PUT IN THE SPECIFIC POINTS AND IN ITS APPROPRIATE SPECTRUM, WHETHER POSITIVE OR NEGATIVE. THE MORE THE POLARITY WILL BE CHANGING, THE BETTER. IF IT DOES NOT WORK, THINK ABOUT THE PLOT OF THE COMIC AGAIN, AND DO NOT BE AFRAID OF REWORK IT.

SCENARIO

FINALLY, WE CAN START WITH THE SCENARIO. DUE TO THE FACT THAT FOR MY COMICS I CHOSE THE COMIC FORM WITH THREE LINES, I CAN MAKE A SCENARIO SAMPLE ACCORDING TO A SINGLE PAGE. I DECIDED THAT I AM NOT STRICTLY KEEPING THE NINE POLE SAMPLE AND THE LINES WILL BE THE MAIN GUIDELINES. SOME EXCEPTIONS WILL APPEAR, BUT WHEN IT COMES IT WILL MAKE SENSE. SO NOTHING CAN STOP FROM WORKING ON THE SCENARIO WHICH WILL FOLLOW THE ORIGINAL PLOT. AGAIN, I DO NOT KNOW YOU STORY, SO I AM PRESENTING MINE. WE WILL BE DISCUSSING A FIVE PAGE INTRODUCTION TO THE COMIC BOOK ROBIN AND ARCHETYPE ISLAND. IN FACT, IT HAS A NARRATOR'S ARC. I AM ABLE TO DEMONSTRATE SOME TRICKS WHICH WILL COME IN HANDY FOR YOU.

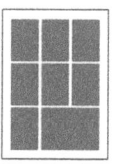

3 x 3 Watchman model

SCRIPT OF ROBIN AND ARCHETYPE ISLAND COMIC BOOK

BOARD 1

PANEL	DESCRIPTION	DIALOGUES	NOTE
1	LARGER PANEL OVER TWO LINES. WE CAN SEE A MYSTERIOUS GRAVEYARD SURROUNDING A RUNDOWN CHATEAU. EVERYTHING GIVES AN IMPRESSION OF MYSTERY AND SCARY. IT IS SEMI-DARK BUT NOT NIGHT, DEPRESSIVE AND BLUISH ENVIRONMENT. ROBIN AND PEEP ARE CROUCHING IN FRONT OF A GRAVESTONE, CAREFULLY WATCHING WHAT IS HAPPENING AROUND THE CHATEAU. NOTHING IS HAPPENING THERE SO FAR.	PEEP: PEEP? ROBIN (WHISPERING): SHHH. SHUSH. EVERYTHING INDICATES THAT THEY ARE KEEPING ANNA HERE. HOWEVER, WE MUST BE SURE BEFORE WE CALL THE POLICE.	ROBIN IS CLEARLY VISIBLE AT THE BACKGROUND. HE'S GOT A RED JACKET.
2	FINALLY, WE CAN SEE, OVER ROBIN'S SHOULDER, THE ENTRANCE TO THE CHATEAU. TWO HENCHMEN GUARD IT. THEY ARE SITTING BY A BOX AND THEY ARE PLAYING CARDS. THEIR RIFFLES ARE LEANING AGAINST THE BOX.	ROBIN (WHISPERING): I WAS RIGHT. I IDENTIFIED THEM WELL IN THEIR SIGNATURE CALL. TRAIN HONKING BY A NEAR TRAIN CROSSING.	MANY GRAVESTONES BUT JUST A MINIMUM OF RELIGIOUS SYMBOLS. WE WILL DESTROY THEM BUT WE DO NOT WANT TO INSERT A MESSAGE IN THE STORY THAT WE DO NOT WANT.
3	ROBIN IS DIALLING SOMETHING ON HIS PHONE.	NOW QUICKLY AN SMS TO THE POLICE. HOPEFULLY IT'S NOT TOO LATE...	

BOARD 2

PANEL	DESCRIPTION	DIALOGUES	NOTE
1	ROBINS IS TALKING TO PEEP	ROBIN: PEEP, FLY ALL AROUND THE CHATEAU AND TRY TO FIND ANNA.	
2	ROBIN AND IKAR ARE WATCHING PEEP AS HE FLIES AWAY. AT THE BACKGROUND, WE CAN SEE A COUPLE OF THE GUARDS DISTRACTED BY THE GAME.	ROBIN TO IKAR: SOMETHING IS WRONG, IKAR. GUARD 1 – WHAT KIND OF ACE IS THAT? WHAT DO YOU THINK WE HAVE BEEN PLAYING HERE ALL THE TIME? GUARD 2 – WELL...WHAT DO YOU MEAN? POKER!	
3	ROBIN IS LOOKING AT THIS MOBILE PHONE. ON THE SCREEN, THE GUARDS ARE HAVING A ROW.	GUARD 1: POKER IS NOT PLAYED LIKE THIS, YOU FOOL!	
4	PEEP FLIES BY THE GUARDS UNNOTICED. HE SEES A WINDOW.	GUARD 1: AND WE ARE PLAYING MAU – MAU!	NO BRAND OF THE MOBILE PHONE! NOBODY PAID US FOR IT SO WHAT?
5	ON THE MOBILE SCREEN, THERE IS A WINDOW. IKAR IS LOOKING OVER ROBIN'S SHOULDER.	ROBIN: THIS IS IT, PEEP! GUARDIAN 2: I PREFER THE CONCENTRATION GAME!	ABOVE THE WINDOW, THERE IS A GARGOYLE OVER WHICH A ROPE WILL BE ABLE TO THROW.
6	INSIDE VIEW, WE CAN SEE PEEP FLYING IN THE WINDOW.		
7	ON THE MOBILE SCREEN, WE CAN SEE ANNA TIED TO A CHAIR WITH A GAG IN HER MOUTH.	ROBIN: HMM, THOSE SCOUNDRELS BUT IT SEEMS THAT SHE IS OK. ANNA, DON'T BE AFRAID, HELP IN COMING!	
8	DUKE OF LAUTERNITZ APPEARS AT THE DOOR OF THE CHATEAU YELLING AT THE GUARDS.	LAUTERNITZ: WHAT ARE YOU DOING HERE, YOU FOOLS? YOU SHOULD BE GUARDING!	

TASK: CREATE YOUR SCENARIO

COMIC BOOK SCENARIO ....
BOARD ....

PANEL	DESCRIPTION	DIALOGUES	NOTE
1			
2			
3			
4			
5			
6			
7			
8			
9			
10			
11			
12			

BOARD 3

PANEL	DESCRIPTION	DIALOGUES	NOTE
1	SHOT OF ANNA. PEEP IS POINTLESSLY TRYING TO PECK OFF THE CUFFS. VOICES FROM THE OUTSIDE ARE BEING HEARD.	GUARD 1: EXCUSE ME, DUKE OF LAUTERNITZ, BUT THIS FOOL HERE.... LAUTERNITZ: I DO NOT CARE!	ANNA – BETWEEN 5 AND 8 YEARS OLD. CUTE, SCARED.
2 + 2a	DUKE OF LAUTERNITZ IN DETAIL. AN INSERTED PICTURE OF SHOCKED ROBIN. WE WILL INFRACT THE LAYOUT IN ORDER TO EXPRESS TWO SIMULTANEOUS EVENTS AND SIMULATE QUICK CUT.	LAUTERNITZ: BOTH OF YOU ARE FOOLS! THE FAMILY OBVIOUSLY DON'T WANT TO PAY THE RANSOM! LET'S GO UPSTAIRS, LET'S FINISH THIS WITH THE GIRL AND LET'S GET OUT OF HERE!	LAUTERNITZ IN ALL WHITE WITH A GOLD BUCKLE INSTEAD OF A TIE.
3	THE DUKE WITH GUARDS IS COMING IN THE DOOR OF THE CHATEAU. IN THE BACKGROUND WE CAN SEE ROBIN RUNNING BEHIND THEM FROM THE OTHER SIDE, IN THE DIRECTION WHERE PEEP HAD FLOWN.	LAUTERNITZ – YOU STAY AND GUARD.	
4	ROBIN IS LOOKING THROUGH THE WINDOW AND NOTICES THE GARGOYLE ABOVE IT.		IT IS POSSIBLE TO MERGE IT WITH PANEL 5.
5	ROBIN PULLS OUT HIS MULTIPURPOSE GADGET FROM IKAR'S BAG. HE IS LOOKING IN THE DIRECTION WHERE HE WANTS TO THROW IT. HE IS SPINNING IT LIKE WITH A LASSO.	THIS IS A TIME RACE, IKAR!	
6	ROBIN THROWS UP THE LEASH HANDLE.		
7	THE HANDLE FLIES OVER THE GARGOYLE ABOVE THE WINDOW AND FALLS DOWN.		
8	ROBIN CATCHES THE HANDLE AND TURNS TO IKAR.	ROBIN: NOW, HOLD!	

BOARD 4

PANEL	DESCRIPTION	DIALOGUES	NOTE
1	ROBIN IS CLIMBING UP AND IKAR IS BITING AND HOLDING A TREE BRANCH WITH ALL HIS MIGHT. ROBIN'S WEIGHT IS LIFTING HIM IN THE AIR.		ROBIN IS CLIMBING LIKE ADAM WEST DID WHEN PLAYING BATMAN.
3	ROBIN IS CLIMBING AROUND THE BOTTOM WINDOW. IN THE WINDOW, WE CAN SEE THE SCOUNDRELS RUNNING UP THE STAIRS.	LAUTERNITZ: UFF! THESE STAIRS...WE SHOULD HAVE BURIED THE GIRL RIGHT AWAY!	
4	ROBIN IS FINALLY AT THE WINDOW. HE IS INDICATING PSSST TO ANNA.		
5	WHILE THE GUARD ABOVE HEARS A SOUND AND GOES TO CHECK IT OUT IN IKAR'S DIRECTION.		
6	WE CAN SEE THE DOOR HANDLE BLOCKED BY ANNA'S CHAIR.	HOW COME THAT IT IS LOCKED? WHAT ARE YOU LOOKING AT? SMASH THE DOOR!	
7	GUARD 2 SMASHES THE DOOR. THE CHAIR FALLS TO PIECES.		SFX: CRACK
8	A LOOK AT LAUTERNITZ. HE IS SHOCKED. GUARD 2 IS RUBBING HIS PAINFUL SHOULDER.	LAUTERNITZ SHOCKED: WHAT...	

COMIC BOOK SCENARIO ....
BOARD ....

PANEL	DESCRIPTION	DIALOGUES	NOTE
1			
2			
3			
4			
5			
6			
7			
8			
9			
10			
11			
12			

BOARD 5

PANEL	DESCRIPTION	DIALOGUES	NOTE
1	WIDE LOOK AT ROBIN HANGING ON THE LEASH BEHIND THE WINDOW. ANNA IS HOLDING HIS SHOULDERS. LAUTERNITZ IS POINTING ANGRILY AT ROBIN. GUARD 2 IS STILL SHOCKED.	LAUTERNITZ: CATCH THEM YOU FOOL! ROBIN: IKAR, RELEASE!	DO NOT FORGET ABOUT PEEP, HE IS FLYING SOMEWHERE OVER THERE!
2	IKAR RELEASES THE BRANCH AND DUE TO THE PULLEY, THE BRANCH IS GOING UP AND ROBIN DOWN. IKAR IS PULLING OUT HIS TONGUE AT GUARD 1	GUARD 1: ?	
3	ROBIN FALLS ONTO THE GUARD.	ROBIN: THIS IS WHAT I CALL A SOFT LANDING.	
4	IKAR RUNS BY THE CONFUSED LAUTERNITZ.	LAUTERNITZ:?	
5	ROBIN CATCHES IKAR.	ROBIN: NOW, LET'S GET OUT OF HERE, IKAR! I CAN ALREADY HEAR POLICE SIRENS BEHIND THE DOOR. WE CAN'T GIVE THOSE SCOUNDRELS AN ADVANTAGE.	
6	LAUTERNITZ, RED WITH ANGER, LEANING OUT OF THE WINDOW, IS SHOUTING.	LAUTERNITZ: WHY DO YOU HAVE THOSE RIFLES FIRE!	
7	IKAR IS PULLING ROBIN ON THE LEASH. HE HAS ACTIVATED ROLLING SKATES. ANNA IS HANGING ON HIS BACK AND ALL OF THEM ARE WHOOSHING OUT OF THE REACH OF THE VILLAINS. GUNSHOTS ARE BEING HEARD. EXCITED FACES INDICATE THAT THE HEROES ARE ALREADY OUT OF DANGER.	ROBIN: FLY, IKAR! FLY!	SFX: BANG! BANG! BANG!

THIS IS A SAMPLE OF THE PUREST FORM OF SCENARIO. OF COURSE, THERE ARE MANY MORE OF THEM BUT I PREFER THIS ONE. IT IS SIMPLE, CLEAR AND THE AUTHOR MUST THINK IN A COMIC MANNER. THIS IS A PROBLEM OF THE CONTEMPORARY (AND IN PARTICULAR OF THE CZECH) COMIC BOOK SCRIPT WRITERS. IN FACT, THEY CREATE SCENARIOS IN THE FORM OF A SHORT STORY. COMMON FICTION SPEAKS A COMPLETELY DIFFERENT LANGUAGE THAN COMIC BOOKS. WE HAVE ALREADY GONE THROUGH THIS. IF THE CARTOONIST DOES NOT RECEIVE THE SCENARIO DIVIDED INTO SINGLE BOARDS AND PANELS, THEY ARE FORCED TO ADAPT IT. AND BECAUSE A COMIC BOOK HAS ITS EXPRESSIVE TOOLS, THEY WILL HAVE TO MAKE SOME CHANGES BECAUSE IF THEY KEPT THE ORIGINAL PATTERN, IT WOULD NOT WORK.

IT WILL ALL REMAIN SOMEWHERE HALFWAY.

IF THE SCRIPT WRITER WRITES A SCENARIO AS A SHORT STORY, THEY CAN'T POSSIBLY KNOW HOW LONG THE COMIC BOOK WILL BE. MOREOVER, IF IT HAS A PREDETERMINED NUMBER OF PAGES, A PROBLEM WILL APPEAR, WHICH THEY WILL BLAME THE CARTOONIST FOR. ALTHOUGH IT MIGHT SOUND GOOD IN A SHORT STORY, THE CARTOONIST CAN EMPHASISE OTHER SCENES THAN THE ONES WHICH WERE INTENDED BY THE SCRIPT WRITER AND IT ALL STOPS WORKING. COMIC BOOKS **ADAPTED** IN THIS MANNER DO NOT HAVE THE RIGHT PACE.

IF YOU ARE HONOURED TO WRITE A SCENARIO, BE CAREFUL ABOUT THE WAY THE CARTOONIST WILL DEAL WITH YOUR PIECE OF ART. THE MORE PRECISE YOU PLAN THE COMIC BOOK, THE BETTER YOUR INTENTION WILL WORK OUT. IF YOU DARE, YOU CAN EVEN MAKE A ROUGH SKETCH OF THE WHOLE BOARD.

THAT IS BETTER THAN THOUSANDS OF WORDS, BELIEVE ME. THE CARTOONIST WILL BE ABLE TO WORK MUCH FASTER AND MORE PRECISELY. YOU DO NOT HAVE TO WORRY ABOUT MISUNDERSTANDING OF YOUR IDEA.

HOWEVER, IF YOU GIVE THE CARTOONIST JUST A ROUGH DRAFT OF THE SHORT STORY, YOU CANNOT POSSIBLY THINK YOU CONTRIBUTED ENOUGH TO THE SCENARIO. YOU MIGHT HAVE CONTRIBUTED WITH THE TOPIC OF THE STORY, BUT THE CARTOONIST WILL HAVE TO PUT SCENARIOS TOGETHER ON THEIR OWN. BECAUSE THEY HAVE TO RE-CREATE YOUR SCENARIO IN THEIR HEADS, IT MIGHT EVOLVE INTO A MUCH WORSE CASE.

AND ONE MORE THING AND I EMPHASIZE IT. WE ARE LIVING IN THE 21ST CENTURY AND IT SHOULD BE A MATTER OF COURSE.

HAND OUT THE TEXT TO THE CARTOONIST IN ACTIVE TEXT FORM! IT MEANS IN A PROGRAMME FROM WHERE THE CARTOONIST CAN COPY AND PASTE. DO NOT LEAVE IT WITH THE CARTOONIST SO THEY MUST MANUALLY REWRITE IT. IF THEY DO NOT DO LETTERING MANUALLY, OF COURSE. MISTAKES THEN HAPPEN MORE FREQUENTLY, AND THE CARTOONIST.

MUST ACTIVELY SPEND THEIR TIME ON SOMETHING THAT THE SCRIPT WRITER HAS ALREADY DONE.

IT MIGHT NOT SEEM SO IMPORTANT BUT IF YOU ARE A COMMERCIAL CARTOONIST, THE TIME YOU SPEND ON A COMIC BOOK DECIDES IF THE PROJECT WAS SUCCESSFUL OR NOT. DO NOT DO REDUNDANT THINGS AND DO NOT FORCE OTHERS TO DO THEM TOO. WITH LAZINESS, YOU JUST CREATE MORE WORK, WHICH WILL NOT BE PAID BY ANYBODY. ANYWAY, WHY AM I TRYING TO EXPLAIN THAT. YOU WILL STILL DO IT YOUR OWN WAY, RIGHT? WE, ARTISTS, ARE HORRIBLE RIFF-RAFF.

> "ALWAYS SUBMIT THE SCENARIOS IN THE ACTIVE TEXT!"

COMIC BOOK SCENARIO ....
BOARD. ....

PANEL	DESCRIPTION	DIALOGUE	NOTE
1			
2			
3			
4			
5			
6			
7			
8			
9			
10			
11			
12			

Board 133

ABSTRACT AND SYNOPSIS

THE THINGS YOU ARE GOING TO DEAL WITH, IDEALLY AT THE END, ARE SYNOPSIS AND ABSTRACT. IT IS A BRIEF SUMMARY OF THE THAT SHOULD CATCH THE READER'S EYE. SUCH LURE CAN BE FOUND ON THE BACK BOOK COVER AND IT IS USED FOR PUBLISHERS TO PUBLISH THE BOOK. BUT BE CAREFUL. SYNOPSIS FOR PUBLISHERS WILL LOOK DIFFERENT!

WHILE IN A READER'S SUMMARY YOU NEED TO MAKE SURE YOU DO NOT REVEAL TOO MUCH FROM THE STORY PLOT, YOU MUST NOT HIDE ANYTHING IN THE PUBLISHER'S VERSION. IN THE EDITORIAL OFFICE THEY MUST KNOW EXACTLY IN ADVANCE WHAT THEY ARE GOING TO DEAL WITH. IT CAN HAPPEN THAT THEY WILL INTERFERE IN THE PLOT AND THEY WILL ASK FOR EDITING IT. THIS IS PRECISELY THE REASON WHY WE ARE PREPARING JUST A TEASER AND NOT THE COMPLETE COMIC BOOK AS AN OFFER FOR THE PUBLISHER. EVERY EDITORIAL OFFICE WILL TURN THEIR BACK ON A NON-EDITABLE COMPLETE PIECE OF ART. SO, I AM PRESENTING AN EXAMPLE OF WHAT IT SHOULD ROUGHLY LOOK LIKE.

ABSTRACT FOR THE READER:

ROBIN AND HIS TWO INSEPARABLE FRIENDS, A DOG IKAR AND SPARROW PEEP, HAVE FOUND AN AGENCY FOR HIRED ADVENTURERS AND JUST ONE OF THE FIRST CONTRACTS TAKES THEM FAR TO A MYSTERIOUS ISLAND FROM WHERE THERE IS SEEMINGLY NO WAY OUT. HOWEVER, THEY MIGHT HAVE BIT OFF MORE THAN THEY CAN CHEW. TO ESCAPE THE CLAWS OF DEATH, THEY DON'T HAVE ANY OTHER CHOICE THAN REVEALING THE SECRET OF THE CREEPY ISLAND OF ARCHETYPE!

SYNOPSIS FOR THE PUBLISHER:

THE STORY IS ABOUT ROBIN, A HERO IN THE MANNER OF TINTIN. HIS AGE IS NOT SPECIFIED AND HE DOES NOT HAVE ANY STRONG SYMBOLS SO READERS, ROUGHLY FROM 9 TO 35 YEARS OLD, COULD IDENTIFY WITH HIM. ROBIN HAS FRIENDS – A DOG AND A SPARROW WHO PROVIDE HIM WITH TECHNICAL COVERAGE. TOGETHER THEY ESTABLISH AN AGENCY R.I.P. (ACRONYM OF THEIR NAMES – ROBIN, IKAR AND PEEP) WITH THE SLOGAN: "LEAVE ADVENTURE ON US, YOU REST IN PEACE". THEY COULD BE HIRED AS ADVENTURERS AND STORIES COME EASILY TO THEM.

IN THE FIRST PART, RIGHT AFTER THE PROLOGUE THAT IS ATTACHED, ROBIN IS HIRED BY AN UNKNOWN FRAGILE-LOOKING MAN. HE TELLS ROBIN THAT KIDNAPS ARE SPREADING AROUND THE WHOLE WORLD. AT FIRST SIGHT, THOSE KIDNAPS HAVE NOTHING IN COMMON BESIDES THE FACT THAT TRACES ALWAYS END AT A LOCAL AIRPORT AND THEN NOBODY HEARS ABOUT THE KIDNAPPED PEOPLE ANYMORE. THE TRACES LEAD ROBIN TO AN AIRPLANE. HE GETS ON BOARD. HE FIGHTS THE PILOTS. EVENTUALLY, THE PLANE CRASHES ON A MYSTERIOUS ISLAND OF ARCHETYPE. ROBIN FINDS ALL THE KIDNAPPED PEOPLE AND HE, STEP BY STEP, FINDS OUT THAT A SECRET ORGANIZATION DEALS WITH IMPORTING VARIOUS PERSONALITIES TO THE ISLAND (DETECTIVES, SCIENTISTS, KINGS OF THIEVES, ADVENTURERS, HEROES OF CATASTROPHES) IN ORDER TO SAVE THE FROM THEM BECAUSE IT IS BELIEVED THAT THEIR AURA CAUSES THE PARTICULAR CATASTROPHES). AND ROBIN IS ONE OF THEM AND WAS INTENTIONALLY LURED HERE.

THE ISLAND OF ARCHETYPE RESISTS THEIR POWER AND PREVENTS THEM FROM ESCAPING. ON THE ISLAND, ROBIN AND THE OTHERS FINALLY FIND A TEMPLE THAT CAUSES IT.

HOWEVER, THE MAIN VILLAIN WHO IS BEHIND ALL OF THIS, TURNS OUT TO BE THE FRAGILE MAN WHO HIRED ROBIN. AN ACTION SCENE BREAKS OUT. THE MAIN VILLAIN BECOMES AN ARCHETYPAL VILLAIN WHO ABSORBS THE ENERGY THAT WAS BEING ABSORBED BY THE ISLAND FROM THE LOST PEOPLE. THE MAIN VILLAIN BECOMES A DEMON AND ROBIN BEATS HIM IN A COMBAT.

FINALLY, EVERYONE FLIES AWAY IN A HELICOPTER WHICH WAS LEFT THERE BY THE VILLAIN. THE RESCUED ADVENTURERS COME BACK TO THEIR HOMES ALL AROUND THE WORLD, WHICH MAKES SURE THAT INTERESTING THINGS MIGHT HAPPEN IN THE FUTURE AGAIN.

AGE READER FOCUS: 9 +
SUGGESTED NUMBER OF PAGES: 30 – 40 + COVER
GENRE: ADVENTURE, ACTION
OTHER SPECIFICATION: NO VULGARISMS, PROPER JOKES, NO BLOOD, NO CORPSES, VIOLENCE REALLY MODERATE ONLY
COLOUR: FULL COLOURED, 4/4 CMYK
SIZE: APPROX. A4 FORMAT
TIME TO FINISH FROM THE ASSIGNMENT SUBMITTED: 3 MONTHS
CHARGE: COMPLETE AUTHOR'S SERVICE UP TILL THE PRINT
CONTACT: WWW.PETRKOPL.CZ

TASK
CREATE BOTH SYNOPSES BOTH FOR THE READER AND THE PUBLISHER IN THIS ORDER, IF POSSIBLE. WRITE THE READER'S ONE AS ATTRACTIVE AS YOU CAN. YES, YOU MUST NEGOTIATE EVEN WITH THE PUBLISHER IN ORDER TO CATCH THEIR EYE. DO NOT COUNT ON THEM WANTING TO MEET YOU.

ABSTRACT FOR THE READER:

SYNOPSIS FOR THE PUBLISHER:

AGE READER FOCUS:
SUGGESTED NUMBER OF PAGES:
GENRE:
OTHER SPECIFICATION:
COLOUR:
SIZE:
TIME TO FINISH FROM THE ASSIGNMENT SUBMITTED:
CHARGE:
CONTACT:

Protective zone - no text - 5 mm
Bleed 5 mm

10 LIES ABOUT COMIC BOOK MAKING

I WILL REPEAT MYSELF BUT I HAVE DECIDED TO WRITE DOWN SEVERAL MYTHS ABOUT COMIC BOOKS THAT ARE BEING SPREAD, AND WHICH ONES I HEAR OFTEN, TOGETHER ON ONE PAGE.

1. READING COMIC BOOKS IS EASIER THAN READING BOOKS. I DISCUSS THIS MYTH IN THE INTRODUCTION. SO JUST TO ADD: MAKING A COMIC BOOK IS HARDER THAN MAKING A BOOK, WHICH IS NECESSARY TO DISPROVE THIS LIE.

2. A WELL DRAWN COMIC BOOK IS RECOGNISABLE BY HOW GOOD THE ILLUSTRATION IS. ESPECIALLY WHEN THE CARTOONIST DRAWS REALISTIC BACKGROUNDS AND THE CHARACTERS ARE ANATOMICALLY CORRECT. IT IS THE SAME AS IF YOU SAID THAT PICASSO IS A TINKER BECAUSE HIS PAINTINGS DO NOT FOLLOW A REALISTIC PORTRAYAL OF LIFE. THIS SIMPLY DOES NOT WORK. IT WOULD MEAN THAT CARTOONING IS ONLY ABLE TO MAKE INFERIOR COMIC BOOKS. OF COURSE, THIS IS NONSENSE.

3. IF I DO NOT ENJOY A COMIC BOOK, IT MEANS THAT THE COMIC BOOK IS BAD. OK, THIS IS A REAL NONSENSE. THERE ARE ONLY A FEW COMIC BOOK READERS WHO READ COMIC BOOKS BECAUSE OF THEIR GENRE. SO, IF I READ COMIC BOOKS ABOUT SUPERHEROES. IT IS BECAUSE I LOVE SUPERHEROES. NOT BECAUSE I LOVE THE COMIC BOOK. IF I DO NOT ENJOY LOVE STORY, I WOULD NOT ENJOY A COMIC BOOK ABOUT A LOVE STORY EITHER. HOWEVER, THIS DOES NOT MEAN THAT IT IS A BAD COMIC BOOK. IT MEANS THAT IT IS NOT MY FAVOURITE GENRE. SO, USE ALL YOUR WITS!

4. COPYING A BACKGROUND AND WHOLE PANELS, IS A SIGN OF THE AUTHOR'S LAZINESS. NO! IT IS A COMMON EXPRESSIONAL TOOL. A COMIC BOOK WILL ALWAYS MINGLE A BIT WITH A CARTOON MOVIE. AFTER ALL, YOU DO NOT THINK THAT THE BACKGROUND IN A CARTOON MOVIE IS NOT DRAWN AGAIN IN EACH SINGLE FRAME, DO YOU? WHY NOT USE THE SAME TECHNIQUE IN A COMIC BOOK? OF COURSE, THERE IS A DIFFERENCE IF YOU ARE DRAW A COMIC STRIP OR A LUXURIOUS ARTISTIC ALBUM. HOWEVER, EVEN THEN THERE ARE TECHNIQUES THAT CAN WORK. FOR EXAMPLE, IF YOU WANT THE BEST EXAMPLE, YOU CAN TAKE A LOOK AT THE DEATH OF CAPTAIN AMERICA PUBLISHED IN THE CZECH REPUBLIC (PUBLISHED BY BB ART) AT PAGES 346 – 347. SOMETIMES IT JUST SIMPLY GOES WELL TOGETHER WITH A COMIC BOOK.

5. PHOTO COPYING LOWERS THE ARTIST'S CLASS. WHAT? NO! PHOTO COPYING IS A COMMON TECHNIQUE, AND NOT ONLY FOR COMIC ARTISTS. IT IS ABSOLUTELY ALRIGHT. YOU DO NOT NEED A REALISTIC STREET, YOU CAN FIND AN ACTUAL PHOTOGRAPH OR YOU CAN JUST TAKE A PHOTO OF IT, AND THEN JUST COPY IT. EASY. THE GREATEST NAMES USE THIS TECHNIQUE. YOU DO NOT BELIEVE? CHECK OUT PAGE 28 IN THE TITLED CRIMINAL WHICH WAS PUBLISHED BY BB ART IN THE CZECH REPUBLIC. A GREAT CARTOONIST SEAN PHILLIPS SHOWS HERE HOW HE SIMPLY INSERTED A PHOTOGRAPH IN HIS SKETCH AND THEN HE JUST COPIED IT. DID HE HAVE TO DO IT? DO YOU THINK HE WOULD NOT HAVE DRAWN IT WITHOUT IT? OF COURSE HE WOULD. HOWEVER, HE WOULD HAVE SPENT A COUPLE OF HOURS MORE ON THAT PICTURE IN ORDER TO ACHIEVE THE SAME RESULT, SO WHY WORK MORE THAN NEEDED? BUT BE CAREFUL. YOU NEED TO DO IT WELL. YOU MUST DRAW THE STREET IN THE SAME STYLE AS THE REST OF THE COMIC BOOK. OTHERWISE YOU FAIL.

6. PHOTOS PROCESSED BY A PHOTOSHOP FILTER LOWERS THE QUALITY OF COMIC BOOKS. OF COURSE NOT AGAIN, IT IS A TECHNIQUE USED BY MANY ARTISTS AND THEREFORE, REALLY FORCEFUL PIECES OF ART EMERGE. THERE IS SOMETHING SIMILAR IN ANIMATION. IT IS CALLED ROTOSCOPING, WHICH MEANS A MOVIE EDITED BY A FILTER AND JUST MODERATELY EDITED BY ARTISTS IN ORDER TO FINISH ANY IMPERFECTIONS WHICH CANNOT BE DONE BY THE FILTER. (SEE FILM ALOIS NEBEL 2011). DAREDEVIL BY ALEX MALEEV WAS MADE IN A SIMILAR WAY. (PUBLISHED BY BB ART IN THE CZECH REPUBLIC). WHILE THE BACKGROUND IS ALMOST EXCLUSIVELY A PROCESSED PHOTOGRAPHY, THE CHARACTERS ARE ADDED BY A DRAWING. IT IS THE SAME AS THE PREVIOUS POINT. YOU MUST DO IT WELL AND YOU MUST NOT STRUGGLE WITH THE PHOTOGRAPH!

7. COMIC DRAWING GOES BEST TOGETHER WITH THE AUTHOR'S HANDWRITING. NOT AT ALL. THE FACT YOU DRAW LIKE GOD DOES NOT MEAN THAT YOUR HANDWRITING WILL BE READABLE FOR A PARTICULAR AUDIENCE. HAVE YOU TRIED TO READ ANYTHING BY LEONARDO DA VINCI? IT IS REALLY HARD, RIGHT? WOULD YOU ENJOY PUZZLING OVER SOME HIS COMIC BOOKS? I DON'T THINK SO. THE FONT CHOSEN FOR A COMIC BOOK HAS MORE ASPECTS THAN TO ONLY GO WELL TOGETHER WITH A DRAWING. IT MUST ALSO BE ADEQUATE TO THE AGE OF THE READER FOR WHOM IT IS INTENDED. LAST BUT NOT LEAST, IT MUST FOLLOW ALSO THE STORY GENRE AND NARRATION STYLE. THEREFORE, THERE IS A DIFFERENT FONT IN MORGAVSA AND DIFFERENT IN BREATHTAKING MIRACLE.

8. COMIC BOOKS ILLUSTRATED BY TRADITIONAL METHODS ON A PAPER ARE MORE VALUABLE THAN THOSE WHICH ARE MADE ELECTRONICALLY. THIS IS NOT TRUE EITHER. YES, IF YOU COME ACROSS ORIGINAL VERSIONS OF COMIC BOOKS, THEY REALLY HAVE A HIGH COLLECTOR'S VALUE. HOWEVER, WHEN WE TALK ABOUT PRODUCTS – THESE ARE NOTEBOOKS OR BOOKS. WE DO NOT CARE WHETHER THEY WERE CREATED IN A TRADITIONAL MANNER, ELECTRONICALLY OR A COMBINATION OF BOTH. THE RESULT IS MORE IMPORTANT. WE ASSESS THE IMPRESSION WHICH THE COMIC BOOK LEAVES IN US AND NOT THE TOOLS BY WHICH IT WAS ACHIEVED. 99.9 % OF COMIC BOOKS ARE CREATED IN COMPUTERS OR EDITED IN VARIOUS PROGRAMMES. IN MANY CASES YOU CANNOT EVEN DISTINGUISH IT. IT IS TIME TO RECONCILE.

9. COMICS ARE A DECLINING GENRE. FIRST OF ALL, COMICS IS A MEDIUM, NOT A GENRE. AND YES. THERE ARE ALSO A LOT OF TRASH DIVISIONS. NEVERTHELESS, IT CAN CARRY HIGH ART VALUE OR EVEN BE A DOCUMENTARY. IN ADDITION, WE CANNOT TALK ABOUT ANY DECLINE.

10. COMICS IS FOR CHILDREN. IT SPOILS THEIR STYLE AT THE SAME TIME. COME ON. EITHER IT IS FOR CHILDREN OR NOT. JUST CHOOSE! YES, COMIC BOOKS ARE FOR CHILDREN. OTHER ONES ARE FOR ADULTS AND A LOT OF ADULTS READ THE SMURFS AND THEY DO NOT FEEL ASHAMED BY THAT. I, FOR EXAMPLE. I WOULD REALLY NOT DEAL WITH THIS QUESTION IN THE 21ST CENTURY.

SOME PIECES OF ADVICE FOR CARTOONISTS IN GENERAL

THERE ARE THINGS THAT ARE STILL RELEVANT AND THEREFORE IT IS GOOD IDEA TO REVISE SOME OF THEM. ALTHOUGH, I HAVE DISCUSSED THEM ELSEWHERE IN THIS BOOK. TAKE THE FOLLOWING RECOMMENDATIONS AS SEVEN WELL MEANT PIECES OF ADVICE.

THOU SHALT PRACTISE 8 HOURS A DAY

IT IS JUST THE MINIMUM. A LAYMAN WOULD SAY THAT IT IS A LOT BUT TRY TO MEASURE YOUR DAILY DRAWING TIME. IT IS NOT SO DIFFERENT, IS IT? WELL, UNLESS YOU ARE A MASTER BY NATURE. THE ONE WHO DRAWS LESS, IF THEY ARE NOT GENIUSES, WILL REMAIN AMATEUR. THAT IS TRUE. HOWEVER, THE NEXT PIECE OF ADVICE IS RELATED TO THIS.

THOU SHALT CONCENTRATE NO MORE THAN 3 HOURS A DAY

YES, YOU CAN DOODLE AND KEEP GOING UNTIL YOUR HAND FALLS OFF BUT YOU CAN SERIOUSLY DRAW JUST 3 HOURS A DAY. VIOLIN PLAYERS ALSO PRACTISE MORE THAN 10 HOURS A DAY, BUT THEY CONCENTRATE NO MORE THAN 2. YOU NEED TO PUT YOUR SPIRIT IN THE ART AND WE HAVE A LIMITED AMOUNT OF SUCH ENERGY. IT WILL RECOVER (AFTER 3 HOURS) JUST IN CASE WE OVERDO IT. THE MOST IMPORTANT PIECE OF ADVICE WHICH FOLLOWS IS RELATED TO THIS.

THOU SHALT RELAX ONE DAY A WEEK

DETERMINE ONE DAY A WEEK WHEN YOU STRICTLY FORBID YOURSELF TO EVEN THINK ABOUT DRAWING. THE SAME HAPPENS WITH ABILITIES AS WITH WORKING OUT. EVERY BODYBUILDER CAN TELL YOU THAT RELAXATION IS JUST AS IMPORTANT AS THE WORKOUT ITSELF. THE PITFALL OF THIS PIECE OF ADVICE IS THAT EVEN IF YOU DO NOT RELAX, YOUR ABILITIES WILL IMPROVE. THEY WILL IMPROVE FLUENTLY BUT BY FAR NOT AS FAST AS IF YOU RELAXED. ON THE OTHER HAND, IF YOU REGULARLY RELAX, FOR A LONG TIME IT WILL SEEM THAT NOTHING HAPPENS BUT SUDDENLY YOU LEVELS UP. THEN, ON ONE DAY, YOU WAKE UP AND THE THINGS YOU HAD TO SPEND HOURS ON AND WERE CAUSING YOU DIFFICULTIES WILL BE DONE JUST RIGHT THE FIRST TIME. DO NOT LET YOURSELF WORK WITHOUT REST. BELIEVE ME, I KNOW SOMETHING ABOUT IT.

THOU SHALT STEAL

YES, REALLY. IN ART THERE IS NOTHING WRONG WITH IT. COPY, LEARN FROM OTHERS, COPY OFF THEIR SOLUTIONS. BY COMBINING YOU MIGHT ACHIEVE SOMETHING NEW OR AT LEAST YOU WILL FIND THE EASIEST WAY FOR YOU. HOWEVER, IF YOU INSPIRE YOURSELF WITH SOMETHING, YOU NEED TO CONFESS IT. THERE IS NOTHING MORE AWKWARD THAN WHEN IT WAS REVEALED BY SOMEONE ELSE. YOU ONLY HAVE ONE REPUTATION.

THOU SHALT CONSTANTLY LOOK FOR NEW TECHNIQUES

NEVER STAGNATE IN LOOKING FOR BETTER SOLUTION TO WHICH YOU ALREADY HAVE. THERE ARE ALWAYS SOME. EVEN IF YOU CANNOT FIND IT, STILL LOOK FOR IT. EXPERIMENT AND GO FOR BRAVE RAIDS TO UNDISCOVERED LANDS. IN THE MOMENT WHEN YOU STOP CONQUERING, YOU WILL BECOME SCRAP IRON AND START THE WAY TO FALL INTO OBLIVION.

THOU SHALT SUPPORT NEW COLLEAGUES

WHO DO YOU PREFER TO BE? THE ONE WHO LIVES IN FEAR AND HIDES THEIR TECHNIQUES, METHODS WHICH THEY DEVELOPED WITH GREAT CARE, IN THE SWEAT OF THEIR FACES AND NOT SHARE THEM WITH OTHERS JUST BECAUSE THEY ARE AFRAID THAT SOME LOSER COULD USE THEM? WILL YOU TRAMPLE GERMINATING SPROUTS AND PUSH ASPIRING CARTOONISTS IN THE GROUND BECAUSE STANDING ON THEIR BACKS YOU LOOK ADMIRABLE? OR YOU WILL BE THE ONE WHO GIVES A HELPING HAND TO ENTHUSIASTIC ROOKIES, AND WILL PROVIDE SUPPORT IN THE FORM OF YOUR EXPERIENCE SO THE WHOLE COLOSSUS OF ART WOULD MOVE ONE STEP FORWARD AND DEVELOP FASTER BY IT? THINK ABOUT IT BUT WHAT IS GOOD FOR YOU IS GOOD FOR THEM... BUT MAINLY: WHAT IS RIGHT?

THOU SHALT HONOUR YOUR COLLEAGUES

THIS IS NOT NEITHER A FOOTBALL MATCH NOR A FIGHT BETWEEN SUBURBAN BOYS' GANGS. ART IS NOT A FIGHT. IF YOU DRAW JUST BECAUSE OF YOUR CAREER, YOU WILL NEVER BE GOOD ENOUGH TO HAVE YOUR WORK CAMPAIGNED. DON'T GET ME WRONG. THERE IS NOTHING WRONG WITH A CAMPAIGN TO PROMOTE YOUR NAME BUT IF IT GOES AGAINST SOME STREAM OR EVEN AGAINST SOME PARTICULAR COLLEAGUES, IT IS A DIRTY GAME WHICH WILL EVENTUALLY TURN AGAINST YOU.

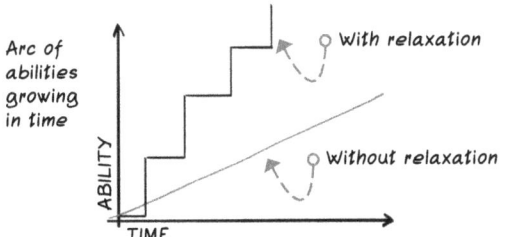

Arc of abilities growing in time

ROUGH SKETCH

FINALLY! AFTER ALL THAT INCREDIBLY LONG PREPARATION, WE ARE GOING TO DRAW! IT TOOK AGES! I KNOW. THERE WERE MANY THINGS THAT HAD TO BE DONE BEFORE YOU DRAW THE FIRST LINE IN YOUR COMIC BOOK. THESE THINGS IN THE BACKGROUND SHOULD NOT BE VISIBLE IN THE RESULT. NOW YOU KNOW THAT BEFORE THE CARTOONIST STARTS DRAWING A COMIC BOOK, THE UNBELIEVABLE AMOUNT OF WORK AND TIME PRECEDES, WHICH WILL NEVER BE SEEN BY A COMMON READER. HOWEVER, YOU NOW, AS A PROFESSIONAL, KNOW THAT THERE ARE DAYS BEHIND THE MERE DEVELOPMENT OF THE MAIN HERO, SO YOU MIGHT APPRECIATE IT.

THERE ARE THINGS WHICH WE WILL DEAL WITH ON THE FLY BUT WE ALREADY HAVE THE PREPARATION. WE HAVE DETERMINED THE ELEMENTARY COMIC BOOK LAYOUT AND WE CAN START DRAWING ACCORDING TO THE SCENARIO. JUST BEAR IN MIND: THE SCENARIO IS NOT GOSPEL.

SOMETIMES, THE PAGE LAYOUT DIFFERS FROM HOW YOU IMAGINED IT. THAT IS WHY WE HAVE ROUGH SKETCHES. THIS WHOLE PAGE SHOULD NOT TAKE YOU MORE THAN HALF AN HOUR. IT IS JUST A FIRST DRAFT MAINLY DUE TO THE COMPOSITION OF PANELS AND OBJECTS IN THEM. IF YOU DEFLECT FROM THE SCENARIO, TAKE THIS VERSION AND GO TO THE AUTHOR AND DISCUSS IT WITH THEM. IT IS YOUR MUTUAL PIECE OF WORK. YOU ARE A TEAM.

HERE ALREADY WE MUST DEAL WITH THE LETTERING FOR MANY REASONS. IF YOU WRITE IT MANUALLY, DRAW IT. IF YOU INSERT IT IN A PROGRAMME, INSERT THE SKETCH FIRST AND FIND OUT WHETHER THERE IS ENOUGH SPACE FOR THE TEXT. THERE NOTHING MORE AWKWARD THAN WHEN YOU ARE TRYING TO SQUEEZE A LOT OF TEXT IN A SMALL BUBBLE OR THE BUBBLE IS TOO BIG. IF YOU COUNT ON A TRANSLATION INTO OTHER LANGUAGES, GIVE THE BUBBLES MORE SPACE BECAUSE GERMAN, FOR EXAMPLE, WILL NEED IT.

Basic comic book layout:
Board mirror: 135 x 190 mm (width is first mentioned in graphics)
Gaps between panels: 3 mm
Line thickness: calligraphy marker # 14 (my personal marking)

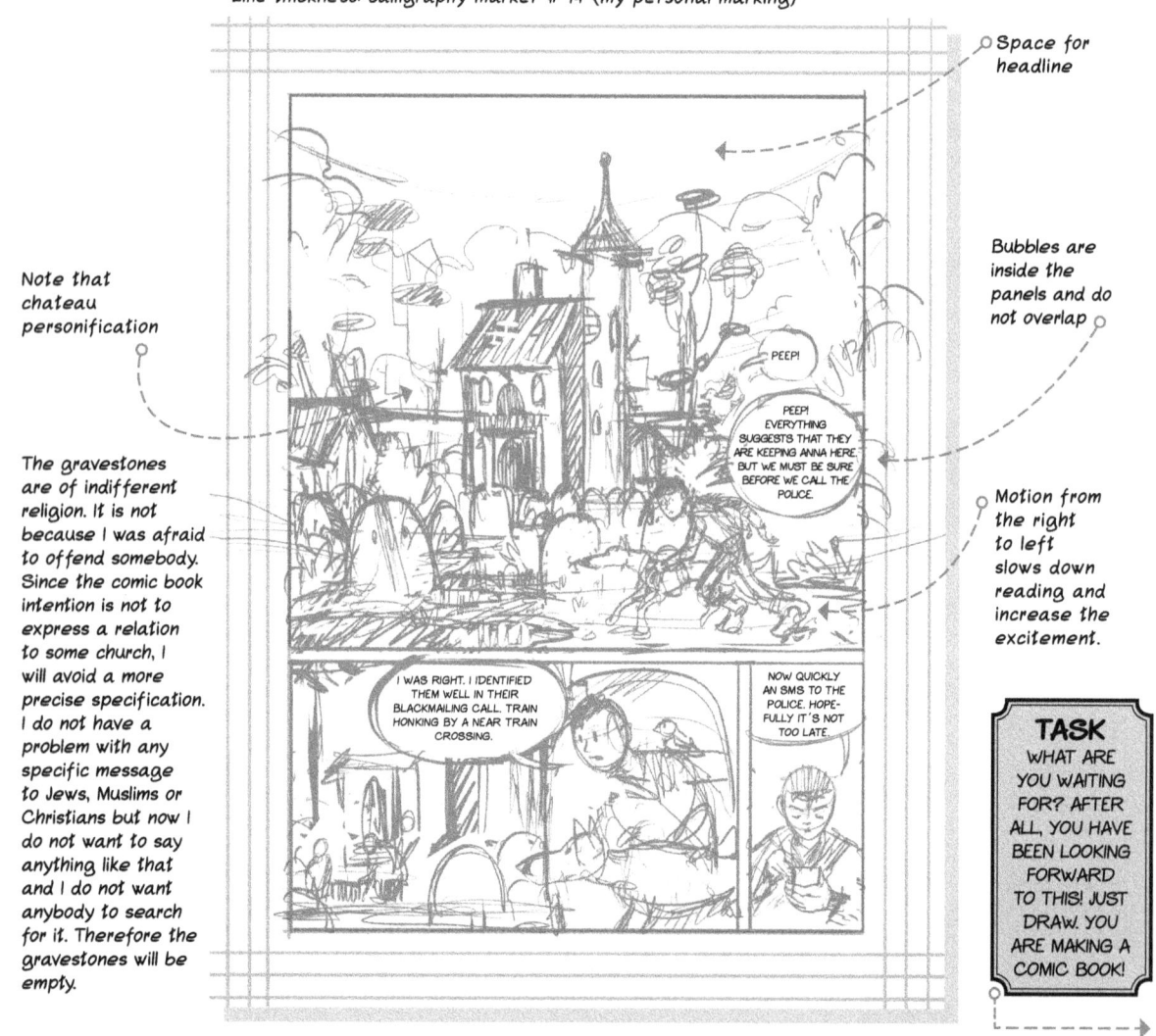

Space for headline

Bubbles are inside the panels and do not overlap

Note that chateau personification

The gravestones are of indifferent religion. It is not because I was afraid to offend somebody. Since the comic book intention is not to express a relation to some church, I will avoid a more precise specification. I do not have a problem with any specific message to Jews, Muslims or Christians but now I do not want to say anything like that and I do not want anybody to search for it. Therefore the gravestones will be empty.

Motion from the right to left slows down reading and increase the excitement.

TASK
WHAT ARE YOU WAITING FOR? AFTER ALL, YOU HAVE BEEN LOOKING FORWARD TO THIS! JUST DRAW. YOU ARE MAKING A COMIC BOOK!

ACCURATE SKETCH

NO, IT IS NOT A DRAWING YET. IT IS NECESSARY TO EDIT A LOT OF THINGS. AS YOU CAN SEE, I HAVE STILL MADE SOME CONCEPTUAL CHANGES. IT CAN HAPPEN MORE THAN OFTEN THAT DURING THE MAKING OF AN ACCURATE SKETCH, YOU WILL FIND OUT THAT THE PICTURES SHOW PROBLEMS WHICH WEREN'T REVEALED IN THE FIRST DRAFT. FOR EXAMPLE, I WAS BOTHERED THAT THE TREE, IMPORTANT FOR THE PLOT, ON THE RIGHT FROM THE CHATEAU, IMAGINARILY GROWS FROM ROBIN'S HEAD. SO, I TRIED TO MOVE THE CHATEAU A BIT TO THE LEFT AND I MADE ROBIN SMALLER. THE CHATEAU IS NOW IN THE CENTRE AND I LIKE IT A GREAT DEAL MORE THAN BEFORE. NOW I AM PUTTING THE SKETCH ASIDE AND I WILL DO SOMETHING ELSE. UNTIL I FINISH SKETCHES OF THE OTHER 4 BOARDS, I WILL COME BACK TO THIS ONE LOOKING AT IT WITH FRESH EYES. ONLY THEN I WILL START TO OUTLINE THE CONTOURS WITH INK.

CLICHÉ!!!

THE GUARDS ARE SITTING AT THE ENTRANCE AND THEY ARE PLAYING CARDS. IT IS A REAL CLICHÉ. AND I SAY: SO WHAT? I PROMISED YOU AN ADVENTUROUS ACTION STORY. CLICHÉS ARE JUST ITS ATTRIBUTES. IF YOU ARE ONE OF THOSE WHO GO TO THE CINEMA TO SEE DIE HARD AND THEN YOU SHAKE YOUR HEAD, LIKE A DOG WATCHING A TABLE TENNIS MATCH, THAT ONE HERO WINS OVER A TREMENDOUS SUPERIORITY, IT MIGHT BE TIME TO START WATCHING SOMETHING MORE DEMANDING. I DID NOT PROMISE A DEEPLY SERIOUS AND HIGH STORY, TO SHOW YOU THAT I AM A CULTURED GUY. I HAVE DETERMINED A MORE DIFFICULT (NOT HIGHER) GOAL. I HAVE DECIDED TO AMUSE YOU. SO, YOU CAN EXPECT HORDES OF SILLY HENCHMEN WITH BAD AIMING, AN UNFLAGGING HERO WHO DOES NOT DEAL WITH COMMON SITUATIONS, MEGALOMANIACAL VILLAINS ADDICTED ON SPEECHES.

IF YOU WORK WITH PAPER AND NOT IN A COMPUTER, I RECOMMEND GETTING A TRANSPARENT SHEET. IT WILL SAVE YOU MUCH WORK AND SPOILED DRAWINGS.

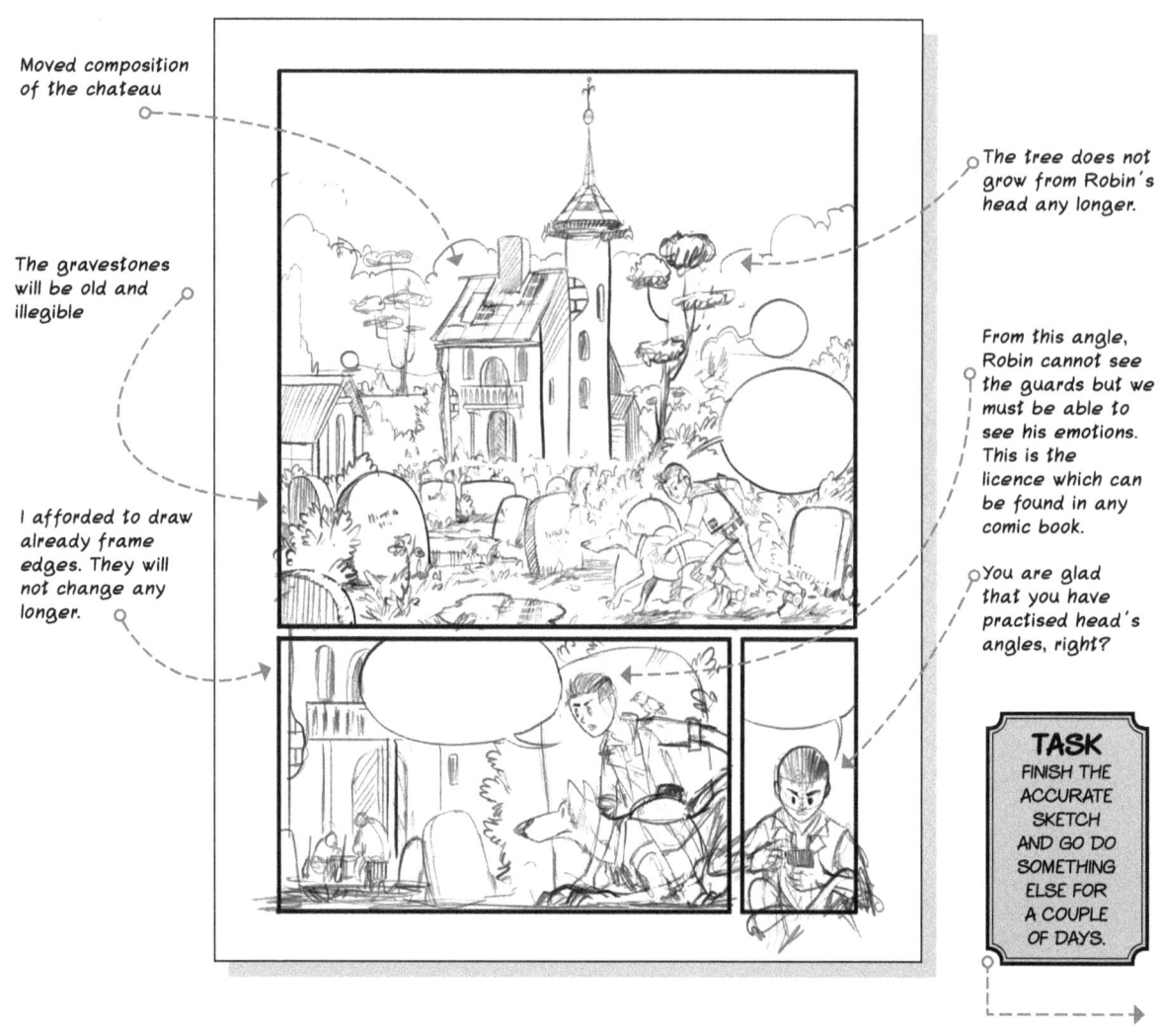

Moved composition of the chateau

The gravestones will be old and illegible

I afforded to draw already frame edges. They will not change any longer.

The tree does not grow from Robin's head any longer.

From this angle, Robin cannot see the guards but we must be able to see his emotions. This is the licence which can be found in any comic book.

You are glad that you have practised head's angles, right?

TASK
FINISH THE ACCURATE SKETCH AND GO DO SOMETHING ELSE FOR A COUPLE OF DAYS.

Protective zone - no text - 5 mm
Bleed 5 mm

OUTLINING

NOW, THE ROUTINE SLOWLY STARTS. IT IS JUST TIME TO OUTLINE THE RIGHT LINES AND ERASE THE BAD ONES. A TRANSPARENT SHEET WOULD BE REALLY HANDY HERE IF YOU WORK MANUALLY WITH PAPER, AND ESPECIALLY WHEN YOU PLAN TO COLOUR THE DRAWING. THE ERASER, NO MATTER HOW USEFUL AND NEEDED IT IS DAMAGES THE PAPER AND EVEN IF YOU ARE TRYING TO MANIPULATE IT AS SOFTLY AS YOU CAN, IT WILL LEAVE AN OILY TRACE, WHICH WILL INFLUENCE THE COLOURS USED. UNDER THE ERASED PART, THE PAPER GETS HARDER AND ANILINE COLOURS REVEAL SUCH PLACE.

I HAVE A SMALL RECOMMENDATION FOR YOU BUT IT IS UP TO YOU WHETHER YOU OBEY IT OR NOT. WHEN YOU FINISH THE DRAWING, SCAN IT INTO THE COMPUTER BEFORE YOU COLOUR IT, EVEN IF THE COLOURS WILL BE FAIRLY TRANSPARENT, THEY WILL INFLUENCE THE LINE. IN MANY CASES THE COLOURS WILL COVER THE LINE DESPITE YOU BEING CAREFUL. IF YOU WANT TO KEEP THE CLEANNESS OF THE LINE EVEN AFTER THE COLOURING, COVER THE UNCOLOURED DRAWING WITH THE COLOURED WHILE INSERTING IT INTO A COMPUTER, SO THAT YOU WILL GIVE THE UNIFIED SHADE TO THE LINE.

PRESERVE SEPARATELY SINGLE STEPS OF YOUR WORK AS MUCH AS YOU CAN. SKETCH – DRAWING – COLOUR. BY THIS, IN CASE OF AN IRREVERSIBLE ERROR, YOU ELIMINATE TIME FOR REWORKING.

NOTE THAT IN THE FOREGROUND, I HAVE USED SLIGHTLY THICKER CONTOURS THAN IN THE BACKGROUND. BY THAT, SIMULATE THE DEPTH OF THE PICTURE. DUE TO THE FACT I AM CREATING THE COMIC BOOK IN A COLOURED VERSION, THE DIFFERENCE IS NOT THAT BIG BECAUSE I AM GOING TO SUPPORT THAT IMPRESSION BY COLOUR. IF I DID NOT PLAN A COLOURED VERSION, I WOULD EMPHASISE THE FOREGROUND WITH A THICKER CONTOUR AND ADD MORE HATCH IN ORDER TO GET DARKER THE THINGS CLOSER TO THE READER. BY DOING THIS, I WOULD CREATE AN ILLUSION OF DEPTH.

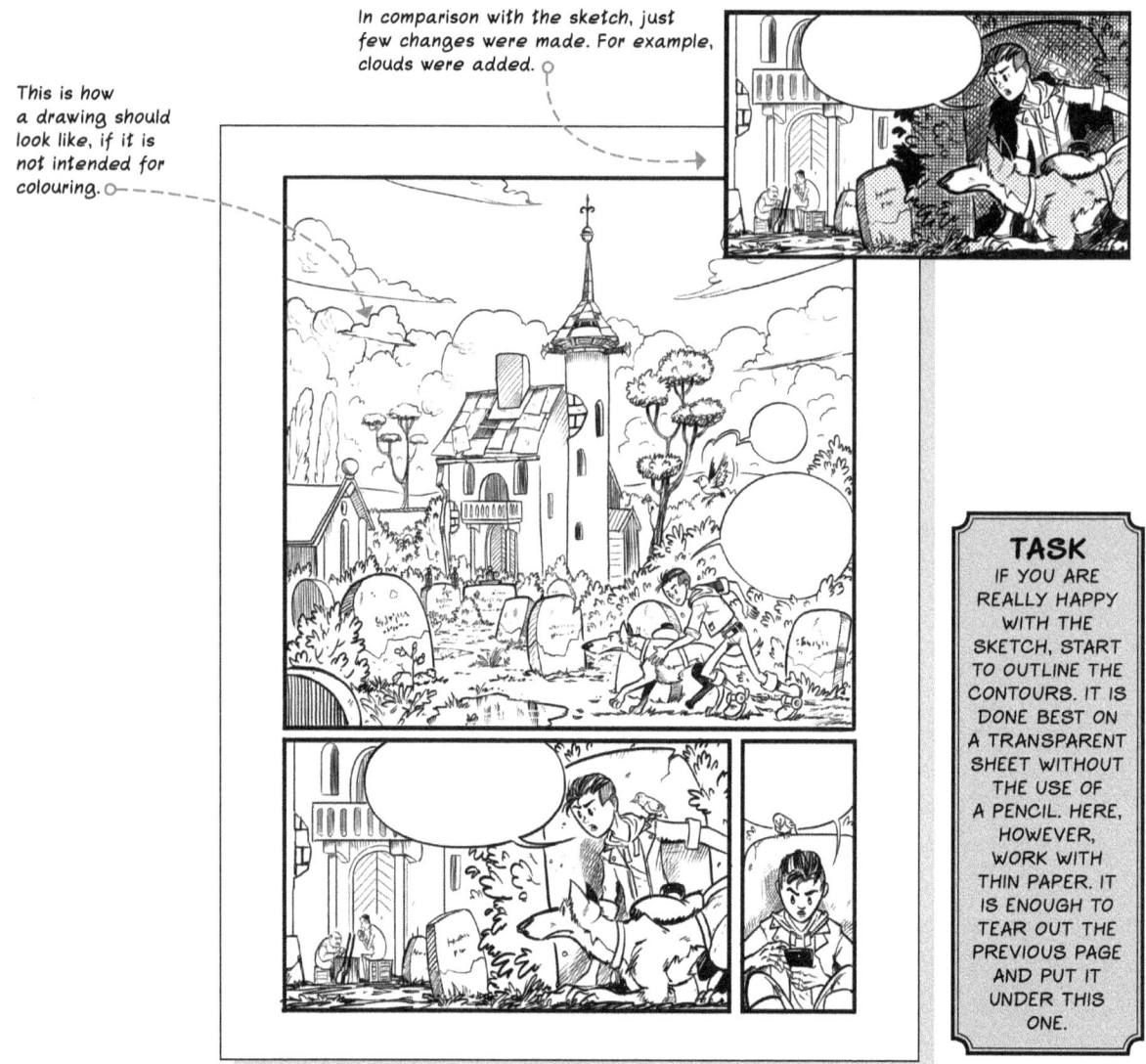

This is how a drawing should look like, if it is not intended for colouring.

In comparison with the sketch, just few changes were made. For example, clouds were added.

TASK

IF YOU ARE REALLY HAPPY WITH THE SKETCH, START TO OUTLINE THE CONTOURS. IT IS DONE BEST ON A TRANSPARENT SHEET WITHOUT THE USE OF A PENCIL. HERE, HOWEVER, WORK WITH THIN PAPER. IT IS ENOUGH TO TEAR OUT THE PREVIOUS PAGE AND PUT IT UNDER THIS ONE.

COLOUR

YOU MUST BE VERY, VERY CAREFUL WITH COLOURS. IF YOU WORK WITH TRADITIONAL METHODS, BEFORE YOU SPOIL A COMPLEX DRAWING BY THE LAST STEP, CREATE A BACKUP AS I RECOMMENDED TO YOU ON THE PREVIOUS PAGE. THIS METHOD HAS PAID OFF TO ME MANY TIMES. EVEN WHEN WORKING WITH A COMPUTER. NOW, SERIOUSLY: BACK UP. I MAKE A BACK-UP EVERY DAY. IT IS MY LIVING. I HAVE NOTHING ELSE. WHAT ELSE CAN BE MORE IMPORTANT?

IN THE SCENARIO, THERE STANDS THAT GRAVEYARD COLOURS SHOULD BE DIMMED AND BLUISH. EVERYTHING SHOULD GIVE THE IMPRESSION OF GLOOM, WHICH IS EVEN MORE EMPHASISED BY THE CHATEAU'S RUIN.

EVEN WHEN I MADE ROBIN'S JACKET A LOT DARKER IN ORDER TO GO WELL TOGETHER WITH THE ENVIRONMENT, IT STILL PROTRUDES NICELY INTO THE FOREGROUND. NO COLOUR IS AS CONTRASTIVE AS THE ONE ON HIS JACKET.

ALSO NOTE THAT THE FURTHER AN OBJECT FROM THE READER IS, THE PALER THE COLOUR IS. THIS IS ONE OF THE TRICKS HOW YOU CAN INDICATE DEPTH. YOU CAN CLEARLY SEE IT ON THE TREE IN FRONT OF THE CHATEAU AND ON THE TREE BEHIND THE WALL OF THE CEMETERY. I INTENTIONALLY USED THE SAME KIND OF THE TREE, SO THAT THE READER RECEIVES INFORMATION ABOUT THE SCALE AND THE IMPRESSION ABOUT THE PERSPECTIVE.

THE BOARD OF THE COMIC BOOK IS BLACK AND WHITE FOR TWO REASONS. FIRSTLY, SO THAT THE BOOK WOULD NOT POINTLESSLY COST ONE POUND MORE AND SECONDLY, COLOUR INTENSITY CAN BE EASILY RECOGNISED ON BLACK AND WHITE AND AS THE INTENSITY FADES AWAY IN THE SPACE. IF YOU ARE NOT SURE ABOUT THE PICTURE, CHANGE IT INTO BLACK AND WHITE. IT IS LIKE A LOOK IN A MIRROR, WHICH I RECOMMENDED TO DO WITH THE DRAWING. YOU CAN IMMEDIATELY SEE WHERE THE PROBLEM IS.

JUST TO MAKE SURE: OBJECTS IN THE FOREGROUND HAVE MORE INTENSE COLOURS THAN OBJECTS IN THE BACKGROUND, WHICH IS EVEN CLEARER IN BLACK AND WHITE VERSION. THIS COMIC BOOK WAS MADE IN A COMPUTER. BEFORE WE DISCUSS SOME TIPS ON HOW TO COLOUR IN A COMPUTER, WE NECESSARILY NEED TO GO THROUGH THE ESSENCE OF COLOUR PRINTING ITSELF. LET'S GET DOWN TO COLOUR THEORY...

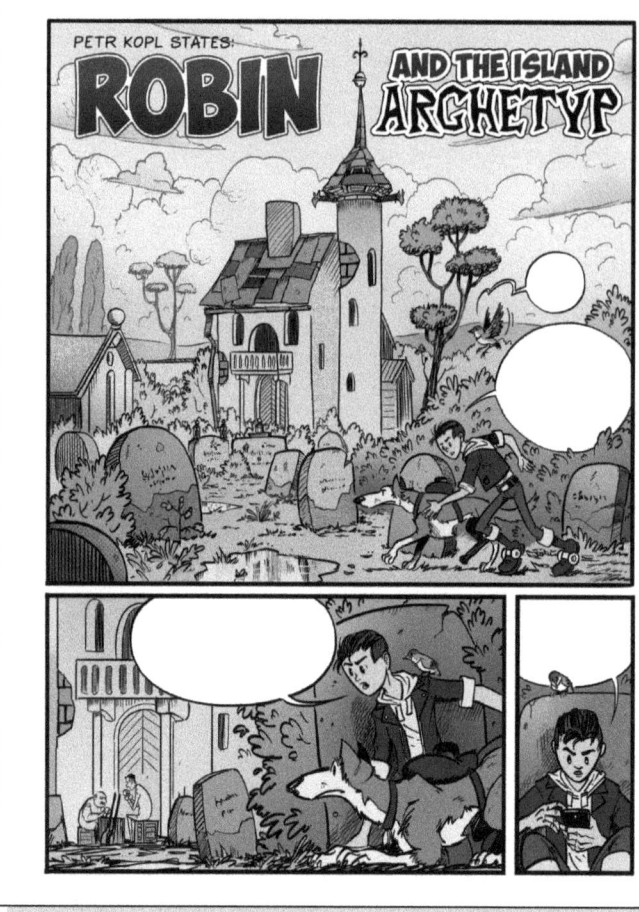

TASK

COLOUR YOUR PIECE OF ART AND BEAR IN MIND THE RULES OF COLOURING. IF YOU ARE NOT SURE, LOOK AT CHAPTERS THEORY OF COLOURS AND SYMBOLISM OF COLOURS IN THIS BOOK. THEN, CARRY ON AND THE FIRST PAGE OF YOUR COMIC BOOK WILL BE DONE.

*IF YOU EVER CREATE A PUBLICATION WHERE SOME PAGES WILL BE COLOURED AND SOME BLACK AND WHITE, PREPARE FOR THE POSSIBILITY THAT THE PUBLISHER WILL WANT THESE SECTIONS DIVIDIBLE BY 16. IF YOU GO THROUGH THIS BOOK, YOU WILL FIND OUT THAT COLOURED PAGES ARE 1 – 16 AND 147 – 160. MUCH MONEY IS SAVED DUE TO THAT FACT AND THE PUBLICATION IS MUCH CHEAPER THAN IF COLOURED AND BLACK AND WHITE PAGES WERE SPREAD IN WHOLE BOOK. THIS IS, HOWEVER, A REALLY ADVANCED PIECE OF ADVICE WHICH EXPLANATION WOULD TAKE A LOT OF SPACE. JUST TAKE IT AS IT IS.

WAYS OF COLOURING A COMIC BOOK

THERE ARE AS MANY WAYS OF COLOURING COMIC BOOKS AS ARTISTIC STYLES. THOSE ARE COUNTLESS. HERE, YOU MUST RELY ON YOUR PERSONAL TASTE. I MOSTLY COLOURING IN A COMPUTER, IN A PHOTOSHOP PROGRAM IN PARTICULAR. IT IS BECAUSE OF A PRACTICAL POINT OF VIEW. IT IS THE FASTEST AND MOST SECURE WAY. IF I DRAW COMMERCIALS, I HAVE THE COLOURS UNDER CONTROL ALL THE TIME AND THE WAY I EXACTLY WANT WITHOUT THE NEED OF SCANNING AND ADDITIONAL MODIFICATIONS, WHICH RESULTS IN MOVING THE COLOURS SOMEWHERE ELSE A BIT.

HOWEVER, IF I WORK MANUALLY, I CANNOT FORGET ABOUT CLASSICAL WATER COLOURS. BELOW, YOU CAN SEE AN EXAMPLE OF SUCH COLOURING. THIS IS JUST ONE OF THE POSSIBILITIES THOUGH. THERE ARE MANY OF THEM. SOME CARTOONISTS, FOR EXAMPLE, COLOUR A SOFTLY DRAWN SKETCH FIRST AND THEN THEY OUTLINE THE PICTURE WITH A BLACK CONTOUR. IT IS SIMPLY A PERSONAL MATTER AND IT CANNOT BE GENERALISED IN ANY WAY. YOU MUST FIND OUT WHAT SUITS YOU BEST. THIS BOOK GIVES YOU JUST A COUPLE OF SIMPLE PRACTICAL PIECES OF ADVICE.

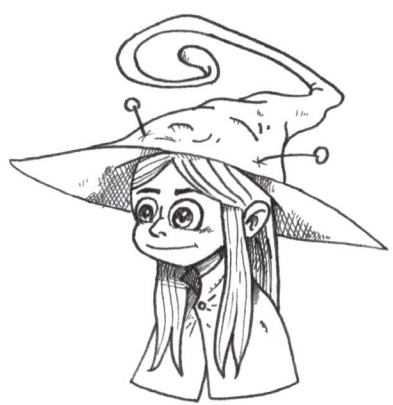
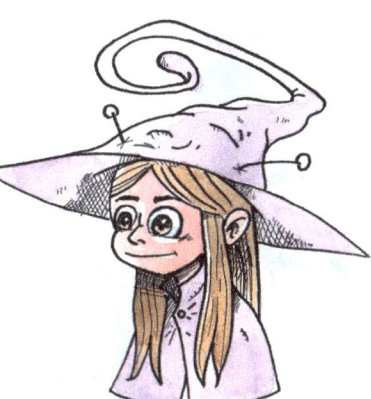
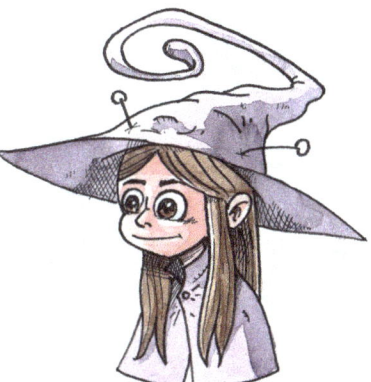

THE CONTOURS ARE DONE. THE SKETCH MADE BY A PENCIL WAS CAREFULLY ERASED.

LET'S APPLY THE BRIGHTEST COLOURS FIRST. IF WE WANT TO KEEP SOME PARTS WITHOUT A COLOUR, WE NEED TO COVER THOSE PARTS WITH A SPECIAL COVERING VARNISH WHICH CAN BE BOUGHT IN ANY SHOP WITH ARTISTIC SUPPLIES.

AFTER THE COLOUR DRIES WE ARE ABLE TO START WITH MORE INTENSE TONES. AT THE END, WE TUNE UP THE DETAILS WITH CRAYONS AND IF ANY CONTOURS DISAPPEARED UNDER THE COLOUR, WE WILL OUTLINE THEM ONCE AGAIN.

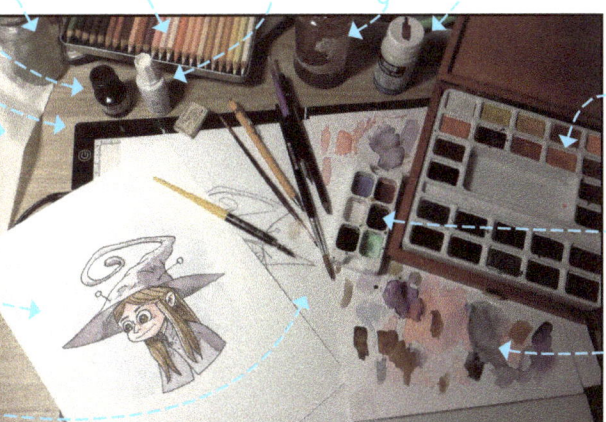

- Jar for flushing brushes
- Transparent board
- Ink
- Crayons
- Corrector
- Jar for water
- Masking liquid
- Quality colours
- Absorbent tissue
- Watercolour palette
- A sheet of paper of minimally 300 grams of weight for watercolour.
- Paper for trying shades
- Sketch on a soft paper

TASK
THERE IS NO BLANK BOARD FOR TRYING ON THIS DOUBLE PAGE. IF YOU WORK WITH COLOURS, TAKE STRONG PAPER FOR WATERCOLOURS AND TRY THE CHARACTERISTICS OF THE COLOURS YOU HAVE CHOSEN. AS I ALREADY SAID: IT IS NOT WORTH SAVING MONEY ON COLOURS AND BRUSHES. AFTER ALL, IT IS NOT WORTH SAVING MONEY ON PAPER EITHER. YOU WILL NEVER ACHIEVE MASTERY WITH TOOLS OF POOR QUALITY.

PRACTICAL THEORY OF COLOURS IN PRINTING

IF YOU WANT TO WRITE ANY STORY, YOU WILL FIND OUT THAT YOU DO NOT HAVE TO BECOME A PALAEONTOLOGIST TO CREATE AN ADVENTUROUS BOOK ABOUT DINOSAURS AND YOU DO NOT HAVE TO BECOME AN ENTOMOLOGIST WHEN YOU WANT A BUTTERFLY TO FLY BY IN YOUR COMIC BOOK. YOUR KNOWLEDGE, HOWEVER, MUST BE A BIT DEEPER THAN READER'S AND A BIT DEEPER THAN YOU PUT IN THE BOOK.

ONE OF MY GOOD TEACHERS AT SCHOOL ALWAYS CLAIMED THAT A MAN SHOULD KNOW A BIT OF EVERYTHING AND EVERYTHING OF SOMETHING. IF YOU WANT TO DEAL WITH COMICS ON A PROFESSIONAL LEVEL, YOU MUST KNOW EVERYTHING ABOUT THE BACKGROUND REGARDING ITS MAKING.

DO YOU THINK THAT SPIELBERG IS JUST AN EXCELLENT DIRECTOR? NO, HE IS A GREAT CAMERAMAN, HE UNDERSTANDS MUSIC, PRODUCTION, TRICKS AND EVERYTHING THAT IS ABOUT FILM.

EVEN YOU ENGAGE ALL YOUR KNOWLEDGE NOT ONLY ABOUT COMICS BUT ALSO ABOUT ITS THE INSERTION, PRINTING, SALES, ADVERTISEMENT AND OTHER THINGS THAT ARE RELATED TO COMICS. ONLY THEN YOU WILL EXACTLY KNOW THE BORDERS OF THE MEDIUM POSSIBILITIES WHICH YOU USE.

AND ONE OF THE RESTRICTIONS THAT YOU WILL COME ACROSS IS COLOUR. IT IS POSSIBLE TO MAKE AN ADVANTAGE OUT OF THIS HANDICAP BUT YOU MUST KNOW THIS ISSUE IN ITS TECHNICAL DETAILS.

EVERYTHING WE CAN SEE AROUND US IS LIGHT. IT WAS PROVEN ALREADY HUNDREDS OF YEARS AGO BY ISAAC NEWTON. THEY ARE REFLECTED PHOTONS FROM ITEMS WHICH STAND IN THEIR WAY. THE STRUCTURE OF THEIR SURFACE DECIDES ABOUT THEIR COLOUR. ITEMS, IN GENERAL, HOLD A PART OF THE LIGHT IN THEM AND THEN WHAT THEY EMIT DETERMINES THEIR COLOUR.

LIGHT HAS THREE ELEMENTS. RED, GREEN AND BLUE. ANYWAY, THAT IS WHY WE HAVE **RGB**. WHEN YOU AIM THESE THREE COLOURS AT ONE POINT, SURPRISINGLY WE GET WHITE LIGHT. IF YOU REMOVE THE COLOURS ONE BY ONE AND IN TURNS, YOU WILL GET SECONDARY COLOURS: YELLOW, PURPLE AND CYAN BLUE. THIS IS HOW LIGHT WORKS.

YOU, HOWEVER, WILL USE A LIQUID COLOUR AND EVEN IF YOUR PIECE OF ART WILL BE CREATED IN A COMPUTER, IT WILL BE PRINTED OUT AND YOU MUST PROVIDE THE PRINTING OFFICE WITH THE INFORMATION FROM WHAT EXACTLY THEY WILL MIX THE COLOURS.

WHEN IT COMES TO LIGHT, YOU WORK WITH THREE ELEMENTS, WHILE IN PRINTING THERE ARE FOUR. THEIR ABBREVIATION IS **CMYK**. IT IS AZURE, PURPLE, YELLOW AND BLACK. BASICALLY, YOU KNOW THIS FROM COMMON DRAWING. OUT OF THESE COLOURS, IT IS POSSIBLE TO MIX NEARLY ANY SHADE IN WATER COLOURS.

BY PROCESSING A PICTURE IN A PRINTING DOCUMENT IN THE CMYK REGIME, YOU ARE INSERTING INFORMATION ABOUT HOW MANY PERCENT OF SINGLE COLOURS IN PARTICULAR PLACES WILL THE PRINTING OFFICE PRINT.

THEREFORE, THE PRINTING OFFICE MUST NOT GET A DOCUMENT IN RGB REGIME BECAUSE RGB HAS A WIDER RANGE OF RESOLUTION OF COLOURS AND THE DOCUMENT CHANGES DURING THE TRANSFER, WHICH WILL BE SURELY REJECTED BY THE PRINTER, WHO WILL GIVE IT BACK TO YOU TO BE REWORKED. THEREFORE, IT IS WORTH CREATING THE COMIC BOOK IN CMYK FORMAT STRAIGHTAWAY.

ANOTHER DIFFICULTY THAT YOU CAN ENCOUNTER IS COVERING POWER OF COLOURS. THE ISSUE IS THAT YOU HAVE 100% OF THE COLOUR TO BE USED IN ONE PLACE. SO, THE SOFTWARE CAN ALLOW YOU TO USE EVEN 400 %. THIS WILL NOT BE ACCEPTED BY ANY PRINTING OFFICE. THE PERCENTAGE REPRESENTS INFORMATION ABOUT THE PHYSICAL AMOUNT OF COLOUR THAT WILL BE PRINTED ON PAPER. THE THICKER LAYER YOU POUR ONTO, THE LONGER IT WILL TAKE TO DRY AND THE MORE DIFFICULT THE MANIPULATION WITH THE PAPER WILL BE. IT WILL SOAK IN WET INSIDE OUT AND TEAR UP AT PLACES WHERE IT IS COLOURED THE MOST.

THE MAXIMUM IS 300 % OF COVERING POWER FOR THE MAJORITY OF DOCUMENTS BUT TRY TO STAY BELOW THIS FIGURE. IF YOU DO NOT KEEP IT AT THAT LEVEL AND ARE NOT WILLING TO MODIFY THE DOCUMENT, SOMEBODY IN THE PRINTING OFFICE MIGHT GET ON THE TASK AND YOU MIGHT NOT APPRECIATE THE FINAL CHANGE. IT IS ANNOYING BUT THIS IS ONE OF THOSE THINGS WHICH YOU MUST KNOW ABOUT ART CREATION IN ORDER NOT TO PUT OBSTACLES TO YOUR PUBLISHER. THEN CONSIDER WHAT IMPRESSION YOU WILL MAKE IF YOU COME UP WITH THE TERM "COVERING POWER OF COLOURS". THIS TERM IS EVEN UNKNOWN TO A NUMBER OF EXPERIENCED GRAPHIC DESIGNERS. YOU BET!

THE ISSUE OF COLOURS IS MUCH MORE COMPLEX, OF COURSE. HERE, WE HAVE JUST DISCUSSED THE PRACTICAL SIDE OF PRINTING.

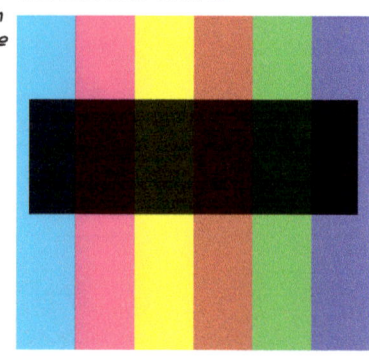

A VIEW OF REPRINT OF 100% BLACK. YOU CAN SEE THAT IT REACTS ON DIFFERENT COLOURS DIFFERENTLY BECAUSE THIS BLACK IS PRINTED AFTERWARDS OVER THE COLOURED STRIPES.

LET US TAKE A LOOK AT IT ILLUSTRATIVELY, SO WE COULD BETTER UNDERSTAND WHAT HAPPENS WITH THE PICTURE WHICH GOES THROUGH PRINTING PROCESS. LET US IMAGINE THAT THE PAPER WHICH WE USE TO PRINT GOES THROUGH FOUR MACHINES. EACH OF THEM PRINTS JUST ONE COLOUR. LIKE THIS, COLOURS ARE PLACED IN LAYERS AS YOU DREW WITH WATER COLOURS TO ACHIEVE A PARTICULAR SHADE. IT WOULD ILLUSTRATIVELY LOOK LIKE THIS:

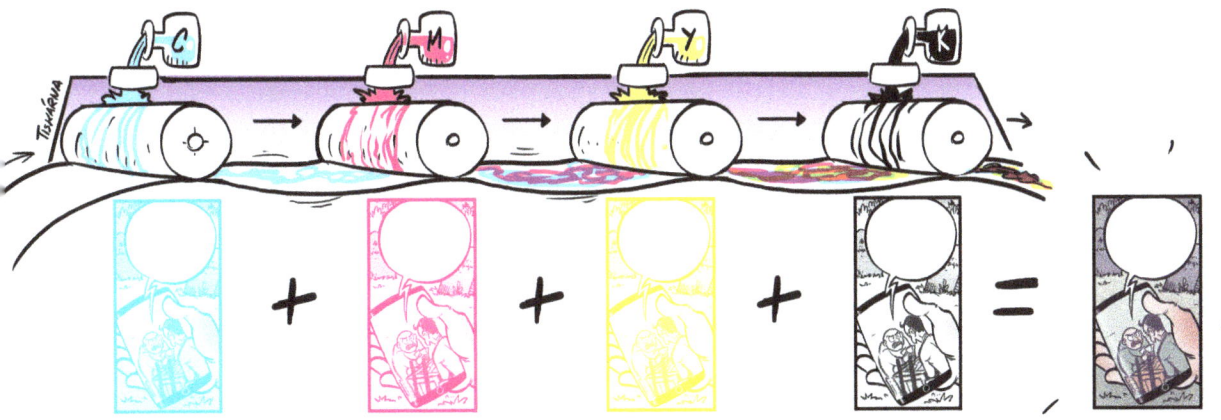

IT IS CLEAR THAT THE SETTINGS OF THESE FOUR COLOURS MUST BE ABSOLUTELY PRECISE. REGARDLESS THE EFFICIENCY OF TODAY'S MACHINES, A CERTAIN DEFOCUSING ALWAYS HAPPENS. EVEN IF IT IS MINIMAL IN HUNDREDTHS OF A MILLIMETRE. SUCH DEFECT IS NOT RECOGNIZABLE IN A PICTURE BUT IT CAN BE A CATASTROPHE IN A TEXT. THEREFORE, I PLACED GREAT EMPHASIZE THAT THE TEXT IN YOUR COMIC BOOK SHOULD BE IN 100 % BLACK IF POSSIBLE. THE THING IS THAT WE SHOULD AVOID ANY OTHER COLOUR THERE. WHY? BECAUSE THERE IS ALSO ONE MORE PRINTER THAT OUR PAPER MUST GO THROUGH. IT IS A MACHINE WHICH DEALS WITH JUST REPRINTED BLACK COLOUR. IT PRINTS OUT JUST 100% BLACK, EVEN OVER COLOURED AREAS OF A COMIC BOOK.

WITH THIS, IT IS ENSURED THAT THE TEXT WILL ALWAYS BE PERFECTLY SHARP AND LEGIBLE. THIS IS ALSO THE REASON, HOWEVER, WHY COLOURS THAT ARE WEAKER THAN BLACK ARE SOMETIMES USED FOR TEXT, BECAUSE IT CANNOT BE COMPOSED FROM MORE SHADES, JUST ONE. LET US BEAR IN MIND THAT WE CHOOSE OTHER COLOURS MORE THOROUGHLY AND SOBERLY DURING COLOUR CHOOSING PROCESS. THE HIGHER THE PERCENTAGE SUM THE COLOUR HAS, THE STRONGER IT WILL BE, AND THEREFORE, MORE NOTICEABLE. IF WANT THE TEXT TO BECOME MORE APPARENT, YOU NEED TO LOWER THE COLOUR INTENSITY.

100% BLACK IS PRINTED APART, EVEN OVER COLOURED AREAS. DO NOT FORGET THAT IN THIS CHOICE, IT WILL INCREASE THE COVERING POWER OF THE COLOUR BY 100%. CHOOSE THE BACKGROUND PRUDENTLY OR MAKE SURE THAT IN THE PARTICULAR PRINTING OFFICE THEY OVERPRINT 100% BLACK COLOUR AFTER THE PAPER DRIES UP. HOWEVER, YOU WILL RARELY HAVE SUCH A POSSIBILITY.

THIS TEXT IS PLACED IN A BLUE STRIPE. AS YOU CAN SEE IT SEEMS TO BE A BIT DARKER THAN THE TEXT ON THE WHITE PLACES ALTHOUGH, IT WAS MADE WITH SAME COLOUR. THE OVERPRINT JUST SIMPLY RECEIVED THE BACKGROUND BLUE.

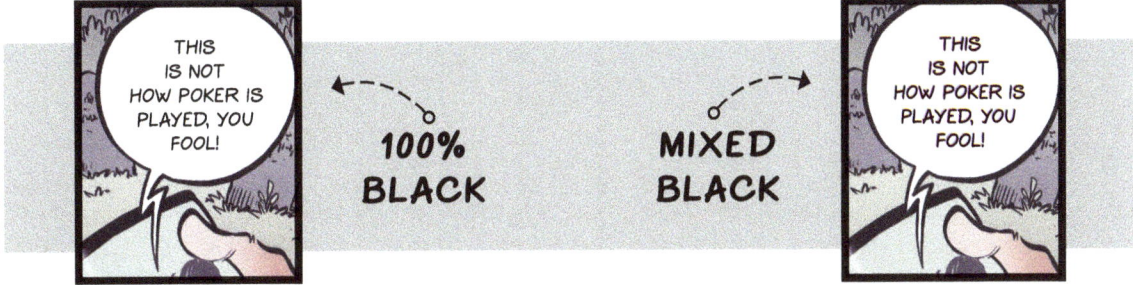

HERE YOU CAN SEE THE DIFFERENCE OF THE TEXT IF IT IS NOT IN 100% BLACK AND THE PRINTER CANNOT MANAGE TO SET THE COLOURS. IT CAN BE TAKEN CARE OF BUT IT IS AN EXTRA SERVICE WHICH IS CHARGED. THEREFORE, I ADVISE YOU, AT LEAST IN THE BEGINNING, TAKE THE EASIER WAY. BY DOING THIS, YOU WILL SHOW THAT YOU UNDERSTAND THE PROBLEMS THAT THE PUBLISHER MUST FACE, AND ALSO YOUR PROFESSIONALISM. IF YOU CREATE COMIC BOOKS MANUALLY ON A PAPER, NOT IN A COMPUTER, I APPEAL TO YOU TO CREATE LETTERING ON EXTRA PIECE OF PAPER AND COMPLETE IT IN INSERTING.

SYMBOLISM OF COLOURS

YES. EVEN COLOURS CARRY A STIGMA OF SYMBOLS. I WILL MENTION JUST A COUPLE OF THEM. THE MOST POPULAR ONES. THE SYMBOLISM IS, HOWEVER, MUCH DEEPER AND IT IS SUBCONSCIOUSLY PERCEIVED BY PEOPLE. ANOTHER WAY SYMBOLISM IS CONDITIONED BY CULTURE. IT MEANS THAT WHILE BLACK IS CONSIDERED A COLOUR OF SADNESS IN OUR CULTURE, ON OTHER CULTURES IT IS, FOR EXAMPLE, WHITE. IN OUR CULTURE, WHITE IS CONSIDERED A COLOUR OF PURITY AND INNOCENCE. THEREFORE, IF YOU NARRATE A STORY DEPENDS ON COLOURS AND THEIR UNDERSTANDING, , IT CAN HAPPEN THAT YOUR COMIC BOOK WILL BE IMPOSSIBLE TO TRANSLATE INTO ANOTHER LANGUAGE.

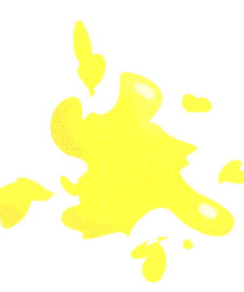

YELLOW IS A COLOUR OF TREASON. IN COMBINATION WITH DARK RED IT GIVES AN IMPRESSION OF LUXURY AS GOLD ON RED VELVET. IT IS SIMILAR TO GREEN SO IT CAN BE A COLOUR OF ILLNESSES OR A WARNING AGAINST A DANGER.

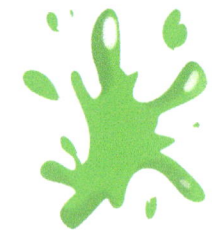

GREEN – A COLOUR OF POISON. IF YOU LET A GREEN GAS INTO YOUR ROOM, YOU DO NOT HAVE TO WRITE IN YOUR COMIC BOOK THAT IT IS POISONED. THE COLOUR TELLS US. HOWEVER, IT IS ALSO A COLOUR OF NATURE AND WITCHES. IT CAN BE A COLOUR OF INTRIGUES AND GOSSIPS BUT ALSO FAVOUR AND COMPASSION.

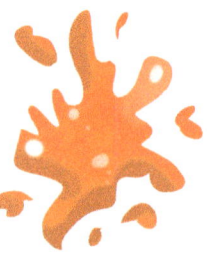

ORANGE EMITS WARMTH, SAFETY, CALMNESS, DELIBERATION, WISDOM AND SIMPLICITY OF THINKING.

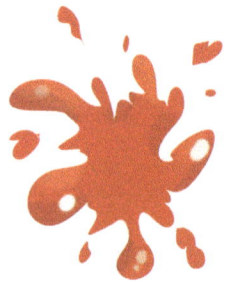

RED IS THE PRIMARY COLOUR OF BLOOD. IT IS ALSO CONNECTED WITH PASSION, ENERGY AND LOVE.

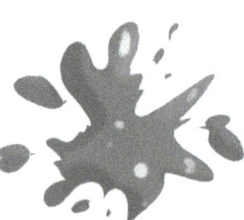

GRAY IS NEUTRAL. HOWEVER, WHEN WE MEAN PALE, IT MEANS DEAD, PALLID OR SICK, INDISTINCTIVE, TOTALITARIAN.

BLUE, MAINLY CONNECTED WITH WHITE IS A COLOUR OF INNOCENCE AND CLEANLINESS. IT IS A COLD COLOUR OF HEAVEN AND WATER, CALMNESS AND PEACE.

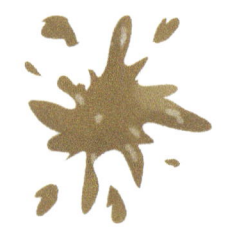

WE EXPRESS SIMPLICITY BY BROWN IN COMBINATION WITH GRAY. IT IS A COLOUR OF THE POOR. IT IS NATURAL AND ORDINARY.

WHITE MEANS PURITY AND ORDER. IT IS CEREMONIAL AND IT IS A COLOUR OF SILVER, MOON. IT FEELS AS IF FROM ANOTHER WORLD.

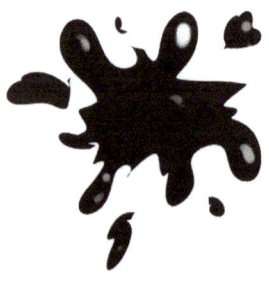

IN OUR CULTURE, BLACK IS THE COLOUR OF SADNESS, AND MAYBE THAT IS WHY IT IS CONNECTED WITH EVIL AND DARKNESS. IN CONNECTION WITH RED IT IS PERCEIVED EVEN SATANIC AND IT SYMBOLISES HELL FIRE.

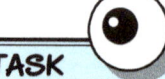

TASK
DRAW A COUPLE OF CHARACTERS IN THE COLOUR OF THEIR NATURE. YOU WILL SEE THAT THE COLOUR WILL NICELY COMPLEMENT THEM AND THE READER WILL NOT EVEN CONSCIOUSLY NOTICE IT.

HOW TO NEGOTIATE WITH PUBLISHERS

IF YOU CAME ACROSS AN IDEA OF TAKING THE FOLDER WITH A HUNDRED-PAGE COMIC BOOK, THROW IT ON THE PUBLISHER'S TABLE WITH WORDS: "SURPRISE, HA?" AND IF YOU REALLY DID IT, I KNOW WHAT THE RESULT WOULD BE. THE ANSWER WOULD BE: "NO".

OR YOU SEND A SHORT LETTER, MAYBE WITH ONE LITTLE SKETCH AND THE LETTER WOULD SAY: "I HAVE GREAT IDEAS; I WILL DRAW A COMIC BOOK FOR YOU." THE ANSWER WOULD BE: "NO", AGAIN.

THIS BOOK SHOULD HELP YOU. IF YOU WENT THROUGH IT REALLY THOROUGHLY AND DID THE TASKS I GAVE YOU PRECISELY, YOU HAVE HANDOUTS FOR NEGOTIATING WITH YOUR PUBLISHERS.

THESE MATERIALS CONTAIN:
1. INTRODUCTION OF YOUR PERSONALITY
2. SYNOPSIS FOR THE EDITORIAL OFFICE
3. SYNOPSIS FOR READERS
4. STORY OUTLINE
5. DETAILED GRAPHIC STORY OUTLINE
6. SAMPLE OF MAXIMUM OF 5 COMPLETED PAGES
7. FURTHER SKETCH SAMPLES, SKETCHES OF CHARACTERS ETC.

We have not gone through this much but we can write a CV, right?

NOTHING CAN STOP YOU FROM TAKING THESE PAGES, PUTTING THEM IN A NICE FOLDER AND YOU HAVE A PROFESSIONAL OFFER OF COOPERATION FROM ANY EDITORIAL OFFICE. AND WHAT FOLLOWS IS YOU, AS A COMMERCIAL CARTOONIST, HAVING ONE ELEMENTARY OBLIGATION. YOUR EFFORT, WHICH YOU PUT INTO THE PROJECT, MUST BE LOWER OR EQUAL TO THE REWARD WHICH YOU RECEIVE FOR THE JOB. THERE IS A FORMULA WHICH FOLLOWS.

EFFORT </= REWARD

THIS FORMULA WORKS IN ANY FIELD OF EXPERTISE OR CRAFT. IT IS CLEAR THAT YOU CANNOT RECEIVE A MONTHLY SALARY FOR A YEAR-LONG JOB.

HERE WE HIT THE POINT WHY CZECH COMIC BOOKS ARE SO RARE. CZECH MARKET IS SO SMALL AND SPECIFIC THAT IF PUBLISHERS PAID ADEQUATE MONEY TO THE AUTHORS, THE BOOKS WOULD BE SO EXPENSIVE THAT NOBODY COULD AFFORD THEM. WE NEED TO TAKE ANOTHER WAY.

AT THE BEGINNING I ENCOURAGED YOU NOT TO BE NARROW-MINDED AND NOT TO BE FOCUSED JUST ON DRAWING. THE TIMES ARE BAD AND YOU NEED TO TAKE THE EASIEST WAY. OFFER THE PUBLISHER NOT ONLY THE DRAWING THE BOOK BUT ALSO THE GRAPHICS AND RELATED THINGS. IT IS NOT SUCH A GREAT EXTRA VOLUME OF WORK. AFTER ALL, YOU INSERT TEXT IN THE COMIC SO WHY SOME GRAPHIC DESIGNER WOULD TAKE THE MONEY FOR THE JOB WHICH IS ALREADY DONE? LEARN HOW TO TAKE YOUR BOOK TO THE PRINTING OFFICE WITHOUT THE NEED OF GIVING IT TO SOME GRAPHIC STUDIO.

THIS IS HOW YOU GAIN YOUR MONEY, WHICH BALANCES A BIT THE BUDGET OF THE BOOK YOU WORK ON. ANOTHER BIG ADVANTAGE IS THAT IF YOU OFFER THAT THE BOOK WILL BE PREPARED FOR CO-EDITION THE PUBLISHER CAN INCREASE THE NUMBER OF COPIES SEVERAL TIMES.

MOREOVER, IF YOU NEGOTIATE GOOD SHARE FROM THE FINAL PRICE, YOU WILL ACHIEVE YOUR FINANCIAL TARGET RESULT.

HOWEVER, IN ANY CASE, DO NOT COUNT ON THE SAME SITUATION THAT CAN HAPPEN ABROAD WHERE AN AUTHOR MAKES A FIFTY-PAGE COMIC BOOK AND THEY LIVE FROM IT FOR THE WHOLE YEAR. (SECRETLY: THIS DOES NOT HAPPEN ABROAD EITHER ANY LONGER, UNLESS YOUR NAME IS ALBERT UDERZO). CZECH MARKET IS NOT BIG ENOUGH. THEREFORE, DO NOT GET RID OF ALL RIGHTS ON YOUR COMIC BOOK AND TRY TO SELL IT ABROAD.

YOUR FIRST ATTEMPTS WILL BE MAINLY AN INVESTMENT FOR THE FUTURE. THE REVENUES FROM BOOKS HAVE PAYBACK PERIOD SOMETHING AROUND FIVE YEARS IF THEY SELL WELL.

ENOUGH OF THEORY. YOU WANT TO HEAR PARTICULAR FIGURES. BELIEVE THAT YOU, AS AN AUTHOR, WILL PROBABLY NEVER HAVE MORE THAN 10 % OF THE RETAIL PRICE AND AS A BEGINNER, YOU WILL APPRECIATE IF YOU ACHIEVE 7 %. DUE TO THE FACT THAT COMIC BOOKS ARE PRINTED IN ROUGHLY 1,500 COPIES, YOU CAN EASILY COUNT HOW MUCH MONEY IT WILL BE IF THEY WERE ALL SOLD OUT.

YOU WILL HAVE TO WORK AS GRAPHIC DESIGNERS AND ILLUSTRATOR. BEAR IN MIND THAT YOU NEED TO BE ABLE TO READ CONTRACTS THOROUGHLY, WHICH IS ANNOYING BUT COUNT ON THE WORST SCENARIO POSSIBLE FROM THE PUBLISHER. THEY WOULD BE FOOLS IF THEY WOULD NOT TRY IT. BUT HOW MUCH SHOULD YOU WANT?

IT IS SIMPLER MORE THAN IT SEEMS. SOONER OR LATER YOU WILL LEARN TO COUNT HOW MUCH TIME YOU SPEND ON PARTICULAR PICTURE. YOU WILL MAKE MISTAKES IN THE BEGINNING BUT IT IS THE PART OF THE EXPERIENCE, WHICH WILL NEVER BE FORGOTTEN. SO, WHEN I KNOW THAT ONE PICTURE WILL TAKE ME ROUGHLY 4 HOURS, I JUST NEED TO REALIZE HOW MUCH I WANT TO EARN A MONTH AND DIVIDE THIS BY THE NUMBER OF HOURS I WANT TO SPEND ON WORKING, AND THERE YOU HAVE THE PRICE FOR ONE PICTURE. EXAMPLE:

I WANT TO EARN 3,000. I WILL WORK 100 HOURS A MONTH. 3,000 : 100 = 30. IF A PICTURE TOOK ME 4 HOURS, IT WILL COST 120. IT IS NOT ROCKET SCIENCE, IS IT? (IT IS JUST AN EXAMPLE!).

BE CAREFUL! IF YOU WORK MAINLY FOR ADVERTISEMENT AGENCIES YOU NEED TO COUNT ON THE FACT THAT THEY WILL WANT TO REWORK THE PICTURES. IN THAT CASE, YOU CERTAINLY NEED TO NEGOTIATE A PRICE FOR MORE WORK. FOR EXAMPLE, IF THE PICTURE REWORKS TAKE MORE THAN ONE HOUR, A NEW PICTURE WILL EMERGE AND THE PRICE WILL DOUBLE. THEY WILL THINK THOROUGHLY IF THEY ARE GIVING YOU A PRECISE AND THOUGHT-THROUGH TASK FROM THE BEGINNING.

TASK
PUT TOGETHER HANDOUTS FOR A PROFESSIONAL OFFER OF YOUR COMIC BOOK, SO THAT YOU WILL BE PREPARED FOR THE FIRST STEP OF A COMIC BOOK AUTHOR'S CAREER.

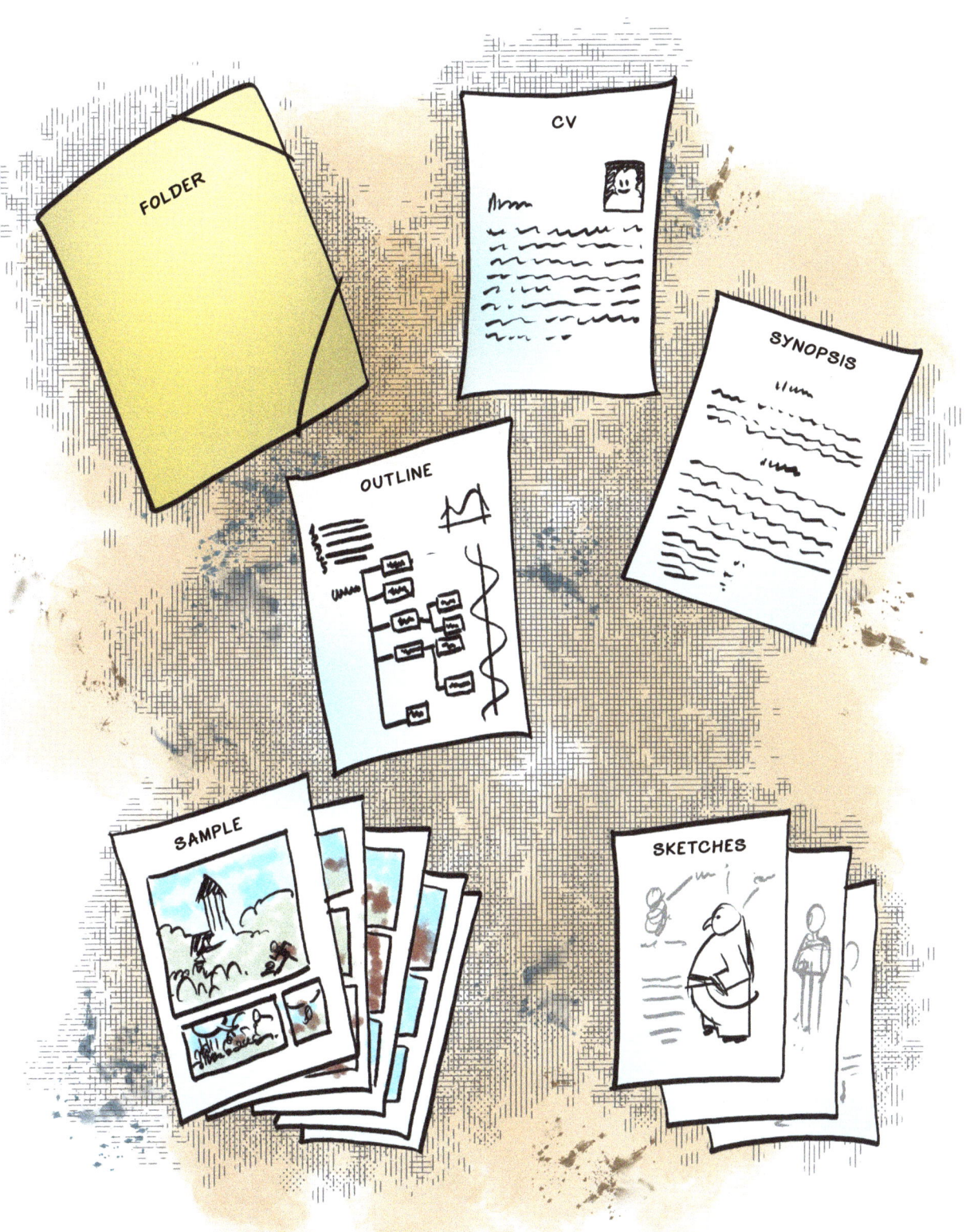

NOTES TO COMIC BOOK II.

THERE IS NOTHING RANDOM IN MOST PANELS IN THE COMIC BOOK YOU READ IN THE BEGINNING. AT DOES NOT MATTER FROM WHICH ANGLE YOU CONSIDER A CHARACTER OR THE POSITION YOU GIVE THEM, THE COMPOSITION AND THE KIND OF PERSPECTIVE HAVE THEIR MEANING. IN THE FOLLOWING COUPLE OF PICTURES, I WILL TRY TO EXPLAIN HOW AND WHY I CHOSE SUCH AN APPROACH. HERE YOU WILL EVENTUALLY SEE THAT A COMIC BOOK IS NOT JUST A PUTTING PICTURES ONE AFTER ANOTHER, AND IT IS A COMPLEX SCIENCE WHERE EVERYTHING MATTERS.

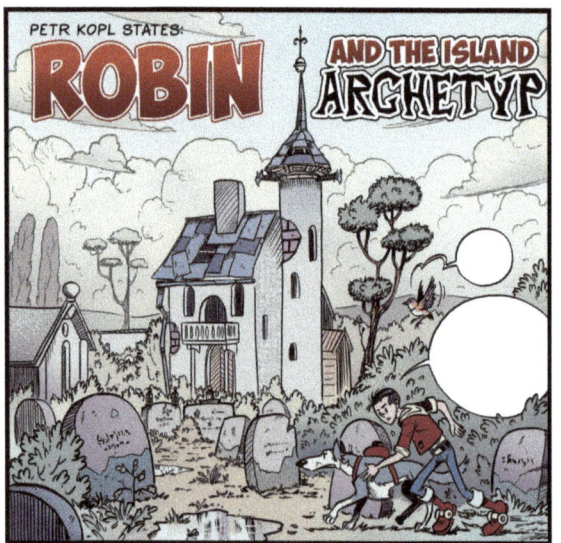

GENERALLY SPEAKING, FIRST PANEL DEALS WITH THE INTRODUCTION OF THE SITUATION OR PLACE. IN MY CASE, IT DEALS WITH BOTH OF THEM, THEREFORE, WE CAN SEE ILLUSTRATED SURROUNDINGS IN ORDER TO INTRODUCE THE READER TO THE ENVIRONMENT WHERE THE COMIC BOOK WILL TAKE PLACE. IT IS A CLASSIC BEGINNING OF MANY COMIC BOOKS BUT IT IS NOT AN UNBREAKABLE LAW BY BREAKING IT, YOU ARE SAYING THAT THE SECRET REGARDING WHERE THE COMIC TAKES PLACE IS THE NARRATOR'S INTENTION. SOME COMIC BOOKS CAN, ON THE OTHER HAND, BEGIN WITH FOCUSING ON DETAIL, HOWEVER SMALL IT IS. IN SUCH CASE, THAT DETAIL WILL HAVE A SYMBOLIC MEANING FOR THE STORY.

IT IS BASICALLY LIKE AT SCHOOL WHERE THE SUBJECTS THAT NEED THE HIGHEST CONCENTRATION ARE SCHEDULED AT THE BEGINNING OF THE DAY NOT TO OVERLOAD THE TIRED MINDS BY PLACING MATH AT THE END. EITHER WAY, IT IS THE EXPOSITION THAT IS CRUCIAL FOR THE NARRATION.

ROBIN INTRODUCES US TO THE SCENE WITH A MONOLOGUE THAT HE WOULD NORMALLY NEVER SAY ALOUD. THIS IS A FEATURE THE READER WILL GLADLY OVERLOOK, AS THEY NEED THIS INFORMATION. IT IS UP TO YOU HOW SMOOTHLY YOU CAN CONVEY THIS TO THEM.

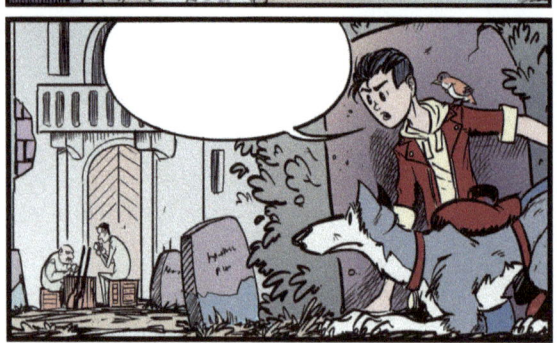

WHY IS ROBIN LOOKING SOMEWHERE ON THE GROUND WHEN THE VILLAINS ARE OBVIOUSLY IN ANOTHER ANGLE? IF YOU DO NOT KNOW, REVISE THE CHAPTER "IT NEVER RAINS IN THE HERO'S FACE".

THE EMOTION WHICH IS EXPRESSED BY ROBIN IS MORE IMPORTANT FOR ME THAN THE ACCURACY OF THE FOCUS THE POINT OF VIEW, PLOT-WISE, IS A LOGICAL SUBJECT OF LICENCE, THAT EVERY GOOD NARRATOR MUST MASTER.

THESE THINGS MUST BE DONE REALLY PRECISELY OTHERWISE IT WILL LOOK STRANGE AND THE WHOLE INTENTION WILL COME IN VAIN.

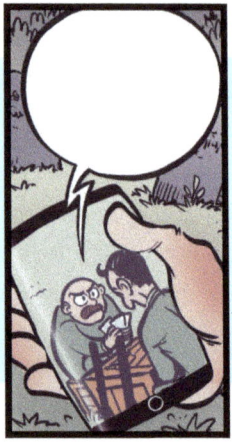

ROBIN IS STILL LOOKING AT HIS CELL PHONE. IT IS ALREADY TIME TO SHOW WHAT IS HE LOOKING AT... DEPENDING ON THE NEXT PICTURE, WITHOUT THE NEED OF A REDUNDANT DESCRIPTIVE TEXT, THE READER ALREADY REALISES THAT PEEP HAS A MINI CAMERA HANGING ON HIS NECK AND ROBIN USES HIM AS AN INTELLIGENT AND MAINLY COMPLETELY INCONSPICUOUS DRONE.

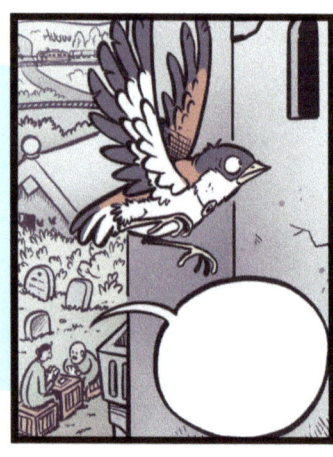

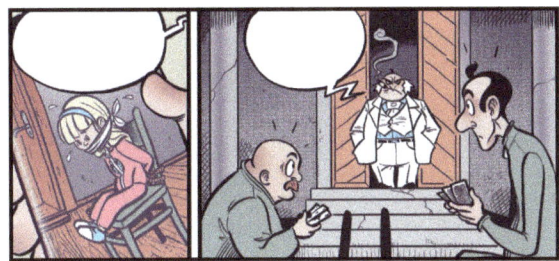

WE HAVE INTRODUCED THE STORY AND WE LET THE READER TAKE A LOOK AT ROBIN, IKAR AND PEEP. THE MAIN HEROES AND SCENERY ARE EXPOSED AND WE ARE READY TO INTRODUCE OTHER STORY CHARACTERS. MAKE SURE THAT EVERY CHARACTER THAT IS SEEN FOR THE FIRST TIME, IS ILLUSTRATED AS CLEARLY AS POSSIBLE, AND IS IN AN APPROPRIATE POSITION. THIS RULE DOES WORK IF YOUR INTENTION IS TO HIDE THE LOOK OF THE CHARACTER. HOWEVER, THIS IS NOT OUR CASE.

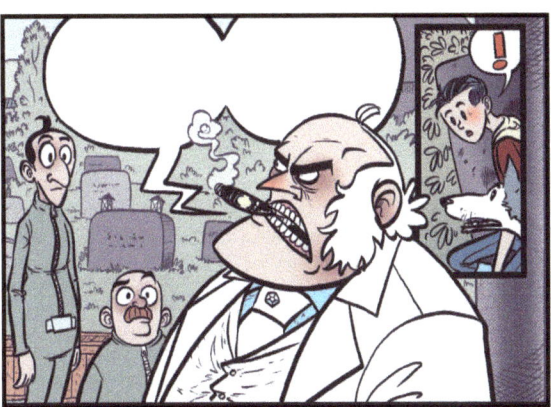

WHEN EVERYTHING IS NICELY PREPARED, ON THE THIRD PAGE THE READER SHOULD KNOW ALL CHARACTERS AND THEIR ROLES. THE READER SHOULD ALSO SUBCONSCIOUSLY KNOW ABOUT THE COMIC BOOKS LAYOUT. THEY ALREADY KNOW THAT THE PANELS WILL HAVE A UNIFIED STYLE, THEY WILL BE DIVIDED BY SAME GAP. THEN, I WILL SUDDENLY BREAK THESE RULES AND INSERT ANOTHER PANEL. THUS, THE READER RECEIVES CLEAR INFORMATION THAT SOMETHING EXTRAORDINARY IS ABOUT TO HAPPEN. HE WILL ALSO COME TO KNOW THAT THE SITUATIONS OF THESE INSERTED PANELS, ARE HAPPENING AT THE SAME TIME. IF THIS WAS NOT THE CASE, WE WOULD DIVIDE BOTH PANELS WITH A WHITE GAP. THIS SHOT IS TELLING THE READER TO IDENTIFY WITH LAUTERNITZ, THE INSERTED PANEL WITH ROBIN, SUCCESSFULLY PREVENTS THAT.

ALSO, THE FACT THAT THE PANEL IS BEHIND THE DUKE'S BACK CLEARLY SHOWS THAT THE VILLAIN HAS NOT SEEN ROBIN YET.

YES, ALL OF THIS WILL BE SUBCONSCIOUSLY PERCEIVED BY THE READER AND YOU NEED TO CONSIDER IT.

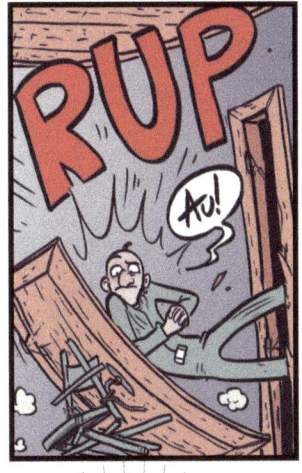

IT WILL REALLY CRACK ON THIS PANEL. I REALLY WANTED THE SOUND TO STICK OUT OF THE PICTURE AND THUS UNDERLINE THE LOUDNESS OF IT. WHY DID I DO THAT? BECAUSE I NEEDED IT. THE STORY WILL ESCALATE A BIT LATER SO, I AM KEEPING THIS EFFECT TO USE WHEN IT WILL HAVE BIGGER FOUNDATION. I MUST NOT SHOW MY BEST BULLETS BEFORE THE END BECAUSE I WOULD LOSE THE TOOLS WHICH WILL BE LATER FOR INCREASING THE EXCITEMENT. SO, IT WAS JUST A GENERAL CRACK, EVEN WITHOUT AN EXCLAMATION MARK.

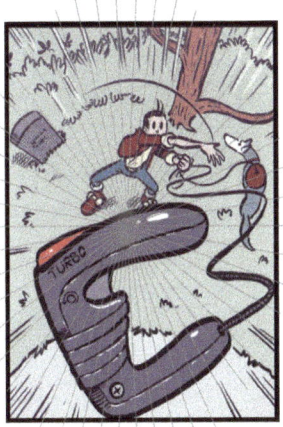

I LOVE PLAYING WITH PERSPECTIVE. ON THE LEFT YOU CAN SEE MY ATTEMPT TO GIVE THE READER THE IMPRESSION THAT THE CAMERA IS MOVING AWAY FROM ROBIN TOGETHER WITH THE HANDLE. AT THE SAME TIME, THE TERRAIN ITSELF BEHIND ROBIN AND IKAR INDICATES THE CURVE OF MOVEMENT OF THE THROWER.

HOWEVER, I WAS DREW THE PICTURE THIS WAY FROM A COMPLETE DIFFERENT REASON. BEFORE YOU CARRY ON READING, TRY TO THINK ABOUT WHAT SPECIAL REASON THIS PICTURE HAS, AND WHY.

YES, I CHOSE THIS EXTRAORDINARY PERSPECTIVE FOR ONE SPECIAL REASON, I NEED THE READER TO FOCUS ON THE GADGET WHICH IS THROWN BY ROBIN. THERE HAS NOT BEEN A PROPER OPPORTUNITY FOR THAT YET. IKAR'S LEASH HAS MORE FEATURES AND I WANTED THE READER TO REMEMBER IT WELL BECAUSE IT IS ONE OF THE THINGS WHICH DEFINES ROBIN, LIKE A BATARANG DEFINES BATMAN.

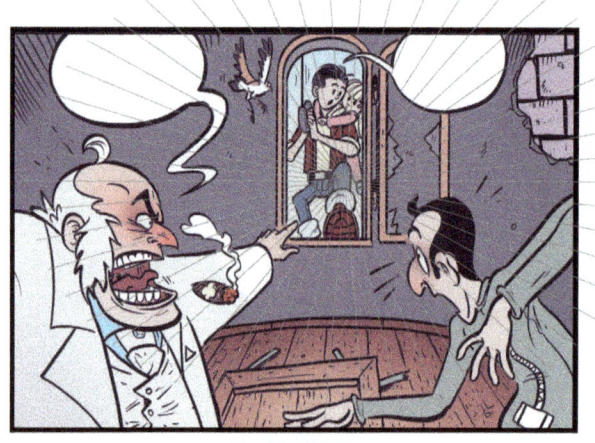

THIS IS A TYPICAL PICTURE WHICH IS BASED ON PERSPECTIVE. AS YOU CAN SEE, ALL LINES LEAD THE READER DIRECTLY TO ROBIN. I WANTED TO CAUSE AN EFFECT AS IF THE CAMERA WAS MOVING FROM THE FRONT TO THE MAIN MOTIVE, WHICH IS ROBIN AND HIS ACTIONS.

NOTE THAT LAUTERNITZ'S HAND DID NOT GO TOGETHER WITH THAT INTENTION. IT IS BECAUSE I DO NOT WANT THIS TRICK TO BE SO OBVIOUS. IT IS LIKE WHEN A MAGICIAN INTENTIONALLY WAVES HIS LEFT HAND TO DISTRACT YOU FROM LOOKING AT HIS RIGHT HAND IN HIS POCKET.

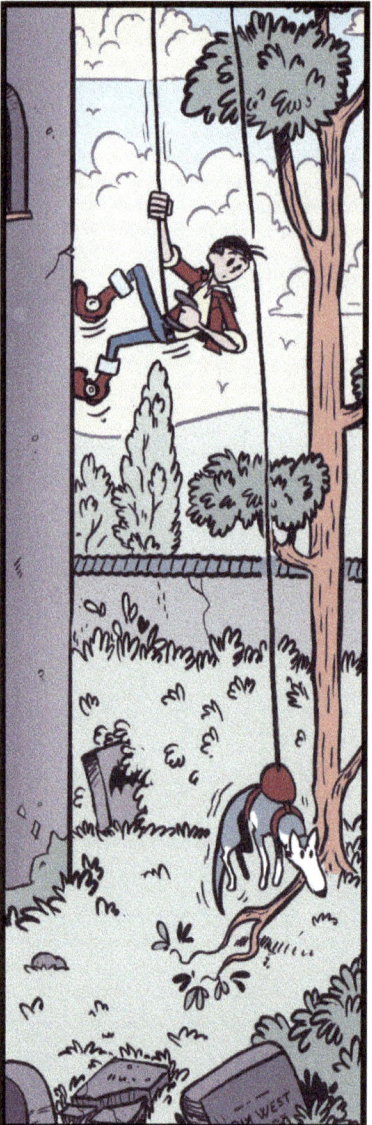

HERE THE PICTURE DEALS WITH LOCALIZATION. THE READER RECEIVES THE WHOLE PICTURE NOT TO LOSE SIGHT ABOUT WHERE THE CHARACTERS ARE. EVEN THE PLACE IS NOT DYNAMICALLY CHANGING YOU SHOULD DO IT ON EACH PAGE ONCE AT LEAST.

THERE IS A HIDDEN MESSAGE IN THIS PICTURE FROM BATMAN SERIES IN THE 70'S, WITH ADAM WEST AS THE LEADING ROLE. THIS IS A WINK TO A KNOWLEDGEABLE READER, AND WOULD BE NOTICED BY MAYBE ONE OUT OF A HUNDRED. IT FOLLOWS THAT IN HIDDEN MESSAGES, THE UNINITIATED READER MUST NOT REALIZE THAT THERE IS A MESSAGE. IF THEY NOTE THAT, THEY START TO THINK ABOUT WHETHER IT IS CONNECTED WITH THE PLOT, THEY START TO BE CONFUSED, A FRUSTRATION COMES, RIOTS IN STREETS, INFERNO, EARTHQUAKE, APOCALYPSE AND, THE END. SO, BE CAREFUL WITH THESE MESSAGES.

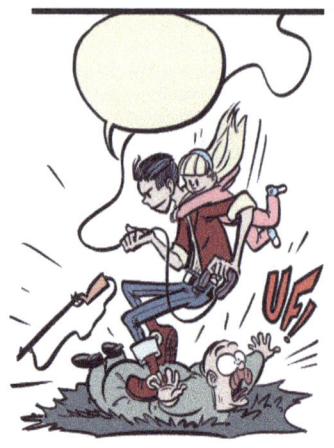

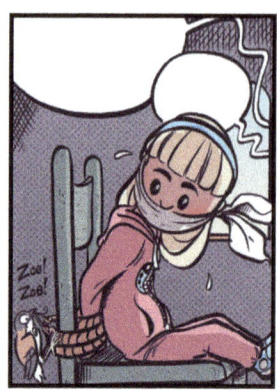

THIS IS ANOTHER LAYOUT DISRUPTION. IN THIS CASE IT IS JUST BECAUSE I WANT TO REFRESH THE PAGE A BIT. NOTE THAT THE BUBBLE IS YELLOW IN COMPARISON WITH THE OTHER ONES. ITS MILD COLOUR ON THE WHITE BACKGROUND IS APPROPRIATE – JUST FOR THE CLEAR ARRANGEMENT.

IF SOMEONE OUT OF THE PICTURE SPEAKS, IT WILL ALWAYS BE CLEAR WHO SAID THAT. IN THIS PICTURE IT IS OBVIOUS FROM THE CONTEXT. THERE IS NO OTHER WAY.

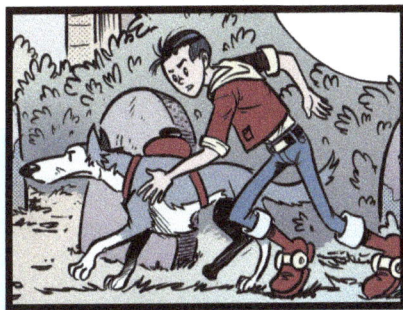 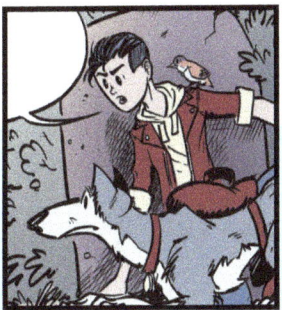 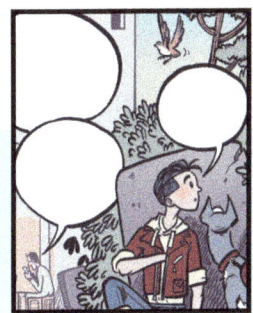 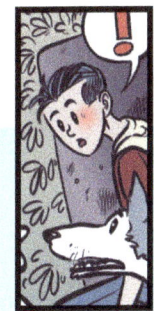

NOTE THAT THE PANELS FOLLOW EACH OTHER, ALTHOUGH SPREAD THROUGHOUT THE WHOLE COMIC BOOK, THEY STRICTLY FOLLOW THE SHOT ANGLE AND COLOURING. I COULD COME UP WITH MANY DIFFERENT ANGLES AND THEY WOULD SURELY BE INTERESTING AND NICE. HOWEVER, THEY WOULD NOT HELP THE READER. IF I WANT TO CARRY THE READER AWAY BY THE STORY, MY AMBITIONS OF ATTRACTING THE USER TO THE PICTURE OR THE SCENES ORIGINALITY SHOULD NOT PREVENT ME FROM DOING SO. THE STORY IS PREFERRED IN THIS COMIC BOOK AND THIS DEPENDS ON MY CONSISTENCY AND ACCURACY. SIMPLY PUT: FOR THE READER, I AM TRYING TO EASE THE ORIENTATION OF THE PICTURE.

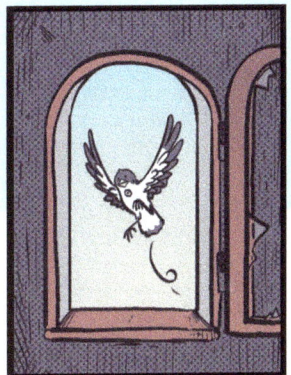 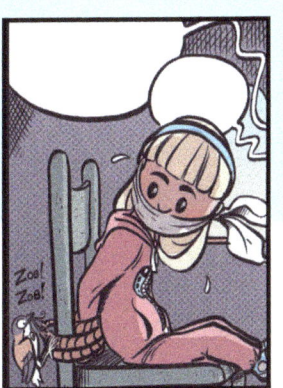 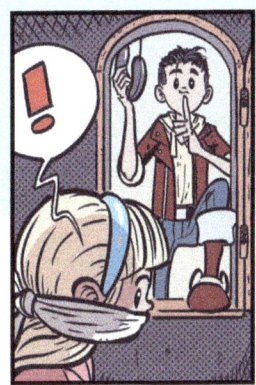 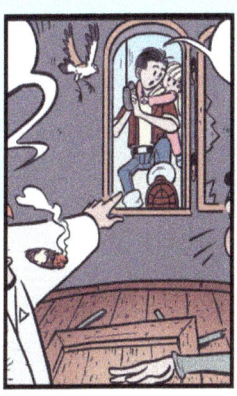

AND HERE COMES THE END OF THE COMIC - ROBIN TRIUMPHS. THERE IS A PANEL INSERTED AGAIN, BUT THE READER IS ALREADY USED TO IT. WHAT IS MORE IMPORTANT, THOUGH, IS THAT I LET IKAR TO RUN OUTSIDE THE PANEL BORDER. THIS HAS NEVER HAPPENED BEFORE. IT IS PART OF THE STORY'S CLIMAX. THE READER WILL START REALISING THAT THE MORE BROKEN THE PANELS ARE, THE MORE DRAMATIC THE STORY WILL BE.

I EXPRESS THE SPEED IN A COUPLE OF WAYS. FIRST OF ALL, THE MOTION HAPPENS FROM LEFT TO RIGHT WHICH IS ((SUPPOSEDLY? SEE PAGE 122) AN EFFECT SUPPORTED BY OUR WAY OF READING. HOWEVER, THIS WOULD NOT BE ENOUGH. THEREFORE, I DEFOCUSED THE BACKGROUND AND EXAGGERATED ROBIN AND IKAR'S PERSPECTIVE. YOU HAVE CERTAINLY NOTICED THAT ROBIN HAS SUDDENLY UNNATURALLY LONG ARMS AND LEGS. ALL OF THAT SHOULD SUPPORT THE IMPRESSION OF SPEED AND ACCELERATION, WHICH THIS PICTURE SHOULD HAVE.

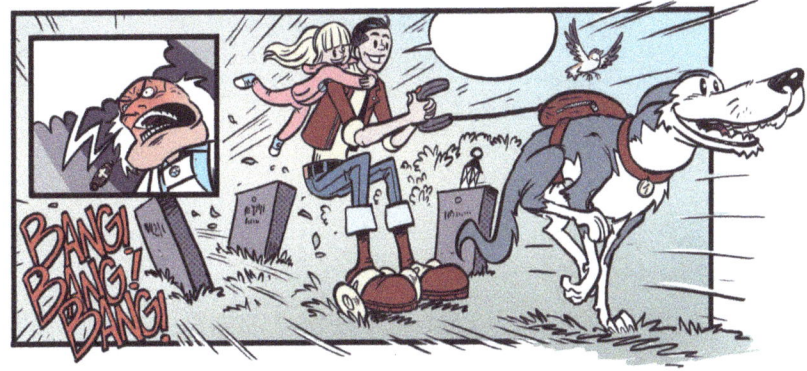

TASK
GO BACK TO THE CHAPTER NOTE TO COMIC BOOK I. COMPARE YOUR INITIAL NOTES WITH THIS DESCRIPTION. HAVE YOU REVEALED ALL OF MY TRICKS?

LAST TASK

HERE WE ARE. LAST TASK. LAST MISSION BEFORE YOU START AN INFINITE ADVENTURE WHICH IS OFFERED BY CARTOONING.

IF YOU STUDIED THIS BOOK THOROUGHLY AND FOLLOWED IT PROPERLY, IT COULD GIVE YOU A LOT, WARN YOU FROM MISTAKES, WHICH YOU COULD HAVE EXPERIENCED AND PAID FOR. HOPEFULLY, I HAVE BEEN USEFUL REGARDING THESE ISSUE AND REINFORCED YOU IN ALL THE RIGHT PLACES.

IT IS IMPORTANT THAT I MENTION MANY PITFALLS WHICH ARE STILL WAITING FOR YOU.

FIRST OF ALL, YOU WILL HAVE TO FACE CRITICS. THE CZECH REPUBLIC IS REALLY SMALL, THEREFORE, THERE IS A LOT OF COMPETITION. CRITICAL REVIEWS WILL HURT YOU. IT ALWAYS DOES. THE PROBLEM IS THAT SUCH A PERSON RARELY REALIZES HOW POWERFUL THEY ARE. THEY ARE EVEN CAPABLE OF STOPPING AN ARTIST. THEY ARE SO POWERFUL, IN FACT, NOBODY CAN AFFORD TO CRITICIZE A CRITIC. YES, EVEN CRITICISM IS A DISCIPLINE WHICH MUST BE DONE WELL. SO, WHEN SOMEBODY TELLS YOU THAT CARTOONING IS SOMETHING WHICH IS DONE BY LAZY ILLUSTRATORS AND CAN BE, IN FACT, DONE BY ANYONE... THOSE PEOPLE'S OPINIONS ARE NOT SOMETHING YOU SHOULD TAKE CARE OF.

CRITICISM FROM COLLEAGUES HURTS THE MOST. IN FACT, THE WAY HOW CERTAIN CRITICISM IS COMMUNICATED REALLY MATTERS. IF ANY OF YOUR COLLEAGUES PUBLISHES A REVIEW OF YOUR PIECE OF WORK, YOU CAN BE SURE THAT IT IS NOT A REVIEW BUT A CAMPAIGN. EVEN IF THEY PRAISE YOUR PIECE OF WORK, THEY ARE, IN FACT, PROMOTING THEMSELVES OVER THE CRITICISED PERSON TO THE POSITION OF A TEACHER, WHO DECIDES WHAT IS GOOD WHAT IS NOT.

THERE IS SOMETHING WHICH IS CALLED PROFESSIONAL ETHICS. IT SAYS THAT COLLEAGUES MUST NOT BE CRITICISED IN PUBLIC SPACE. HAVE YOU EVER HEARD THAT KAREL GOTT RECORDED A REVIEW OF MICHAL DAVID'S MUSIC? OF COURSE NOT! DO YOU THINK HE HAS NOT DONE IT BECAUSE HE DOES NOT HAVE AN OPINION ABOUT HIS MUSIC? NOT AT ALL. HE HAS NOT DONE IT BECAUSE IT IS NOT PROFESSIONAL. DO NOT EVER LET YOURSELF BE LURED BY THIS IMPULSE. PEOPLE WILL ASK YOU FOR YOUR OPINION. BE DIPLOMATIC AND AVOID DIRECT ANSWERS.

EXAMPLE:
JOHN BLABLA IS A SUCCESSFUL CARTOONIST AND YOU DO NOT LIKE HIS WORK TOO MUCH BECAUSE HE MAKES TRIVIAL MISTAKES, WHICH YOU CANNOT STAND. PEOPLE WANT TO HEAR YOUR OPINION THOUGH.

QUESTION: "WHAT IS YOUR OPINION ON JOHN BLABLA'S WORK?"

YOUR ANSWER: "JOHN IS A REAL PROFESSIONAL."

DONE. FULL STOP. IF YOU REALLY CARE THAT JOHN DRAWS BADLY. GET IN CONTACT WITH HIM AND WRITE HIM. DO NOT TALK ABOUT HIS WORK IN PUBLIC. HELP HIM PRIVATELY. DO NOT BE THE ONE WHO DEGRADES THE LESS SKILFUL ONES. YOU CAN BE THE ONE WHO HELP THEM GROW BECAUSE, BE SURE THAT WHAT YOU SOW, YOU HARVEST. IN FACT, REPUTATION IS THE ONLY THING THAT A COMMERCIAL ARTIST HAS.

YOU WILL NEVER HAVE A FEELING THAT YOU RECEIVE WHAT YOU DESERVE FOR YOUR WORK. GENERALLY PUT, THE MORE YOU GIVE TO IT, THE MORE YOU RECEIVE BACK. HOWEVER, NOT EVERYTHING. IT GOES LIKE THAT. IF YOU PLANT TWENTY OAK TREES, ONLY TWO OF THEM GROW UP. DOES IT MEAN THAT IT IS NOT WORTH PLANTING OAK TREES? YES, YOU PLANTED EIGHTEEN OAK TREES FOR NOTHING. BUT THE TWO OF THEM THAT GREW UP START TO GIVE ACORNS AND THAT IS WORTH IT, ISN'T IT? SO, WHEN YOU OFFER HELP, SOMEONE WILL BE GRATEFUL TO YOU AND THEY WILL GIVE IT BACK TO YOU. SIMPLY PUT, WHEN YOU PLANT TWENTY OAKS, YOU CAN BE SURE THAT WHEN YOU NEED TO, YOU CAN LEAN ON SOME OF THEM. HOWEVER, IF YOU SOW ANGER AND HATE, IT WILL SPREAD OUT LIKE A CANCER. YOU WILL NOT FEEL RIGHT ABOUT IT. A TUMOUR DOES NOT HURT RIGHT AWAY EITHER. YOU WILL FIND OUT THAT YOU HAVE CLOSED DOORS IN MANY PLACES JUST BECAUSE YOU RECORD VIDEOS WHERE YOU SPILL ON THE WORK OF THE PEOPLE WHICH THEY WORK WITH.

> "REPUTATION IS THE ONLY THING COMMERCIAL ARTIST HAS"

SO, WE ARE GETTING TO THE MOST IMPORTANT THING WHICH I WANT TO TELL YOU. TODAY YOUR DRAWING ARE ON A CERTAIN LEVEL BUT IN TWO YEARS YOU WILL BE SOMEWHERE ELSE COMPLETELY. YOU WILL BE ASHAMED BY YOUR PREVIOUS WORK. THIS MUST NOT STOP YOU. IF YOU CREATE ACCORDING TO YOUR BEST CONSCIENCE, YOU DO NOT NEED TO REGRET YOUR WORK. ON THE OTHER HAND, IT WILL BE AN INDICATOR HOW FAR YOU'VE COME.

PUBLISHING YOUR ILLUSTRATIONS IS ALWAYS LIKE GOING OUT ON A LIMB. DO NOT TAKE YOURSELF SO SERIOUSLY AND DO NOT PUT IT OFF. NOBODY IS PERFECT. LIFE IS A JOURNEY AND IT WILL NEVER BE DIFFERENT.

YOU CAN ALWAYS DO BETTER! THIS SENTENCE SHOULD IMPRESS AND EXCITE YOU. IF IT SCARES AND FRUSTRATES YOU, ART IS NOT FOR YOU.

THE SAME WORKS FOR THOSE WHO THINK THAT THEY ACHIEVED A PERFECT STYLE AND THAT THEY HAVE NOTHING TO LEARN ANY LONGER. THIS IS A MISTAKE. IT CAN JUST MEAN THAT YOU ARE IN A DEAD-END STREET. WHEN DEVELOPMENT STOPS THE ARTIST DIES.

DRAWING IS NOT ABOUT ACHIEVING A GOAL. IT IS AN ADVENTUROUS EXPEDITION TO PERFECTION. MOREOVER, THE JOURNEY IS NOT THE END BUT JUST DIFFERENT LEVELS. THE JOURNEY ITSELF MUST FULFIL YOU. THE NEVER-ENDING DISCOVERING. YOU CAN LEARN SOMETHING NEW EVERY DAY ALTHOUGH, YOU MIGHT HAVE ACHIEVED A CERTAIN AGE AND LEVEL WHERE YOU RATHER HARVEST THAN SOW. NEVER STOP. EXAMINE NEW METHODS, NEW TECHNIQUES AND TECHNOLOGIES. LIVE!

SO, GOOD LUCK!

PETR KOPL

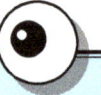

LAST TASK
DO YOU REMEMBER WHEN YOU DREW YOUR FIRST PICTURE IN THIS BOOK? PLEASE, DRAW IT AGAIN WITH COMPLETELY EVERYTHING YOU HAVE LEARNT HERE. CAN YOU SEE THE PROGRESS? TAKE PICTURES OF BOTH OF THEM AND SEND THEM TO ME TO: AUTHOR@PETRKOPL.CZ. I WILL BE REALLY GRATEFUL EVEN FOR A MERE REACTION AND CRITICAL REVIEW OF THIS BOOK. IT WILL MEAN A LOT TO ME. I LOOK FORWARD TO IT!

COMMENTS OF COLLEAGUES

HONZA POTMĚŠIL
SCRIPT WRITER AND YOUTUBER

THE COMIC SKETCH BOOK SHOULD BE AN OBLIGATION FOR EVERY NEW CARTOONIST. THE CONCENTRATION OF CRUCIAL PRINCIPLES OF CARTOONING WILL BE GREAT TRIGGER FOR BEGINNERS AND A PLEASANT INFORMATION COMPLEMENTATION FOR PROFESSIONALS. I PERSONALLY LEAD WORKSHOPS "NARRATION BY COMICS". FULL OF INSPIRATION, AFTER READING THE BOOK, I AM THINKING OF UPDATING AND IMPROVEMENT OF SOME OF ITS PARTS.

MICHAEL PETRUS
COMIC BOOK ILLUSTRATOR
WWW.MICHAELPETRUS.COM

ALL PETR KOPL'S WORK HAVE SOMETHING IN COMMON – AN UNBELIEVABLE LOVE TO THE CRAFT. HERE IT IS NOT DIFFERENT. THE OTHER WAY ROUND. THIS BOOK WAS CREATED MAINLY AS A LOVE LETTER INTENDED TO COMICS AND TO ALL OF THOSE WHO FEEL THE SAME AND THEY MIGHT WANT TO DRAW AS WELL. EVERY PAGE, PANEL AND PENCIL LINE IS AN IMPRINT OF WHAT PETR KOPL MEANS FOR CZECH COMICS.

FROM MY POINT OF VIEW, PETR KOPL IS THE MOST AUTHORISED GUIDE OF THE WORLD OF COMICS. HE LIVES BY COMICS, HIS DRAWING HAS A CLASS AND AS A WRITER HAS THE ABILITY TO PRECISELY TIME THE ACTION AND JOKE. IT FEELS THAT PETR KOPL IS GIFTED FROM GOD BUT AFTER READING THIS BOOK EVEN THE LAST UNBELIEVER REALISES THAT BEHIND HIS GREATNESS, THERE ARE YEARS OF HARD WORK AND THINKING. THANK YOU, PETR, THAT YOU ARE WILLINGLY SHARE YOUR TRICKS, OBSERVATIONS AND EXPERIENCE WITH OTHERS. I WILL BE GLAD TO RECOMMEND THIS BOOK.

FOR ME, PETR KOPL IS A COMIC BOOK MAGICIAN. HE DOES MAGIC WITH THE CONTENT, WORDS AND PICTURES SO EXCELLENTLY THAT HE IS ONE OF THE MOST QUALIFIED ARTIST AND A COMIC BOOK CARTOONIST. I APPRECIATE HIM NOT ONLY FOR HIS CRAFT, HARD WORK AND COLLEGIALITY BUT MAINLY ALSO FOR THAT HE DRAWS WITH HIS HEART AND WILLINGLY SHARES EVERYTHING WITH OTHERS. THIS BOOK IN A FORM OF A GREAT AND PRACTICAL GUIDE FOR BEGINNERS AND PROFESSIONALS IS EVIDENCE OF THAT.

KLÁRA WALKER SMOLÍKOVÁ
WRITER

PETR KOPL IS A "COMIC BOOK MAN". FROM MY POINT OF VIEW, PETR WAS BORN WITH A COMIC BOOK IN HIS HANDS. BEFORE HE STARTED TO SPEAK, HE CERTAINLY COMMUNICATED WITH HIS SURROUNDINGS BY BUBBLES. SINCE THEN, PETR HAS LEARNT NOT ONLY TO SPEAK BUT ALSO TO WRITE AND DRAW, WHICH HE PROVES IN THIS BOOK. HE HAS READ A LOT, WRITTEN A LOT AND DRAWN A LOT. READERS CAN LOOK FORWARD TO BASIC PRINCIPLES AND METHODS OF THE "NINTH" ART AND ALSO A LOT OF JOKES, WISE CRACKS AND PLAYFUL DRAWINGS. I REALLY ENJOYED THIS BOOK AND AS A LAYMAN I AM GIVING IT A LIKE.

BÁRA BUCHALOVÁ
COMIC BOOK CARTOONIST AND ILLUSTRATOR

JIŘÍ WALKER PROCHÁZKA
WRITER AND SCRIPT WRITER

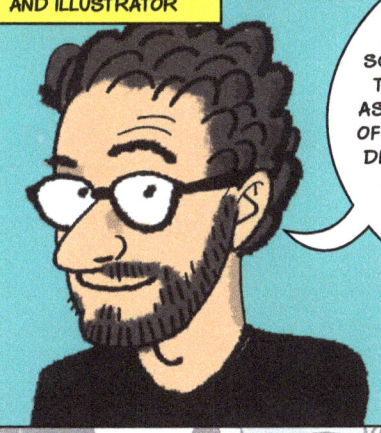

LUKÁŠ FIBRICH
COMIC BOOK CARTOONIST AND ILLUSTRATOR

ON THE MARKET, THERE ARE A GREAT NUMBER OF TITLES "HOW TO DRAW A COMIC BOOK" OR "HOW TO WRITE A SCRIPT" BUT JUST PETR KOPL'S BOOK DEALS WITH BOTH ELEMENTS OF COMICS ART AT THE SAME TIME. COMICS IS A CRAFT AND PETR IS A MASTER OF IT. HE IS A GREAT CARTOONIST AND BRILLIANT SCRIPT WRITER. HE SHOWS THAT FOR A GOOD RESULT IT IS NECESSARY THAT THE SCRIPT WRITER THINKS AS A DESIGNER AND A CARTOONIST AS A WRITER. PETR KOPL IS TALENTED AND HE HAS WORKED THOUSANDS OF HOURS WHICH IS MAYBE MORE INTERESTING THAN TALENT. I HAVE BEEN DEALING WITH COMICS FOR MANY YEARS. I HAVE DRAWN A LOT, STUDIED A LOT AND I AM REALLY HAPPY THAT PETR WITH HIS BOOK LEVELLED ME UP A BIT MORE. IT CANNOT BE STUDIED AT HIGH SCHOOLS OR UNIVERSITIES BUT IF A COMICS DEPARTMENT OPENED AN ACADEMY OF ARTS ARCHITECTURE AND DESIGN IN PRAGUE, PETR KOPL SHOULD BE ITS PROFESSOR AND DOCENT. SERIOUSLY. MOREOVER, THIS BOOK SHOULD BE THE FIRST TEXTBOOK THERE.

PETR KOPL IS ONE OF THE FEW PROFESSIONALS WHO MAKES COMIC BOOKS FOR LIVING IN THE CZECH REPUBLIC. THIS GUIDE IS EVIDENCE THAT HIS SUCCESS IS NOT A COINCIDENCE BUT HE REALLY KNOWS WHAT HE IS DOING AND HE DOES NOT HESITATE TO SHARE HIS METHODS AND TRICKS WITH OTHERS. HE SAVES MANY HOURS TO BEGINNERS, TRYING DEAD END STREETS. FOR EXPERIENCED CREATORS IT REPRESENTS AN INSIGHT BEHIND THE CURTAINS OF CREATIVE PROCESS OF ONE OF THE MOST SUCCESSFUL CZECH COMIC BOOK AUTHORS.

TOMÁŠ KUČEROVSKÝ
COMIC BOOK CARTOONIST AND ILLUSTRATOR
WWW.TOMASKUCEROVSKY.TK

PETR KOPL IS A MAN WHO IS ABLE TO MOTIVATE, EXCITE AND ENCOURAGE THOSE WHO STILL JUST DREAM OF THEIR COMIC BOOK. IN THE CZECH REPUBLIC THERE ARE MANY PROMISING CREATORS WHO JUST NEED TO SEE THE WAY AND PETR HAS ALREADY PROVEN THAT HE KNOWS IT. HE CAN INSPIRE AND HE NEVER GIVES UP. IT IS NOT ONLY THAT, I APPRECIATE HIM AND HIS WORK.

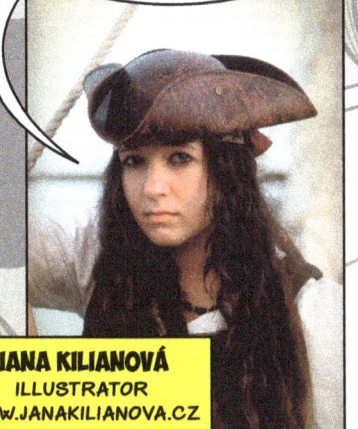

JANA KILIANOVÁ
ILLUSTRATOR
WWW.JANAKILIANOVA.CZ

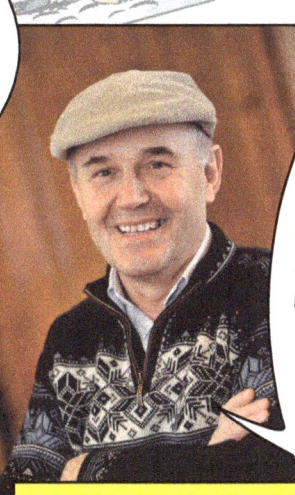

JAROSLAV NĚMEČEK
COMIC BOOK CARTOONIST, ILLUSTRATOR, AUTHOR OF ČTYŘLÍSTEK, A LEGEND

START DRAWING AND DO NOT LET ANY IDEA COOL DOWN. THE SCENARIO IS THE BEGINNING. FIND A FRIEND WHO HAS A LOT OF IDEAS. WRITE STORIES FOR YOUR CHARACTERS WHICH YOU PORTRAY ACCORDING TO YOUR IDEAS LATER ON. I KNOW THAT WRITING A GOOD SCENARIO IS MORE DIFFICULT THAN DRAWING IT. WHEN YOU PRESENT YOUR WORK IN SOME EDITORIAL OFFICE, BRING THIRTY OF THEM STRAIGHTAWAY. MEET DEADLINES. WORK ON MANY PEOPLE DEPENDS ON YOUR PUNCTUALITY. DO NOT COME UP WITH LONG AND COMPLEX STORIES. SIMPLICITY PAYS OFF, THEREFORE, IT IS BETTER TO DRAW A BIT LONGER JOKE WITH FOUR CHARACTERS THAN A LARGE SAGA. A PROPER CARTOONIST IS EASILY DISTINGUISHED BY A CALLUS ON THEIR BUTT... I MEAN, YOU NEED TO DRAW, DRAW AND DRAW.

ACKNOWLEDGEMENT

THANKS TO ALL OF MY COLLEAGUES FOR THEIR COMMENTS AND SUGGESTIONS OF IMPROVEMENT OF MY BOOK AND FOR THEIR BEAUTIFUL COMMENTS ON THE PREVIOUS PAGES, MY EGYPTIAN STUDENTS WHO FIRST TESTED THIS BOOK. THANK HONZA ANDĚL FOR TECHNICAL AND PSYCHICAL SUPPORT AND SELF-SACRIFICING SELF DESTRUCTIVE HELP. THANK BOHOUŠ DVOŘÁK FOR A GREAT LIFE. THANK MOM AND DAD FOR THEY TAUGHT ME WHAT IT MEANS TO LOVE UNCONDITIONALLY. THANK THE LADIES FROM TŘEBÍČ CHARITY FOR THEY INFECTED ME WITH LOVE.

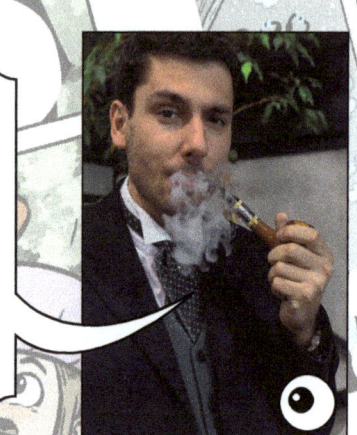

COMIC SKETCH BOOK
PETR KOPL

COPYRIGHT © ZONER SOFTWARE, A. S.
FIRST ISSUE PUBLISHED IN 2018. ALL RIGHTS RESERVED.

ZONER PRESS
CATALOGUE NUMBER: ZRK1711

ZONER SOFTWARE, A. S.
NOVÉ SADY 18, 602 00 BRNO, THE CZECH REPUBLIC
WWW.ZONERPRESS.CZ

MANAGING EDITOR: PAVEL KRISTIÁN
EDITOR IN CHARGE: IVA ŠIŠPEROVÁ
DTP: PETR KOPL
COVER: PETR KOPL
TRANSLATED: JAN RAMÍREZ
PROOFREADING: ASH BEEHARRY AND EVA KROČÁKOVÁ

THE INFORMATION WHICH IS PUBLISHED IN THIS BOOK CAN BE PROTECTED AS PATENT. THE NAMES OF PRODUCTS WERE MENTIONED WITHOUT A GUARANTEE OF THEIR FREE USE. ALTHOUGH, IN CREATING TEXTS AND THEIR PORTRAYAL WAS USED MAXIMAL CARE, POSSIBLE MISTAKES CAN OCCUR. PUBLISHERS AND AUTHORS DO NOT TAKE EITHER LEGAL RESPONSIBILITY AND NOR ANY OTHER GUARANTEE FOR USING WRONG INFORMATION AND FOLLOWING CONSEQUENCES.
ALL RIGHTS RESERVED. NO PART OF THIS PUBLICATION CANNOT BE EITHER REPRODUCED NOR DISTRIBUTED IN ANY OTHER WAY, MEDIA NOR REPRODUCED IN A DATABASE OR OTHER MEDIA WITHOUT AN EXPLICIT AGREEMENT OF THE PUBLISHER WITH THE EXCEPTION OF PUBLISHING SHORT TEXT EXTRACTS FOR THE NEED OF REVIEWS. THIS PUBLICATION DID NOT GO THROUGH A LANGUAGE EDITING.

SEND QUESTIONS REGARDING DISTRIBUTION ON:

ZONER PRESS
ZONER SOFTWARE, A. S.
NOVÉ SADY 18, 602 00 BRNO, THE CZECH REPUBLIC
TEL.: 532 190 883
E-MAIL: KNIHY@ZONER.CZ
WWW.ZONERPRESS.CZ
WWW.FACEBOOK.COM/ZONERPRESS
WWW.FACEBOOK.COM/GROUPS/RAJTVORILKU

ISBN: 978-80-7413-371-8

www.ingramcontent.com/pod-product-compliance
Lightning Source LLC
Chambersburg PA
CBHW040541220526
45473CB00016B/2991